3 I'm the VILLAINESS, so I'm Taming the Final Boss

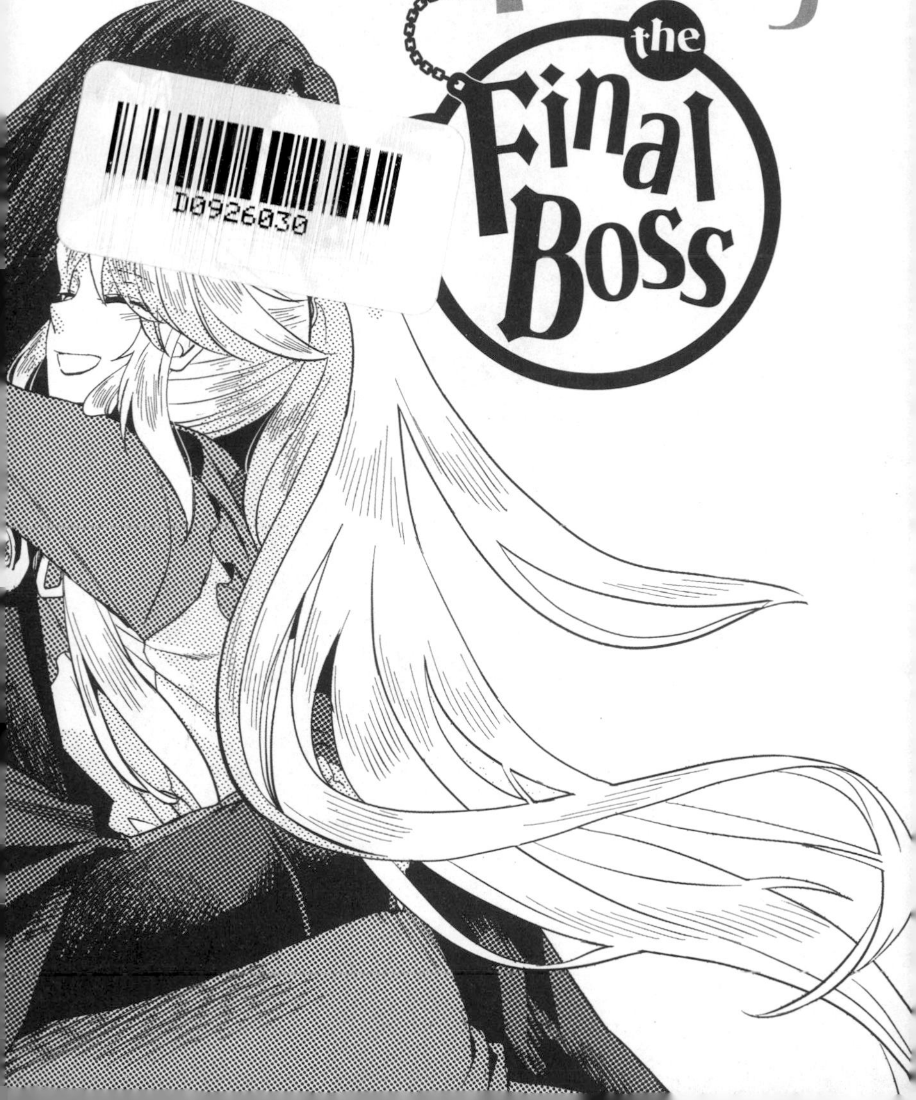

CONTENTS

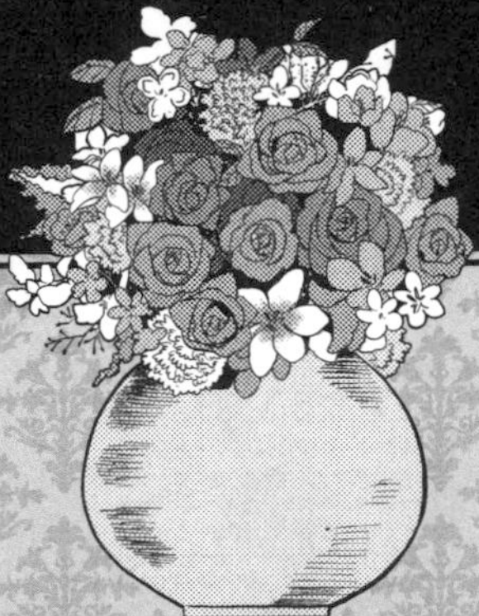

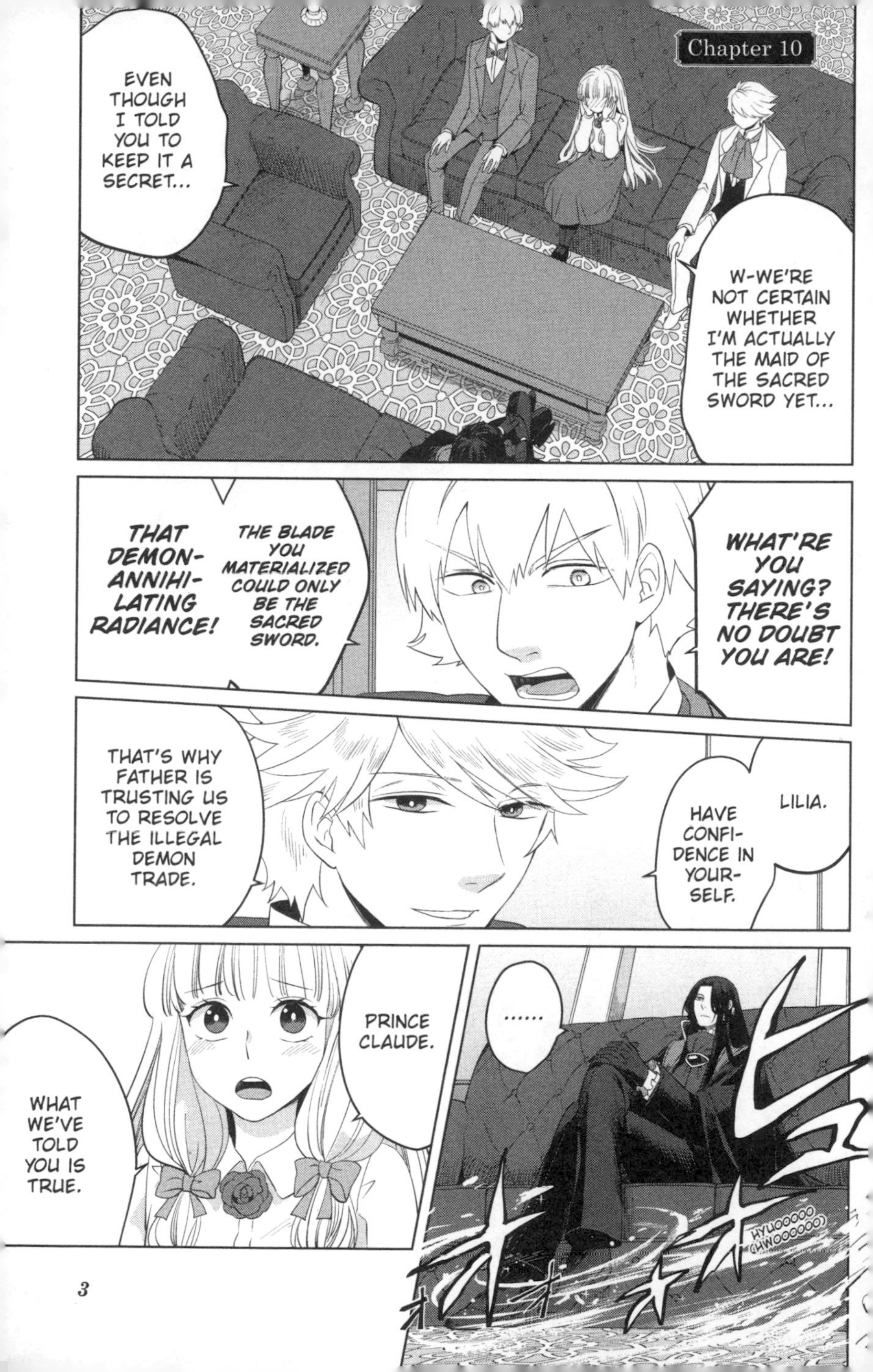
Chapter 10
W-WE'RE NOT CERTAIN WHETHER I'M ACTUALLY THE MAID OF THE SACRED SWORD YET...
EVEN THOUGH I TOLD YOU TO KEEP IT A SECRET...
WHAT'RE YOU SAYING? THERE'S NO DOUBT YOU ARE!
THE BLADE YOU MATERIALIZED COULD ONLY BE THE SACRED SWORD.
THAT DEMON-ANNIHILATING RADIANCE!
LILIA.
HAVE CONFIDENCE IN YOURSELF.
THAT'S WHY FATHER IS TRUSTING US TO RESOLVE THE ILLEGAL DEMON TRADE.
......
HYUOOOOO (CHWOOOOOOO)
PRINCE CLAUDE.
WHAT WE'VE TOLD YOU IS TRUE.

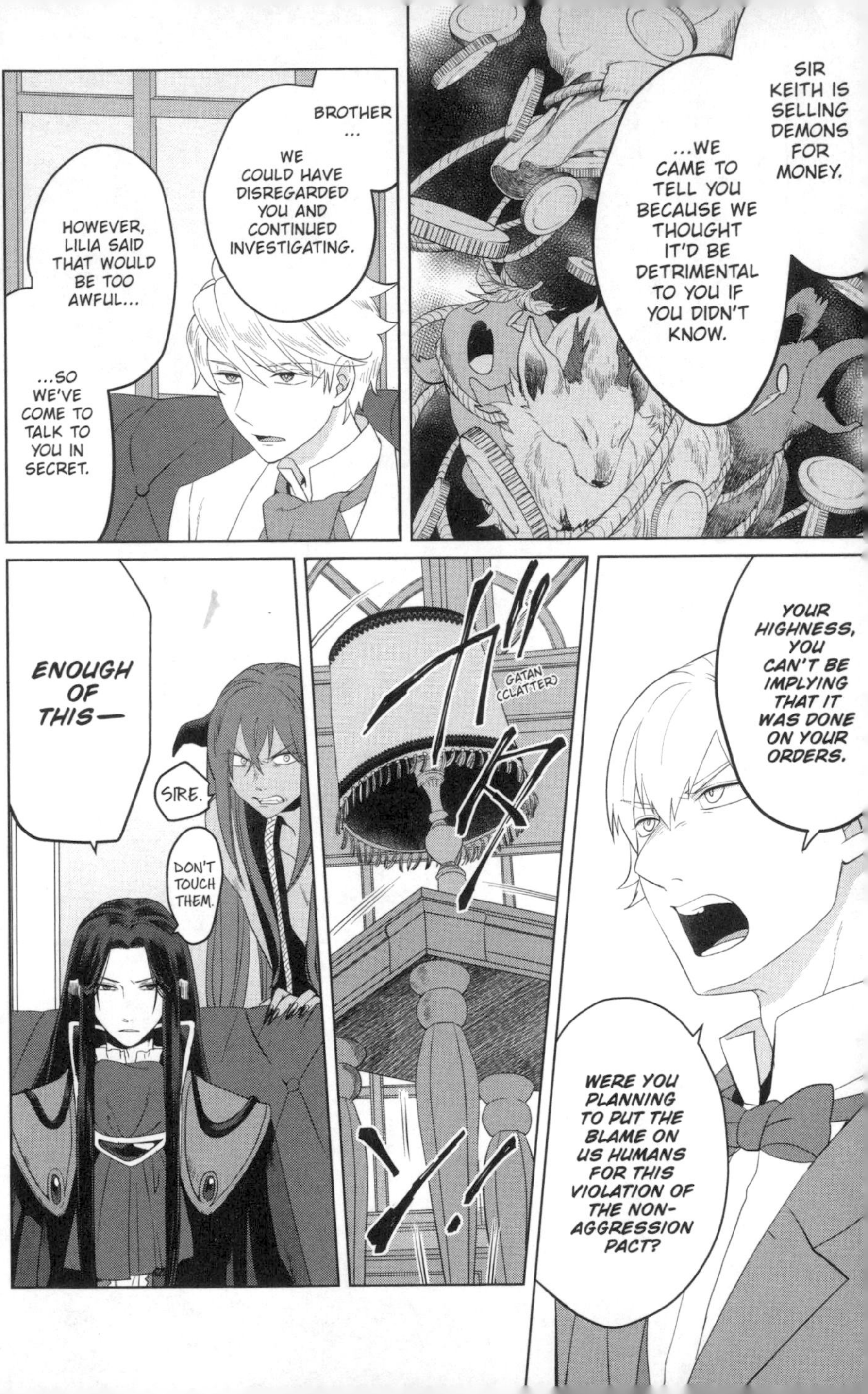
SIR KEITH IS SELLING DEMONS FOR MONEY.
...WE CAME TO TELL YOU BECAUSE WE THOUGHT IT'D BE DETRIMENTAL TO YOU IF YOU DIDN'T KNOW.
BROTHER ... WE COULD HAVE DISREGARDED YOU AND CONTINUED INVESTIGATING.
HOWEVER, LILIA SAID THAT WOULD BE TOO AWFUL...
...SO WE'VE COME TO TALK TO YOU IN SECRET.
YOUR HIGHNESS, YOU CAN'T BE IMPLYING THAT IT WAS DONE ON YOUR ORDERS.
WERE YOU PLANNING TO PUT THE BLAME ON US HUMANS FOR THIS VIOLATION OF THE NON-AGGRESSION PACT?
GATAN (CLATTER)
ENOUGH OF THIS—
SIRE.
DON'T TOUCH THEM.

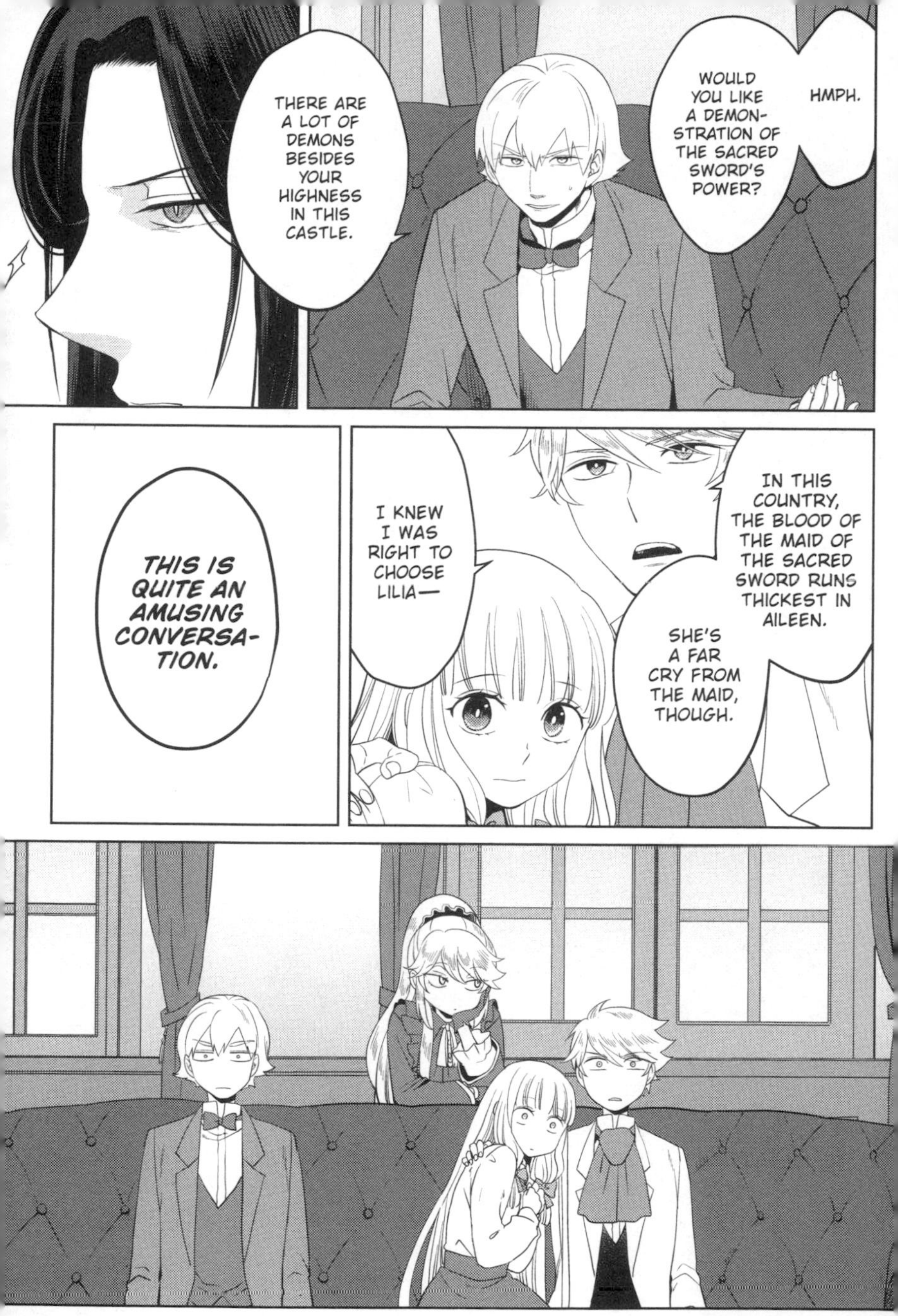
HMPH.
WOULD YOU LIKE A DEMONSTRATION OF THE SACRED SWORD'S POWER?
THERE ARE A LOT OF DEMONS BESIDES YOUR HIGHNESS IN THIS CASTLE.
IN THIS COUNTRY, THE BLOOD OF THE MAID OF THE SACRED SWORD RUNS THICKEST IN AILEEN.
SHE'S A FAR CRY FROM THE MAID, THOUGH.
I KNEW I WAS RIGHT TO CHOOSE LILIA—
THIS IS QUITE AN AMUSING CONVERSATION.

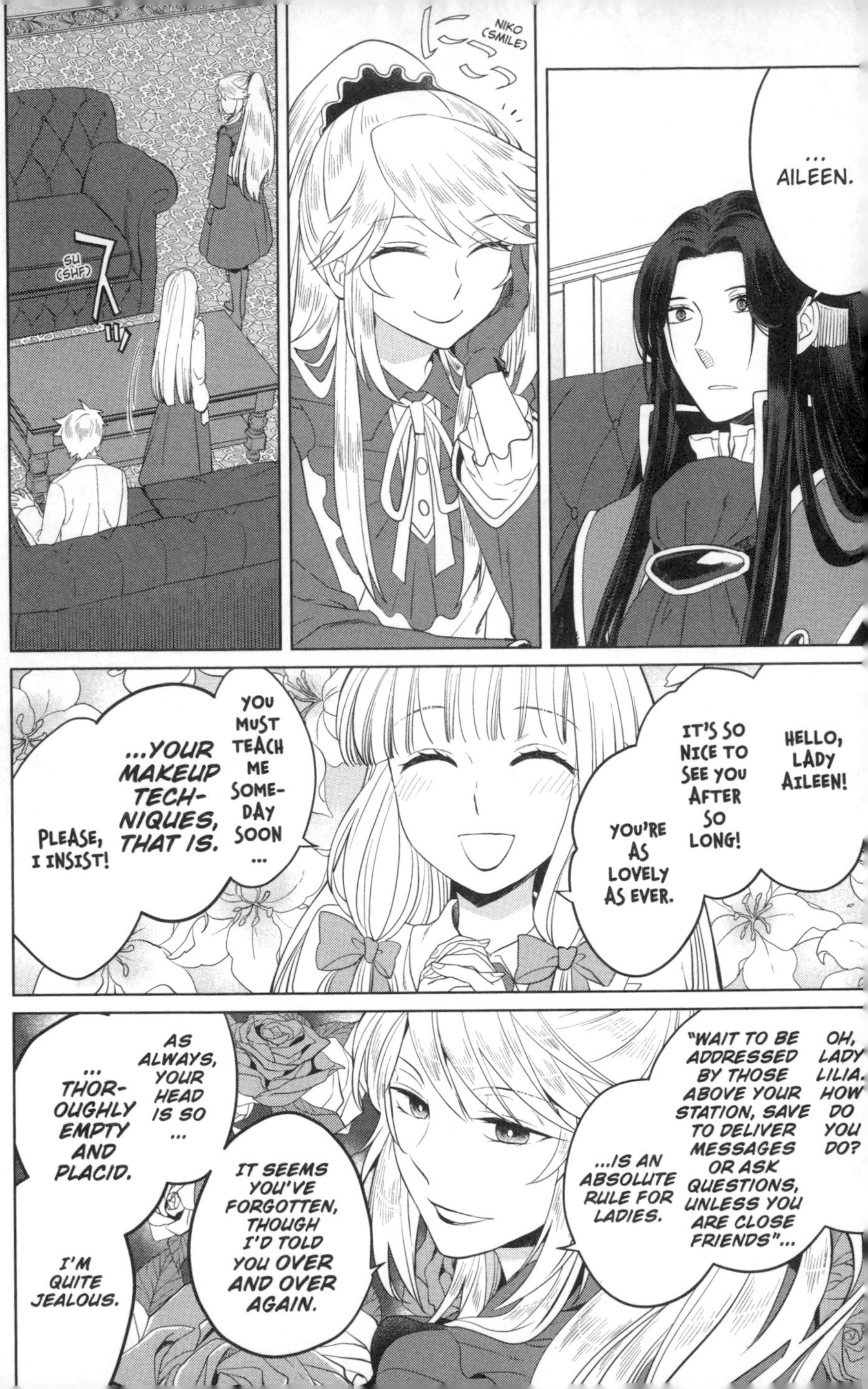
... AILEEN.
NIKO (SMILE)
SU (SHF)
HELLO, LADY AILEEN!
IT'S SO NICE TO SEE YOU AFTER SO LONG!
YOU'RE AS LOVELY AS EVER.
YOU MUST TEACH ME SOME-DAY SOON ...
...YOUR MAKEUP TECH-NIQUES, THAT IS.
PLEASE, I INSIST!
OH, LADY LILIA. HOW DO YOU DO?
"WAIT TO BE ADDRESSED BY THOSE ABOVE YOUR STATION, SAVE TO DELIVER MESSAGES OR ASK QUESTIONS, UNLESS YOU ARE CLOSE FRIENDS"...
...IS AN ABSOLUTE RULE FOR LADIES.
IT SEEMS YOU'VE FORGOTTEN, THOUGH I'D TOLD YOU OVER AND OVER AGAIN.
AS ALWAYS, YOUR HEAD IS SO ...
... THOR-OUGHLY EMPTY AND PLACID.
I'M QUITE JEALOUS.

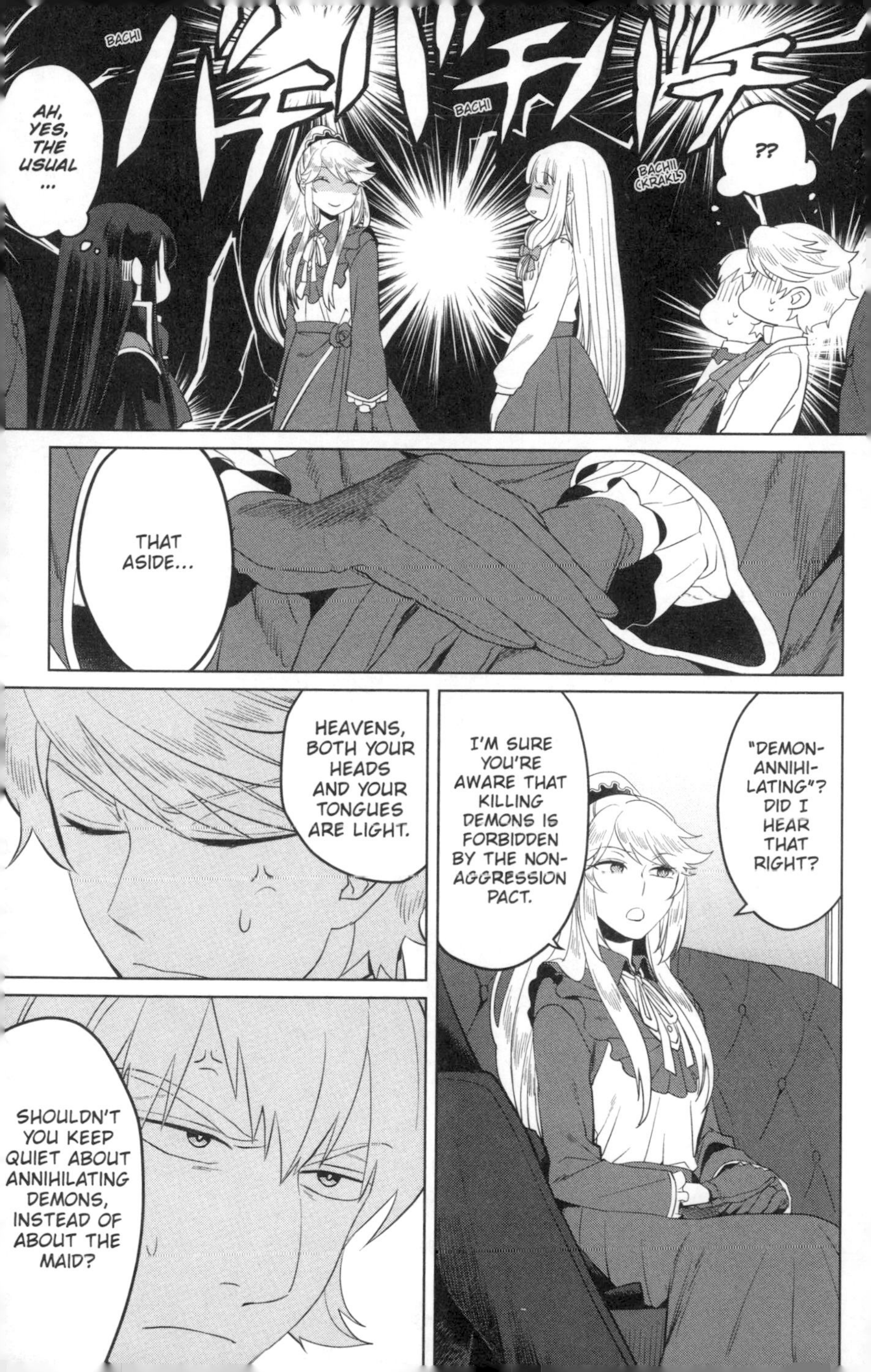
??
BACHII (KRAKL)
BACHI
BACHI
AH, YES, THE USUAL...
THAT ASIDE...
"DEMON-ANNIHILATING"? DID I HEAR THAT RIGHT?
I'M SURE YOU'RE AWARE THAT KILLING DEMONS IS FORBIDDEN BY THE NON-AGGRESSION PACT.
HEAVENS, BOTH YOUR HEADS AND YOUR TONGUES ARE LIGHT.
SHOULDN'T YOU KEEP QUIET ABOUT ANNIHILATING DEMONS, INSTEAD OF ABOUT THE MAID?

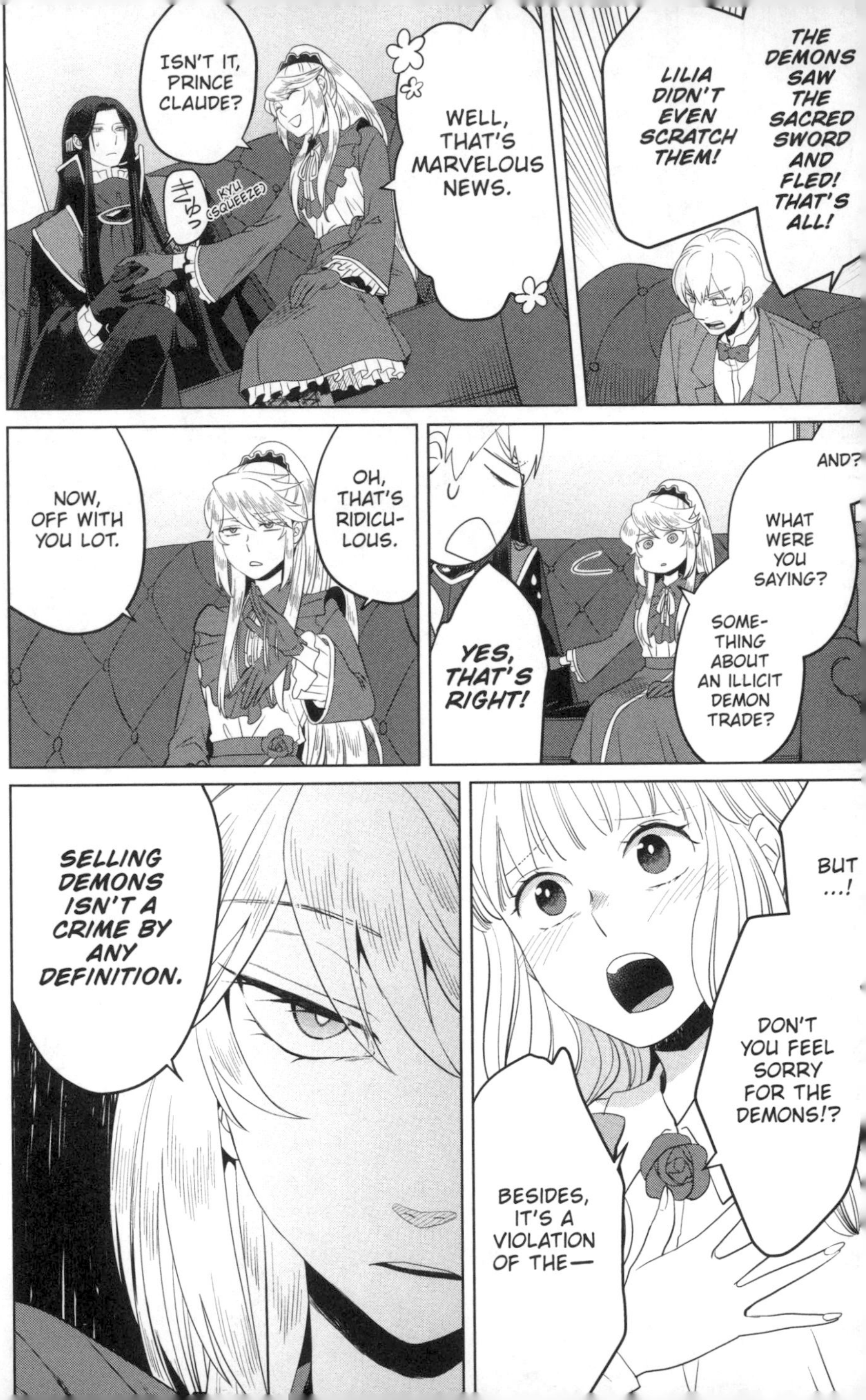
THE DEMONS SAW THE SACRED SWORD AND FLED! THAT'S ALL!
LILIA DIDN'T EVEN SCRATCH THEM!
WELL, THAT'S MARVELOUS NEWS.
ISN'T IT, PRINCE CLAUDE?
きゅっ
KYU (SQUEEZE)
AND?
WHAT WERE YOU SAYING?
SOME-THING ABOUT AN ILLICIT DEMON TRADE?
YES, THAT'S RIGHT!
OH, THAT'S RIDICU-LOUS.
NOW, OFF WITH YOU LOT.
BUT ...!
DON'T YOU FEEL SORRY FOR THE DEMONS!?
BESIDES, IT'S A VIOLATION OF THE—
SELLING DEMONS ISN'T A CRIME BY ANY DEFINITION.

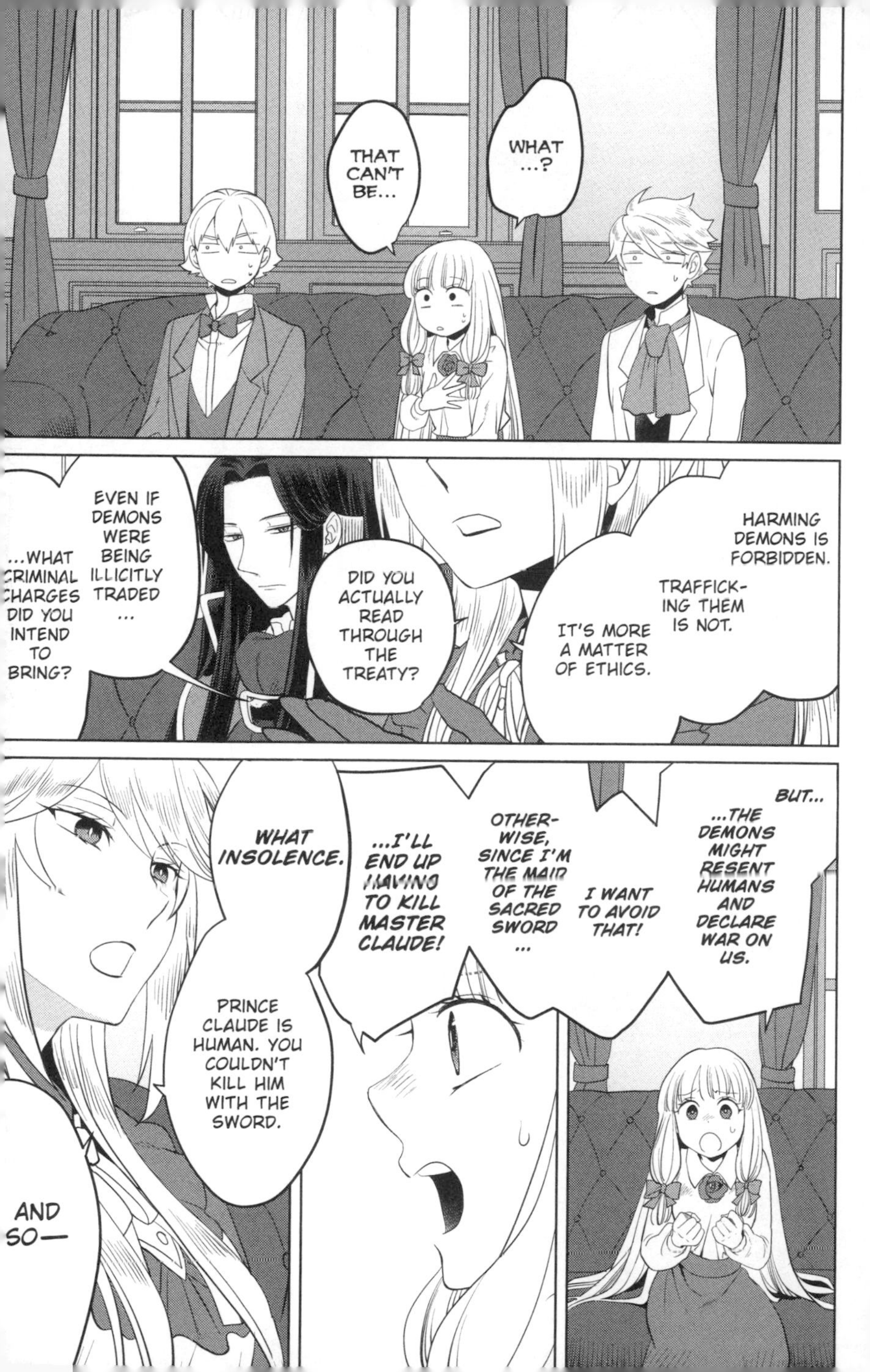
WHAT ...?
THAT CAN'T BE...
HARMING DEMONS IS FORBIDDEN.
TRAFFICKING THEM IS NOT.
IT'S MORE A MATTER OF ETHICS.
DID YOU ACTUALLY READ THROUGH THE TREATY?
EVEN IF DEMONS WERE BEING ILLICITLY TRADED...
...WHAT CRIMINAL CHARGES DID YOU INTEND TO BRING?
BUT...
...THE DEMONS MIGHT RESENT HUMANS AND DECLARE WAR ON US.
I WANT TO AVOID THAT!
OTHERWISE, SINCE I'M THE MAID OF THE SACRED SWORD...
...I'LL END UP HAVING TO KILL MASTER CLAUDE!
WHAT INSOLENCE.
PRINCE CLAUDE IS HUMAN. YOU COULDN'T KILL HIM WITH THE SWORD.
AND SO—

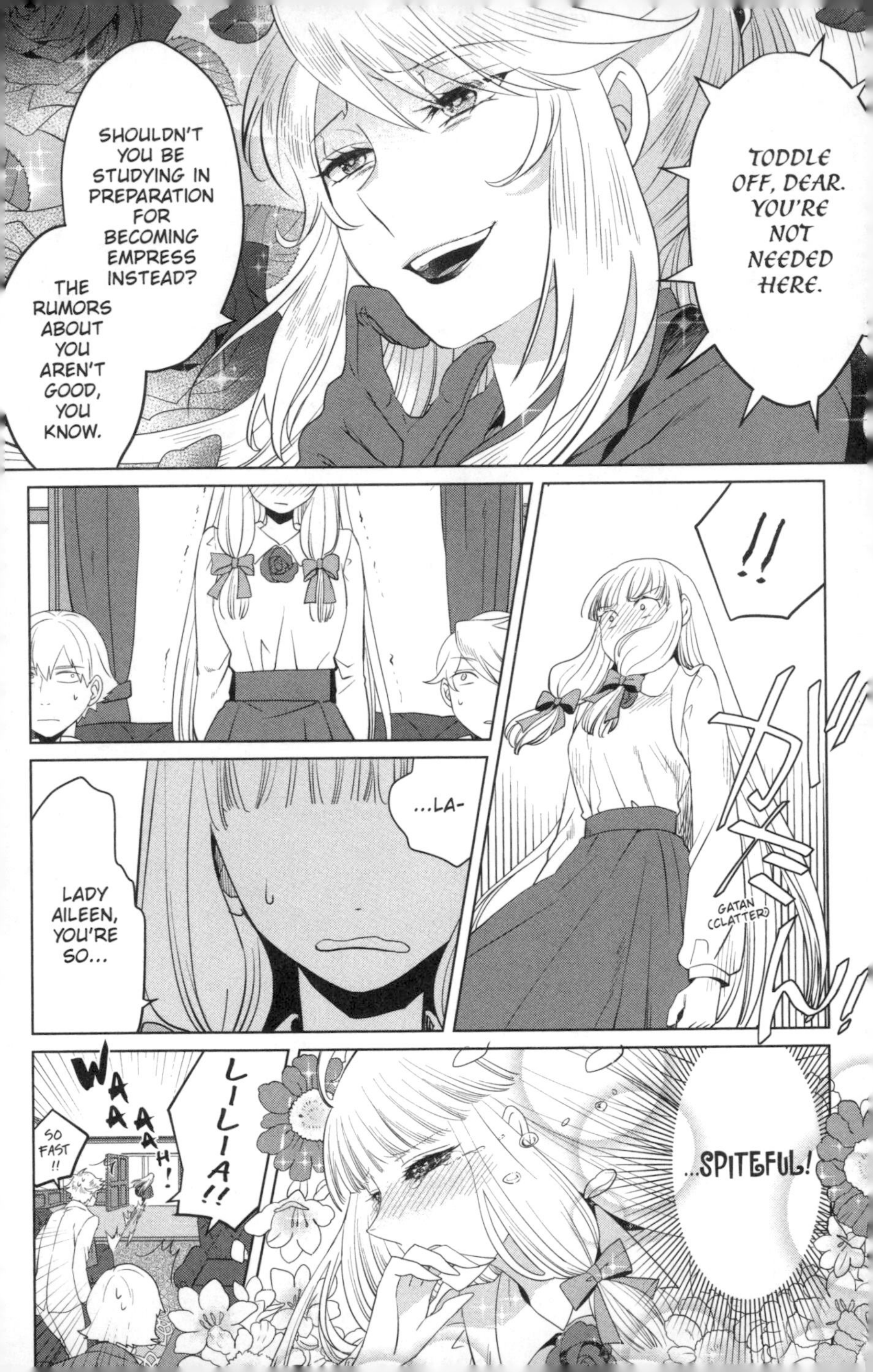
TODDLE OFF, DEAR. YOU'RE NOT NEEDED HERE.
SHOULDN'T YOU BE STUDYING IN PREPARATION FOR BECOMING EMPRESS INSTEAD?
THE RUMORS ABOUT YOU AREN'T GOOD, YOU KNOW.
!!
GATAN (CLATTER)
...LA-
LADY AILEEN, YOU'RE SO...
...SPITEFUL!
LILIA!!
WAAAAH!
SO FAST !!

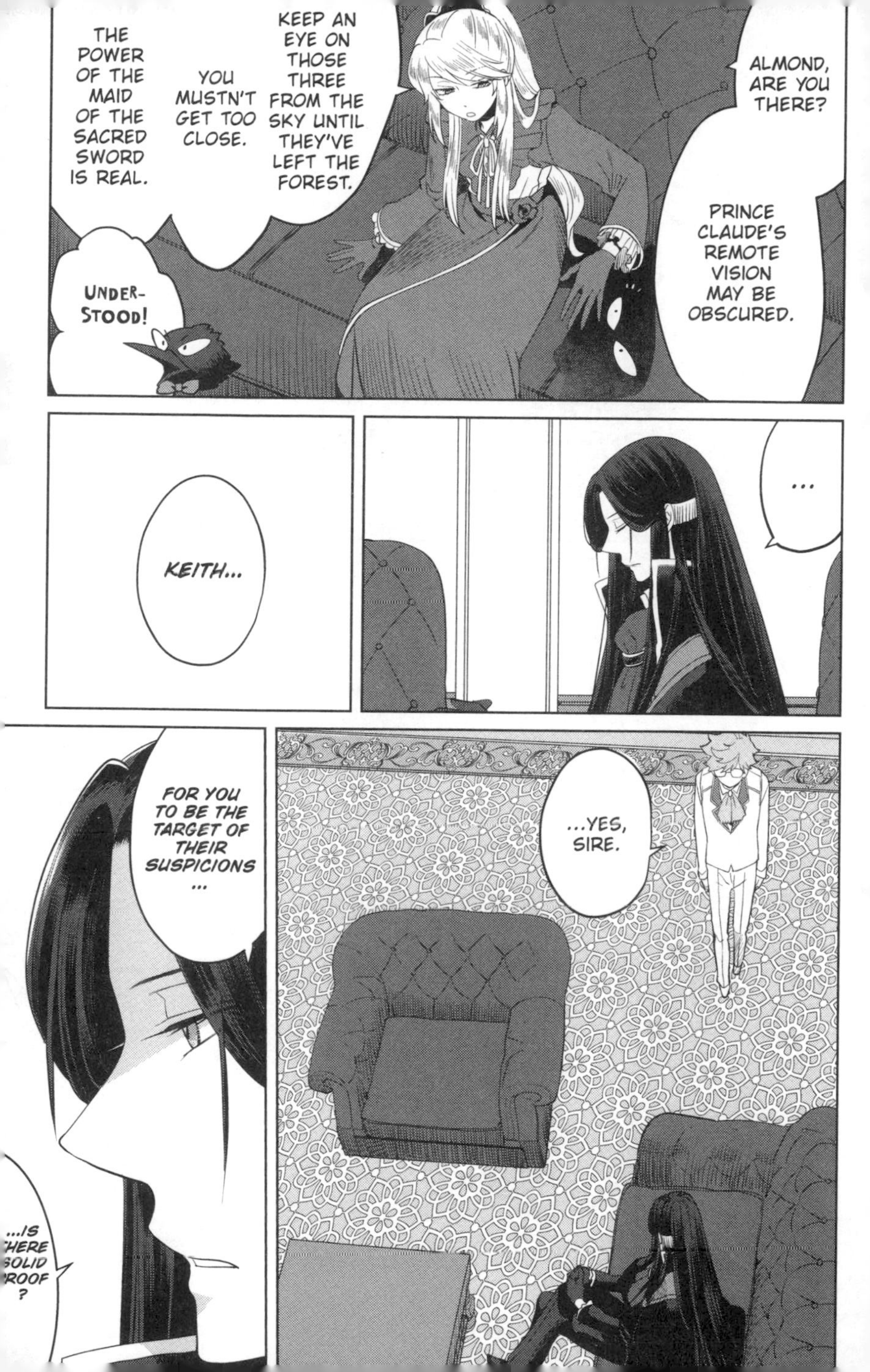
ALMOND, ARE YOU THERE?
PRINCE CLAUDE'S REMOTE VISION MAY BE OBSCURED.
KEEP AN EYE ON THOSE THREE FROM THE SKY UNTIL THEY'VE LEFT THE FOREST.
YOU MUSTN'T GET TOO CLOSE.
THE POWER OF THE MAID OF THE SACRED SWORD IS REAL.
UNDER-STOOD!
...
KEITH...
...YES, SIRE.
FOR YOU TO BE THE TARGET OF THEIR SUSPICIONS ...
...IS THERE SOLID PROOF ?

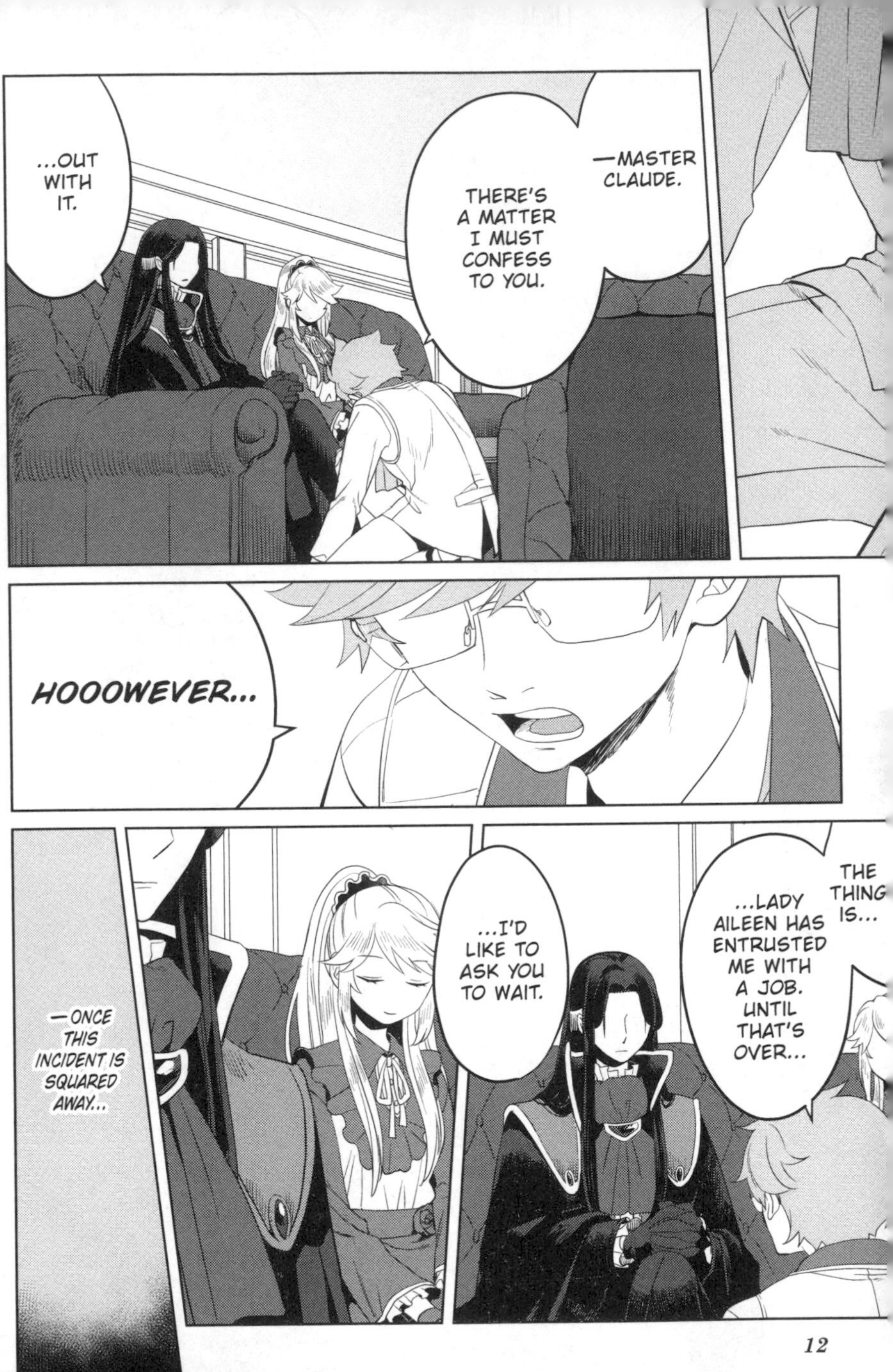
—MASTER CLAUDE.
THERE'S A MATTER I MUST CONFESS TO YOU.
...OUT WITH IT.
HOOOWEVER...
THE THING IS...
...LADY AILEEN HAS ENTRUSTED ME WITH A JOB. UNTIL THAT'S OVER...
...I'D LIKE TO ASK YOU TO WAIT.
—ONCE THIS INCIDENT IS SQUARED AWAY...

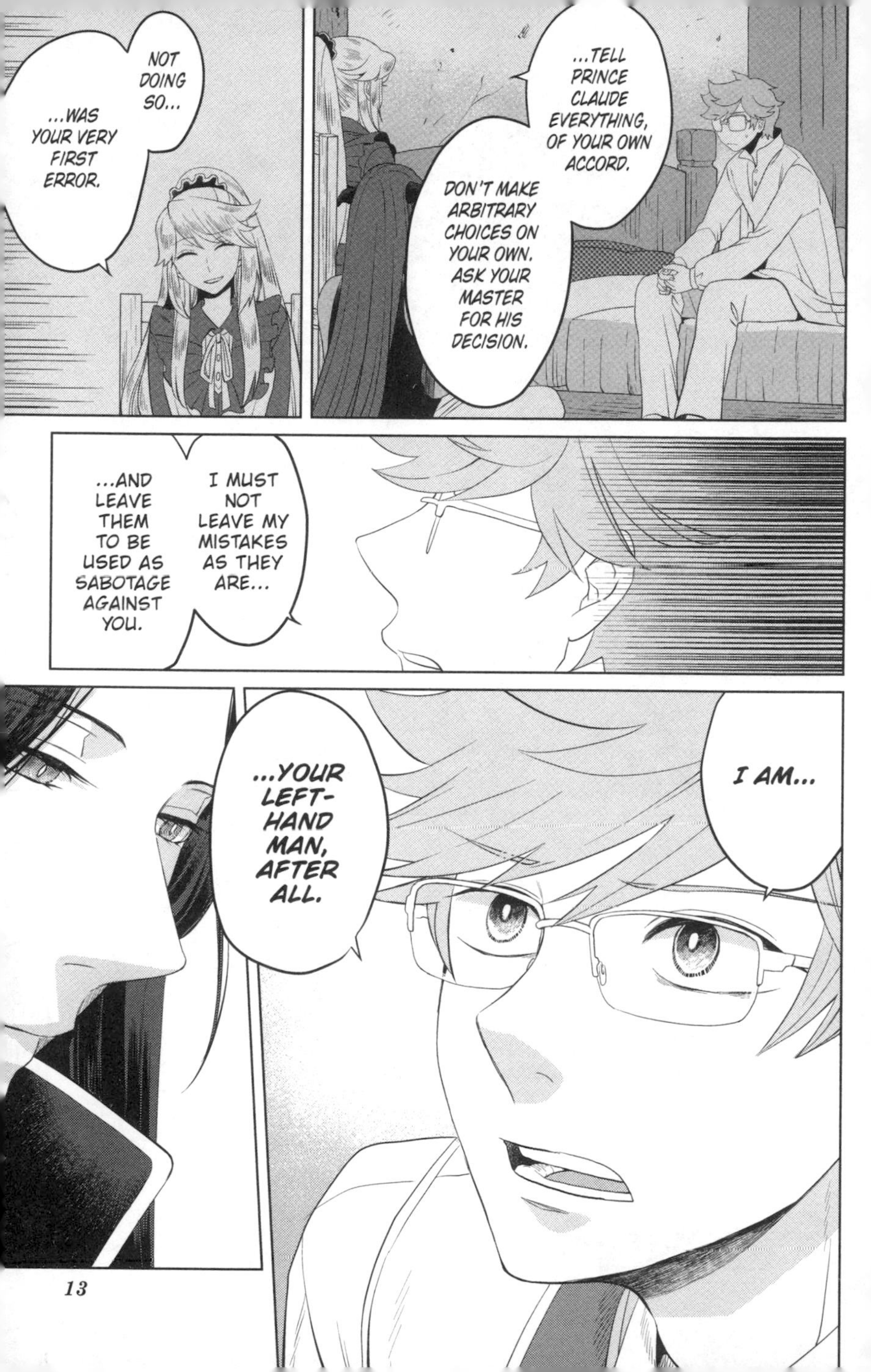
...TELL PRINCE CLAUDE EVERYTHING, OF YOUR OWN ACCORD.
DON'T MAKE ARBITRARY CHOICES ON YOUR OWN. ASK YOUR MASTER FOR HIS DECISION.
NOT DOING SO... ...WAS YOUR VERY FIRST ERROR.
I MUST NOT LEAVE MY MISTAKES AS THEY ARE... ...AND LEAVE THEM TO BE USED AS SABOTAGE AGAINST YOU.
I AM...
...YOUR LEFT-HAND MAN, AFTER ALL.

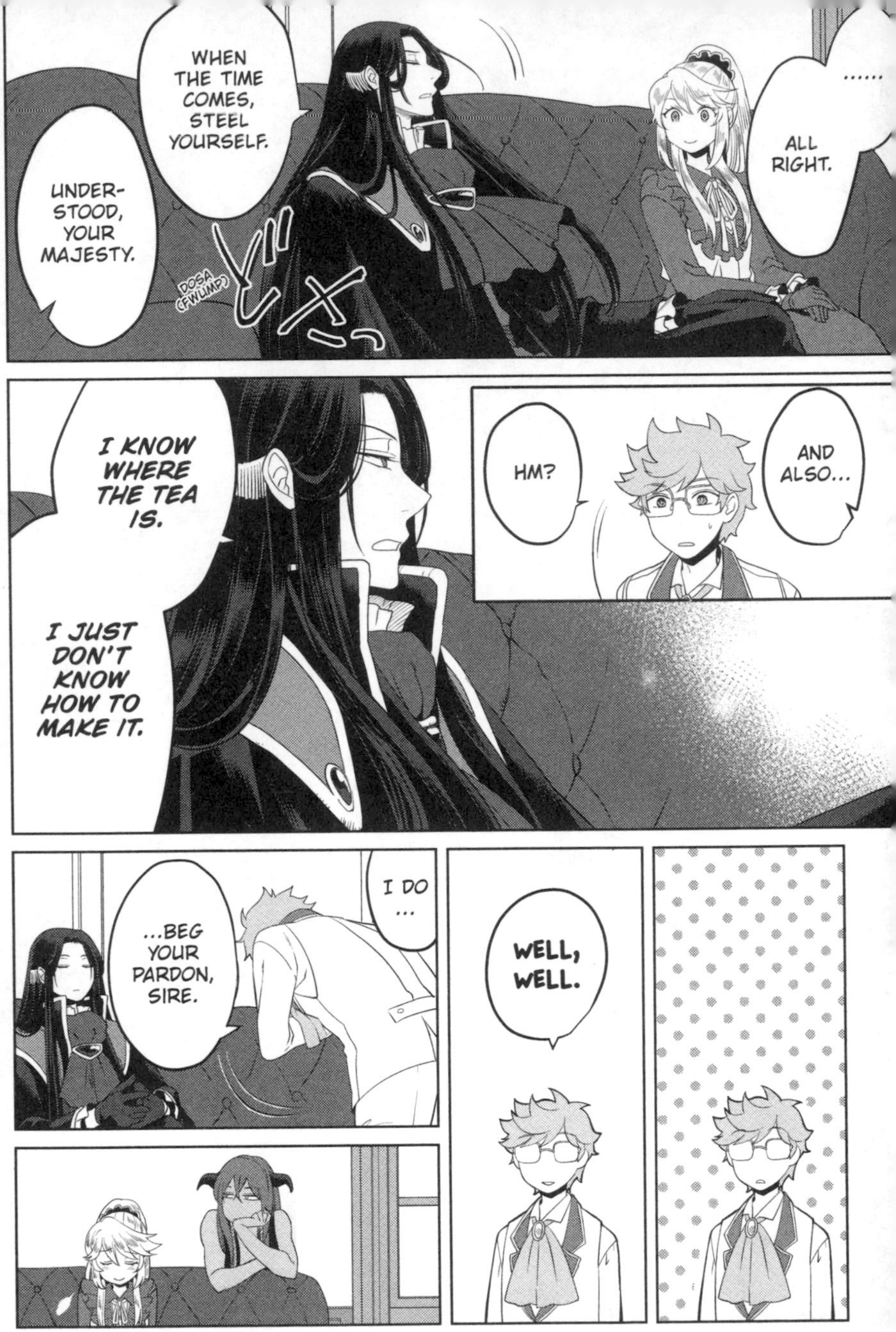
......
ALL RIGHT.
WHEN THE TIME COMES, STEEL YOURSELF.
UNDER-STOOD, YOUR MAJESTY.
DOSA (FWUMP)
AND ALSO...
HM?
I KNOW WHERE THE TEA IS.
I JUST DON'T KNOW HOW TO MAKE IT.
WELL, WELL.
I DO ...
...BEG YOUR PARDON, SIRE.

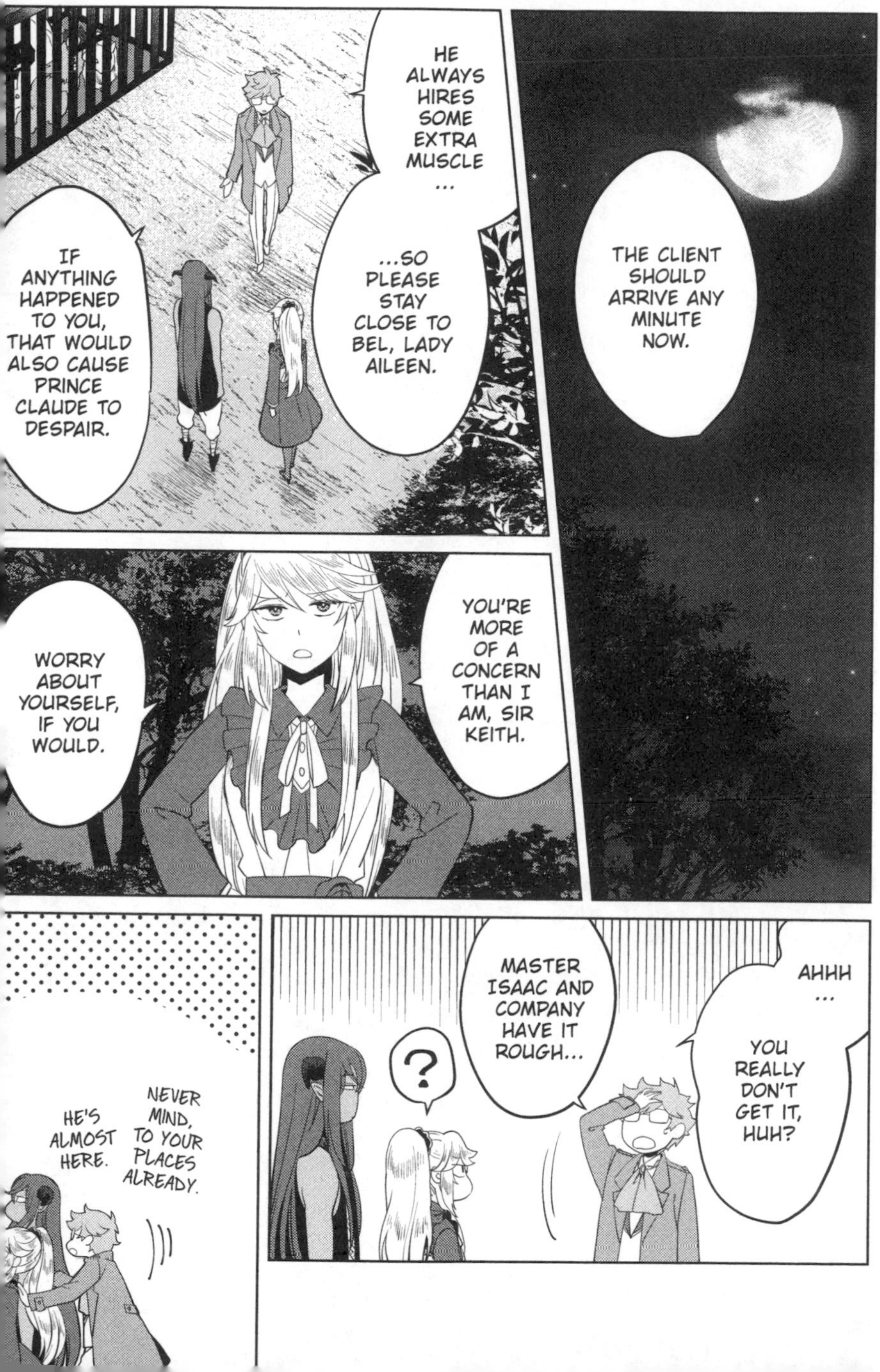
THE CLIENT SHOULD ARRIVE ANY MINUTE NOW.
HE ALWAYS HIRES SOME EXTRA MUSCLE ...
...SO PLEASE STAY CLOSE TO BEL, LADY AILEEN.
IF ANYTHING HAPPENED TO YOU, THAT WOULD ALSO CAUSE PRINCE CLAUDE TO DESPAIR.
YOU'RE MORE OF A CONCERN THAN I AM, SIR KEITH.
WORRY ABOUT YOURSELF, IF YOU WOULD.
AHHH ...
YOU REALLY DON'T GET IT, HUH?
MASTER ISAAC AND COMPANY HAVE IT ROUGH...
?
NEVER MIND, TO YOUR PLACES ALREADY.
HE'S ALMOST HERE.

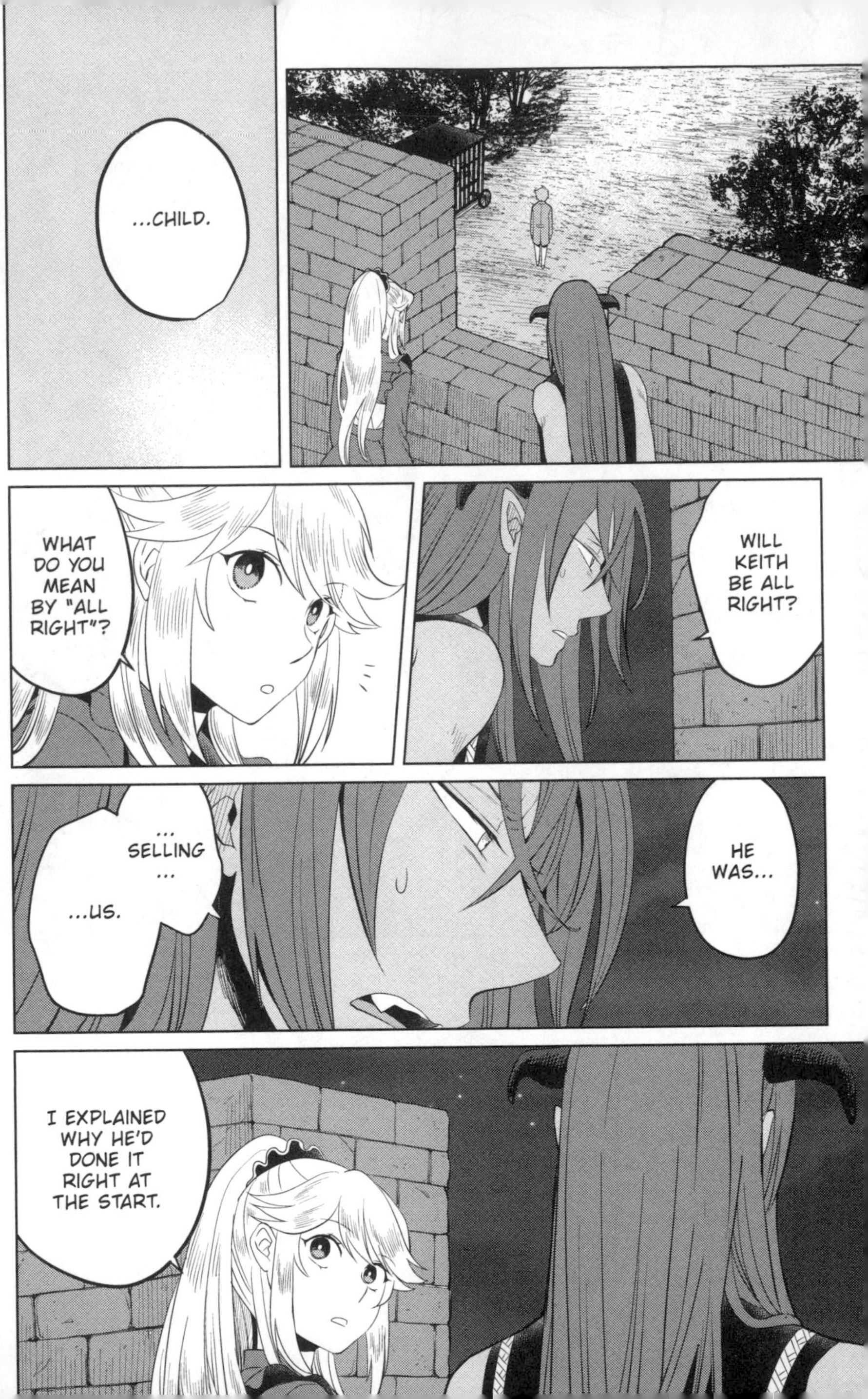
...CHILD.
WILL KEITH BE ALL RIGHT?
WHAT DO YOU MEAN BY "ALL RIGHT"?
HE WAS...
... SELLING ... ...US.
I EXPLAINED WHY HE'D DONE IT RIGHT AT THE START.

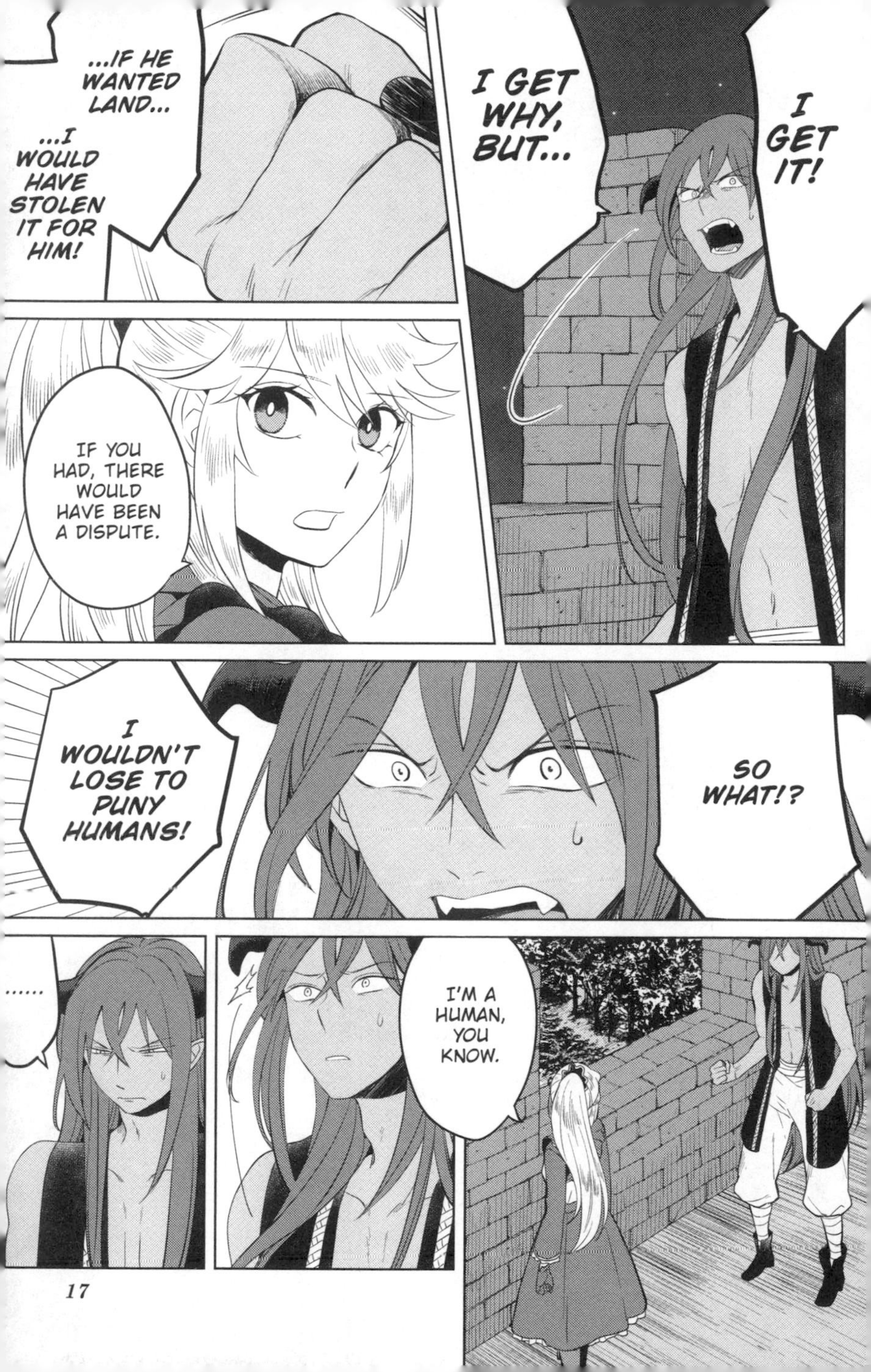
I GET IT!
I GET WHY, BUT...
...IF HE WANTED LAND...
...I WOULD HAVE STOLEN IT FOR HIM!
IF YOU HAD, THERE WOULD HAVE BEEN A DISPUTE.
SO WHAT!?
I WOULDN'T LOSE TO PUNY HUMANS!
I'M A HUMAN, YOU KNOW.
......

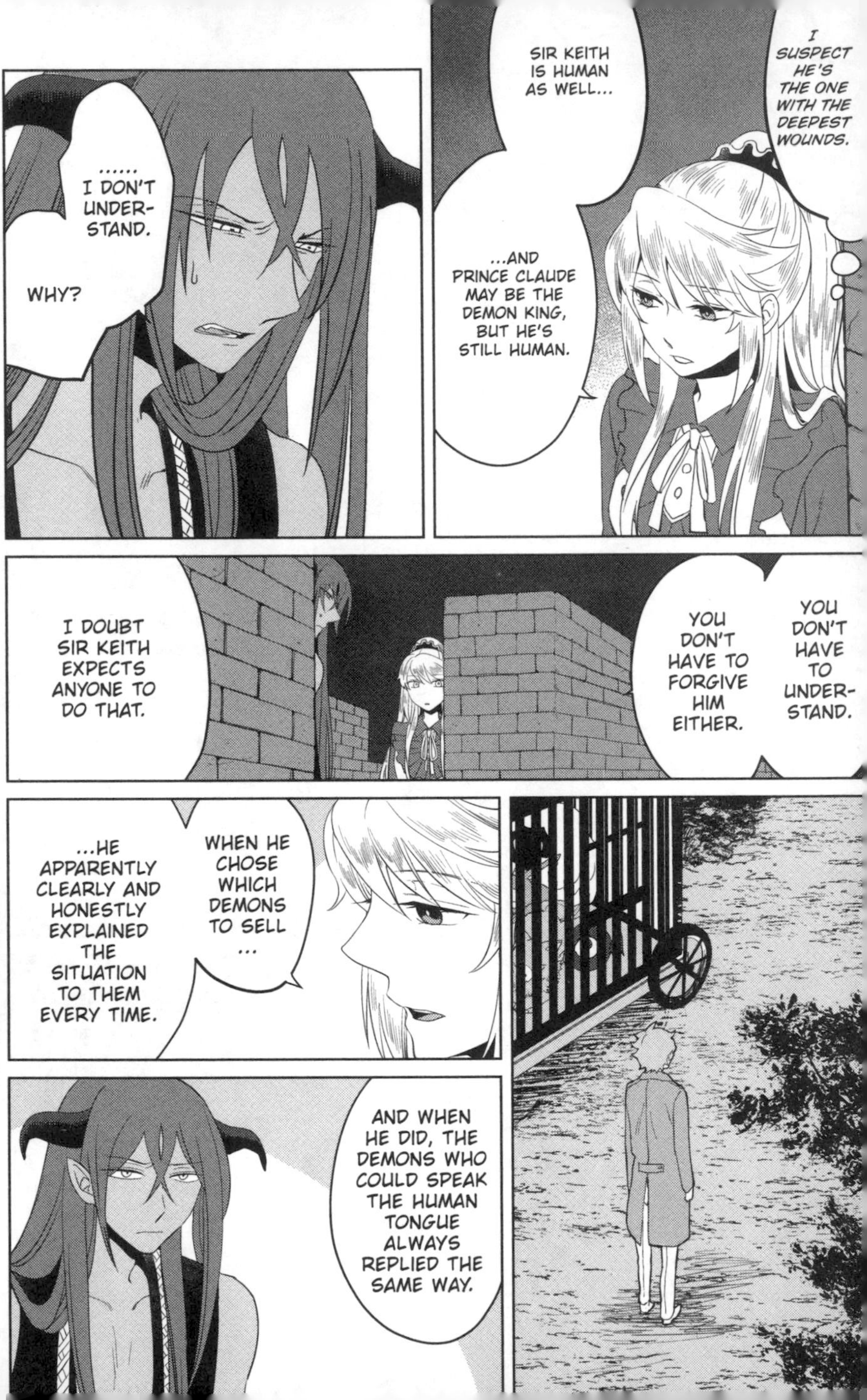
I SUSPECT HE'S THE ONE WITH THE DEEPEST WOUNDS.
SIR KEITH IS HUMAN AS WELL...
...AND PRINCE CLAUDE MAY BE THE DEMON KING, BUT HE'S STILL HUMAN.
...... I DON'T UNDER-STAND.
WHY?
YOU DON'T HAVE TO UNDER-STAND.
YOU DON'T HAVE TO FORGIVE HIM EITHER.
I DOUBT SIR KEITH EXPECTS ANYONE TO DO THAT.
WHEN HE CHOSE WHICH DEMONS TO SELL...
...HE APPARENTLY CLEARLY AND HONESTLY EXPLAINED THE SITUATION TO THEM EVERY TIME.
AND WHEN HE DID, THE DEMONS WHO COULD SPEAK THE HUMAN TONGUE ALWAYS REPLIED THE SAME WAY.

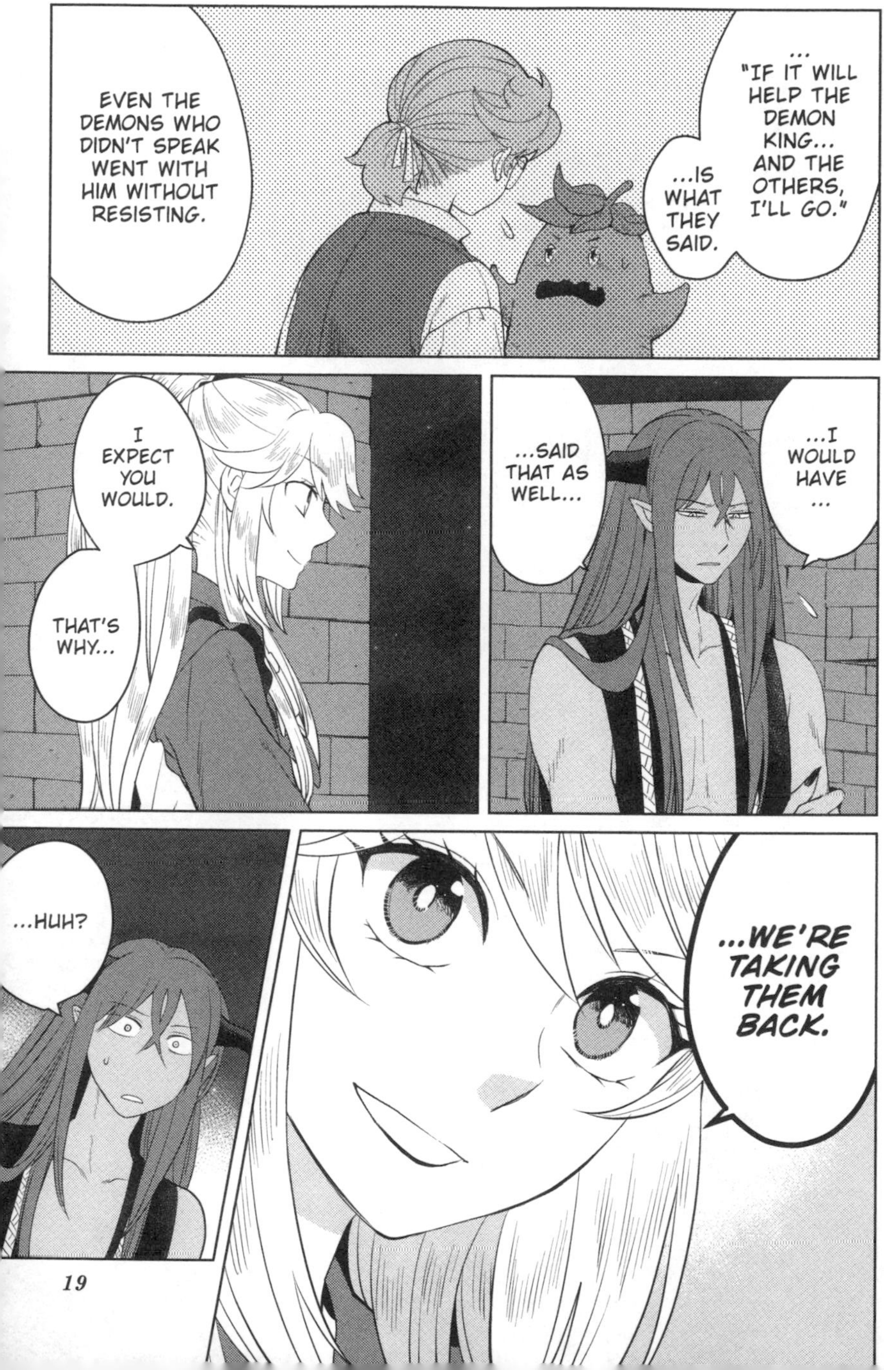
... "IF IT WILL HELP THE DEMON KING... AND THE OTHERS, I'LL GO."
...IS WHAT THEY SAID.
EVEN THE DEMONS WHO DIDN'T SPEAK WENT WITH HIM WITHOUT RESISTING.
...I WOULD HAVE ...
...SAID THAT AS WELL...
I EXPECT YOU WOULD.
THAT'S WHY...
...WE'RE TAKING THEM BACK.
...HUH?

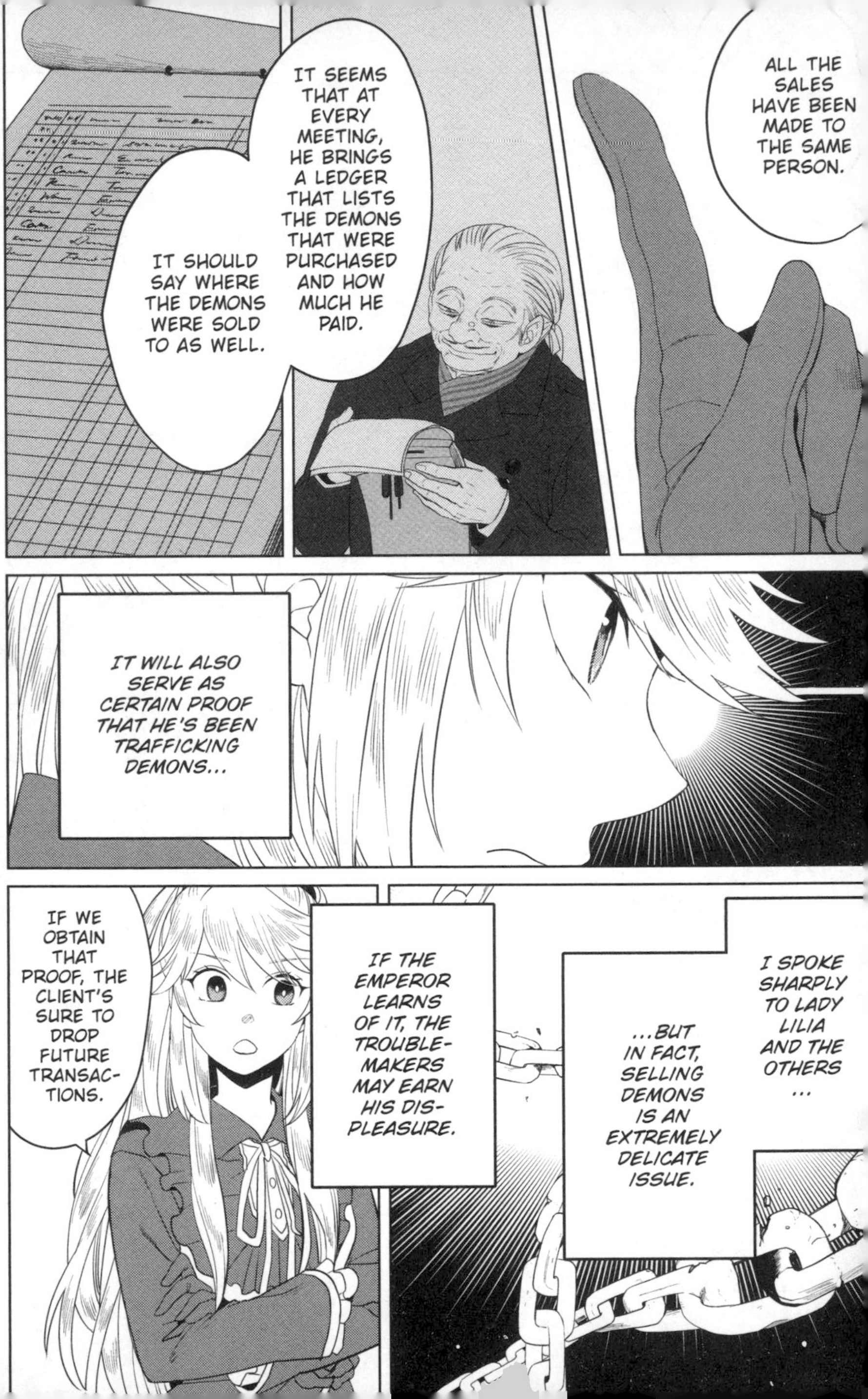
ALL THE SALES HAVE BEEN MADE TO THE SAME PERSON.
IT SEEMS THAT AT EVERY MEETING, HE BRINGS A LEDGER THAT LISTS THE DEMONS THAT WERE PURCHASED AND HOW MUCH HE PAID.
IT SHOULD SAY WHERE THE DEMONS WERE SOLD TO AS WELL.
IT WILL ALSO SERVE AS CERTAIN PROOF THAT HE'S BEEN TRAFFICKING DEMONS...
I SPOKE SHARPLY TO LADY LILIA AND THE OTHERS ...
...BUT IN FACT, SELLING DEMONS IS AN EXTREMELY DELICATE ISSUE.
IF THE EMPEROR LEARNS OF IT, THE TROUBLE-MAKERS MAY EARN HIS DIS-PLEASURE.
IF WE OBTAIN THAT PROOF, THE CLIENT'S SURE TO DROP FUTURE TRANSAC-TIONS.

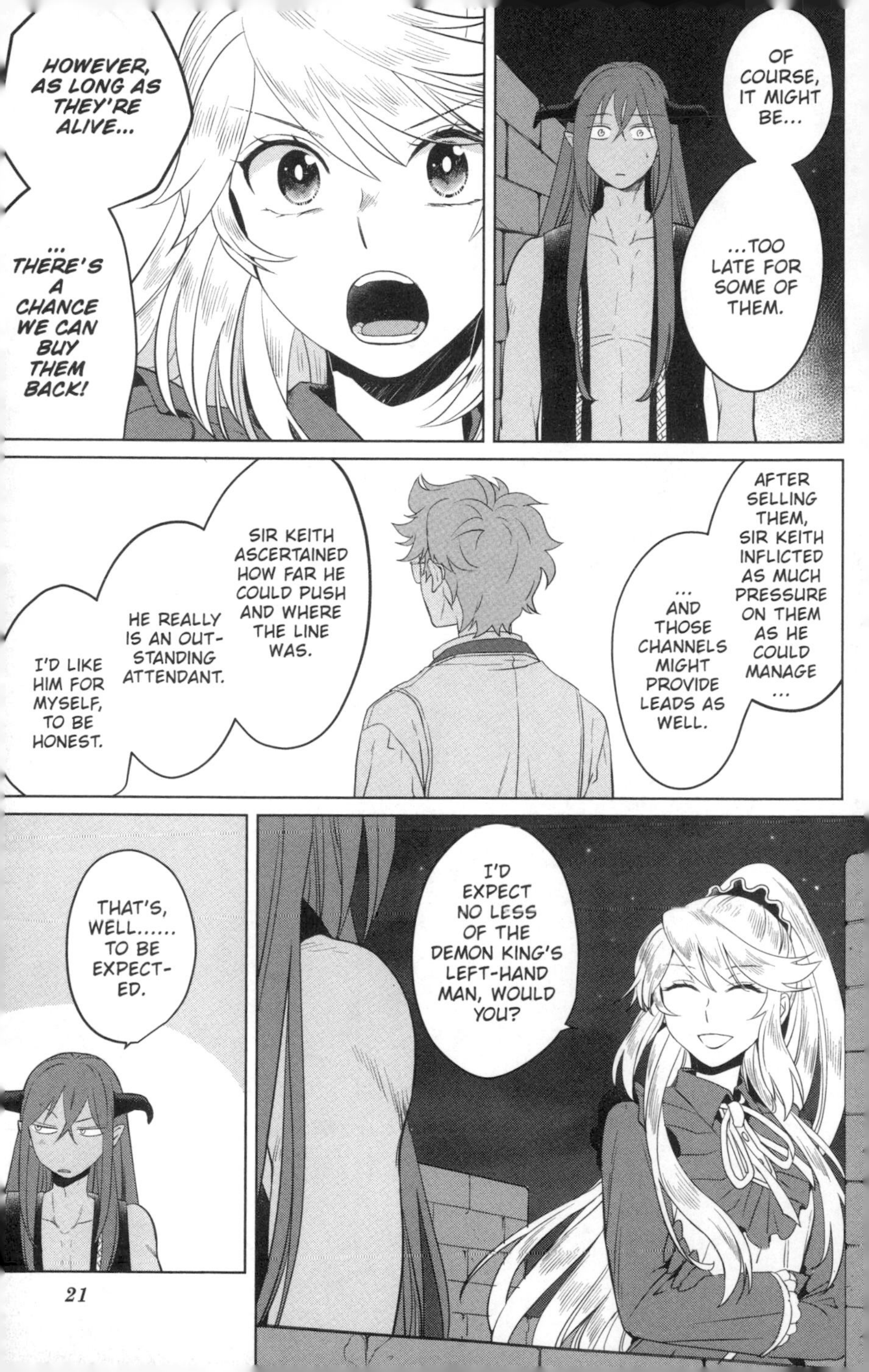
OF COURSE, IT MIGHT BE...
...TOO LATE FOR SOME OF THEM.
HOWEVER, AS LONG AS THEY'RE ALIVE...
...THERE'S A CHANCE WE CAN BUY THEM BACK!
AFTER SELLING THEM, SIR KEITH INFLICTED AS MUCH PRESSURE ON THEM AS HE COULD MANAGE...
...AND THOSE CHANNELS MIGHT PROVIDE LEADS AS WELL.
SIR KEITH ASCERTAINED HOW FAR HE COULD PUSH AND WHERE THE LINE WAS.
HE REALLY IS AN OUT-STANDING ATTENDANT.
I'D LIKE HIM FOR MYSELF, TO BE HONEST.
I'D EXPECT NO LESS OF THE DEMON KING'S LEFT-HAND MAN, WOULD YOU?
THAT'S, WELL...... TO BE EXPECT-ED.

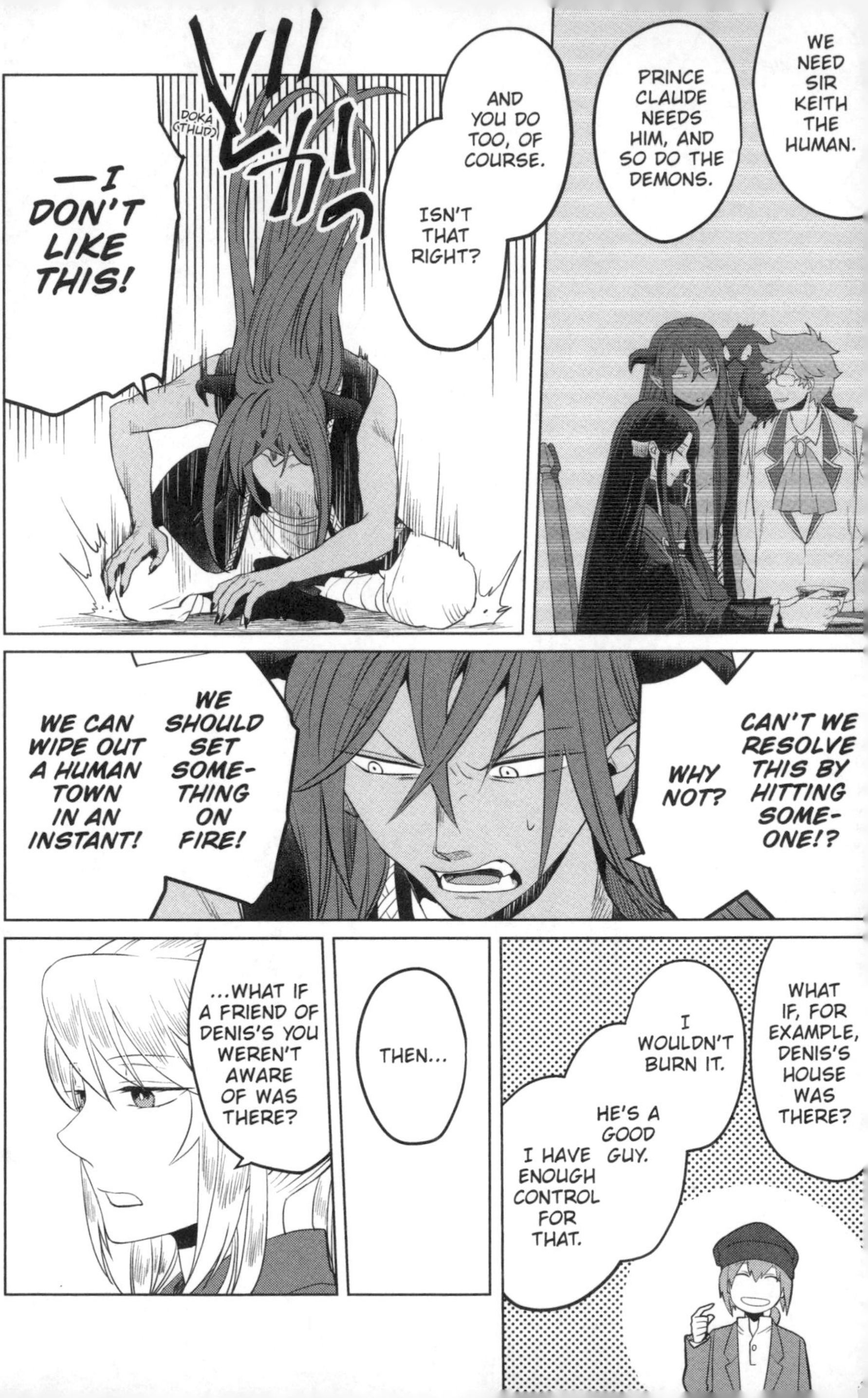
WE NEED SIR KEITH THE HUMAN.
PRINCE CLAUDE NEEDS HIM, AND SO DO THE DEMONS.
AND YOU DO TOO, OF COURSE.
ISN'T THAT RIGHT?
DOKA (THUD)
—I DON'T LIKE THIS!
CAN'T WE RESOLVE THIS BY HITTING SOME-ONE!?
WHY NOT?
WE SHOULD SET SOME-THING ON FIRE!
WE CAN WIPE OUT A HUMAN TOWN IN AN INSTANT!
WHAT IF, FOR EXAMPLE, DENIS'S HOUSE WAS THERE?
I WOULDN'T BURN IT.
HE'S A GOOD GUY.
I HAVE ENOUGH CONTROL FOR THAT.
THEN...
...WHAT IF A FRIEND OF DENIS'S YOU WEREN'T AWARE OF WAS THERE?

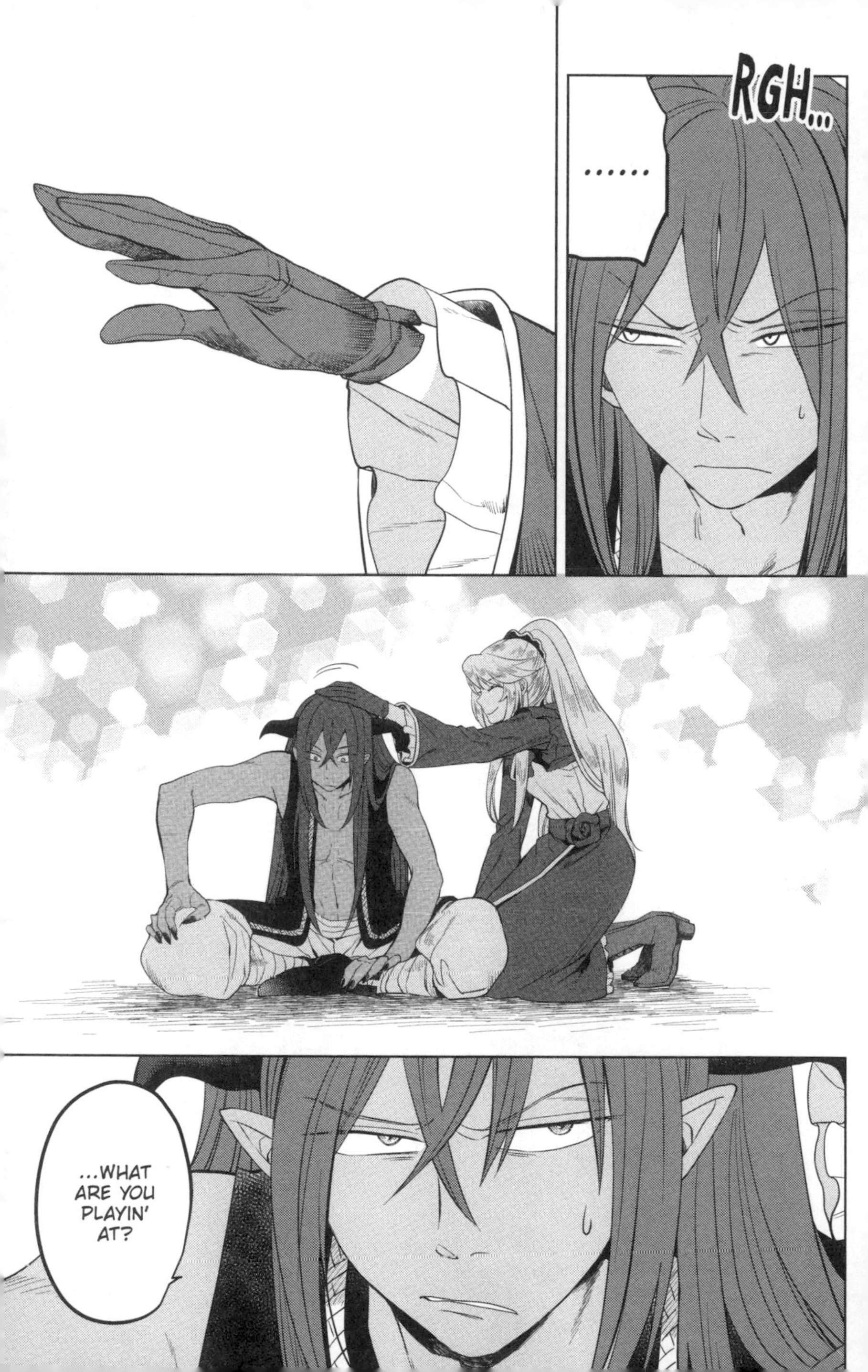
RGH...
......
...WHAT ARE YOU PLAYIN' AT?

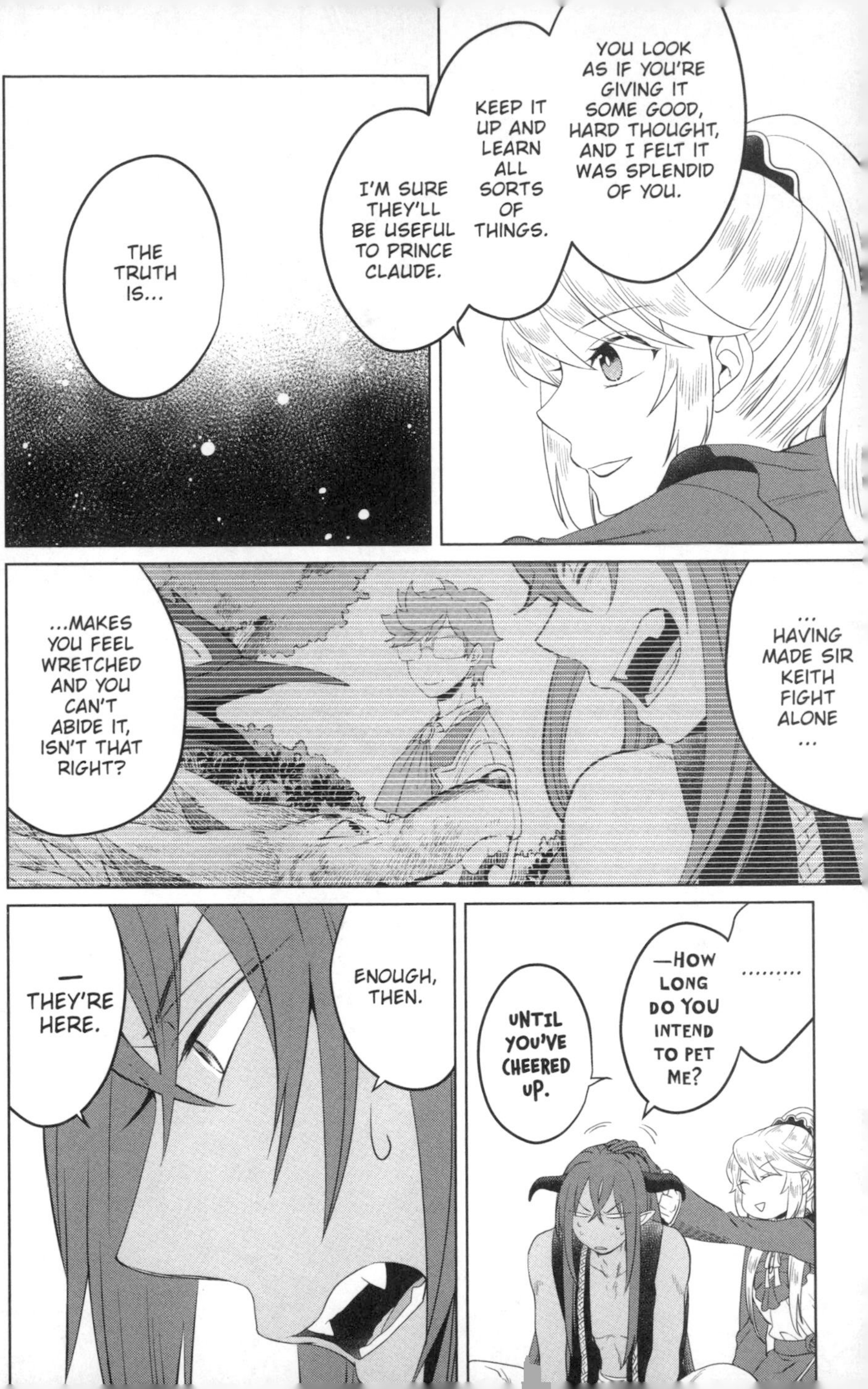
YOU LOOK AS IF YOU'RE GIVING IT SOME GOOD, HARD THOUGHT, AND I FELT IT WAS SPLENDID OF YOU.
KEEP IT UP AND LEARN ALL SORTS OF THINGS.
I'M SURE THEY'LL BE USEFUL TO PRINCE CLAUDE.
THE TRUTH IS...
...HAVING MADE SIR KEITH FIGHT ALONE...
...MAKES YOU FEEL WRETCHED AND YOU CAN'T ABIDE IT, ISN'T THAT RIGHT?
....
—HOW LONG DO YOU INTEND TO PET ME?
UNTIL YOU'VE CHEERED UP.
ENOUGH, THEN.
—THEY'RE HERE.

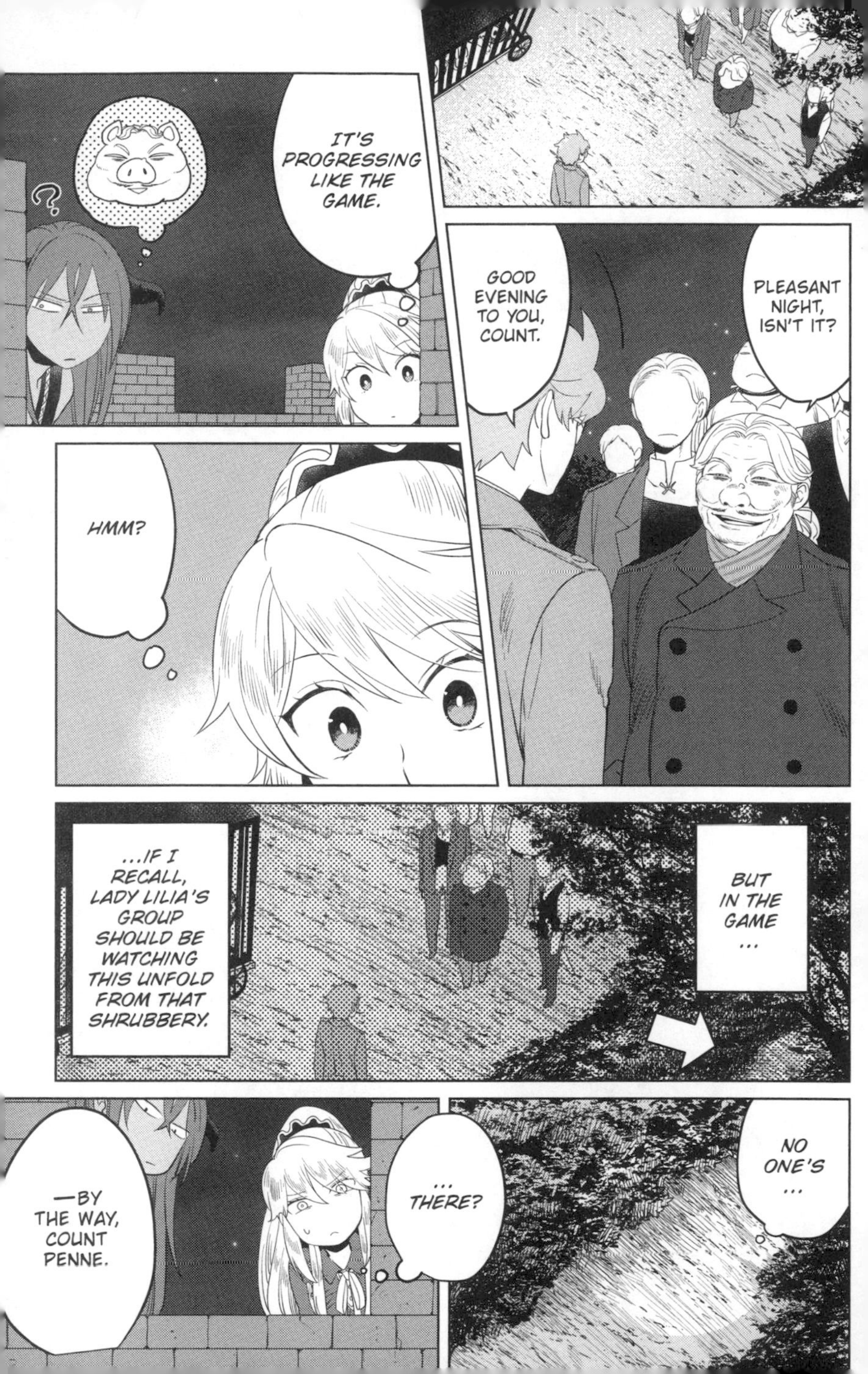
IT'S PROGRESSING LIKE THE GAME.
PLEASANT NIGHT, ISN'T IT?
GOOD EVENING TO YOU, COUNT.
HMM?
BUT IN THE GAME...
...IF I RECALL, LADY LILIA'S GROUP SHOULD BE WATCHING THIS UNFOLD FROM THAT SHRUBBERY.
NO ONE'S...
...THERE?
—BY THE WAY, COUNT PENNE.

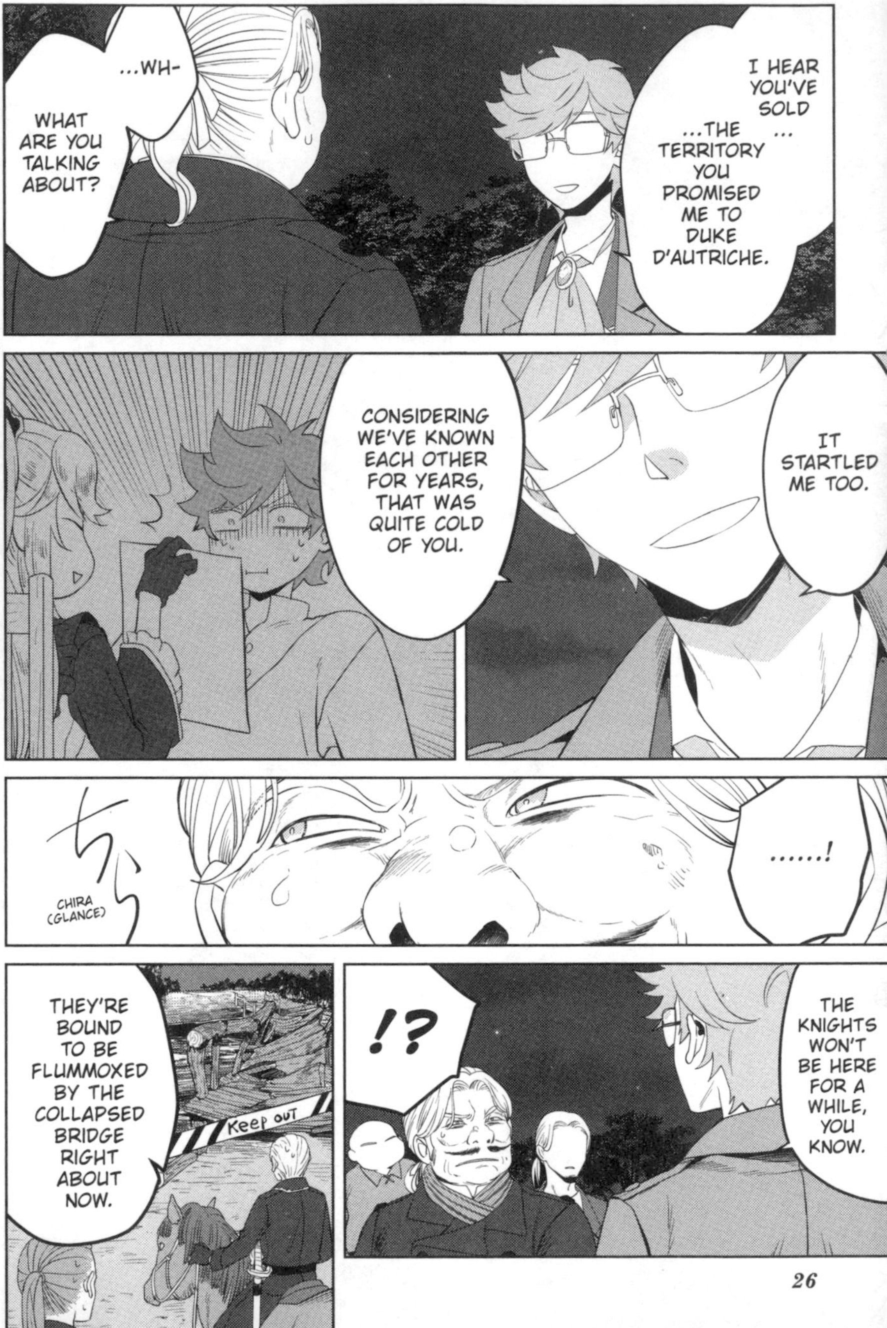
I HEAR YOU'VE SOLD ...
...THE TERRITORY YOU PROMISED ME TO DUKE D'AUTRICHE.
...WH-
WHAT ARE YOU TALKING ABOUT?
IT STARTLED ME TOO.
CONSIDERING WE'VE KNOWN EACH OTHER FOR YEARS, THAT WAS QUITE COLD OF YOU.
......!
CHIRA (GLANCE)
THE KNIGHTS WON'T BE HERE FOR A WHILE, YOU KNOW.
!?
THEY'RE BOUND TO BE FLUMMOXED BY THE COLLAPSED BRIDGE RIGHT ABOUT NOW.
Keep out

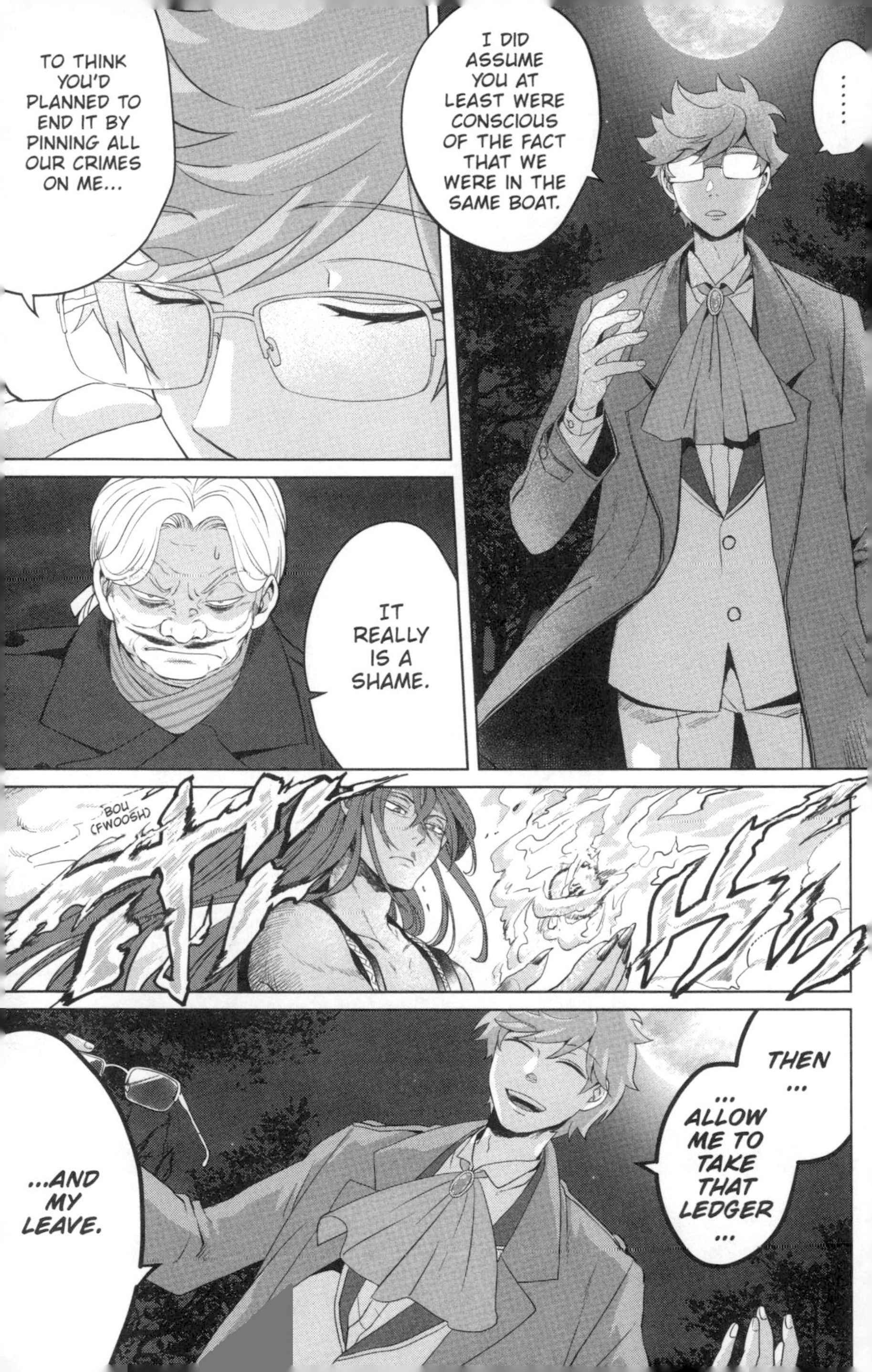
......
I DID ASSUME YOU AT LEAST WERE CONSCIOUS OF THE FACT THAT WE WERE IN THE SAME BOAT.
TO THINK YOU'D PLANNED TO END IT BY PINNING ALL OUR CRIMES ON ME...
IT REALLY IS A SHAME.
BOU (FWOOSH)
THEN... ...ALLOW ME TO TAKE THAT LEDGER...
...AND MY LEAVE.

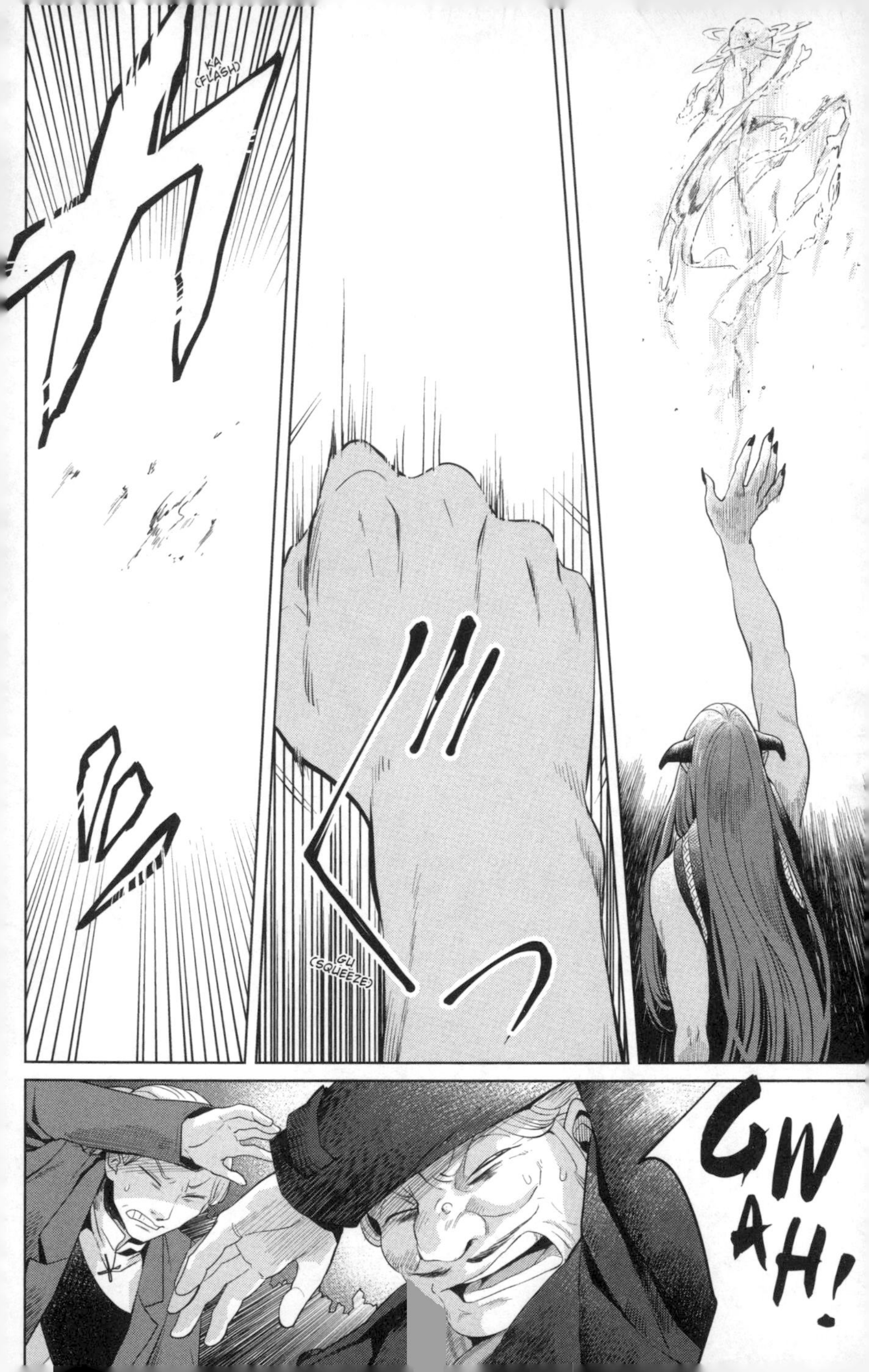
GU
(SQUEEZE)
KA
(FLASH)
GWAH!

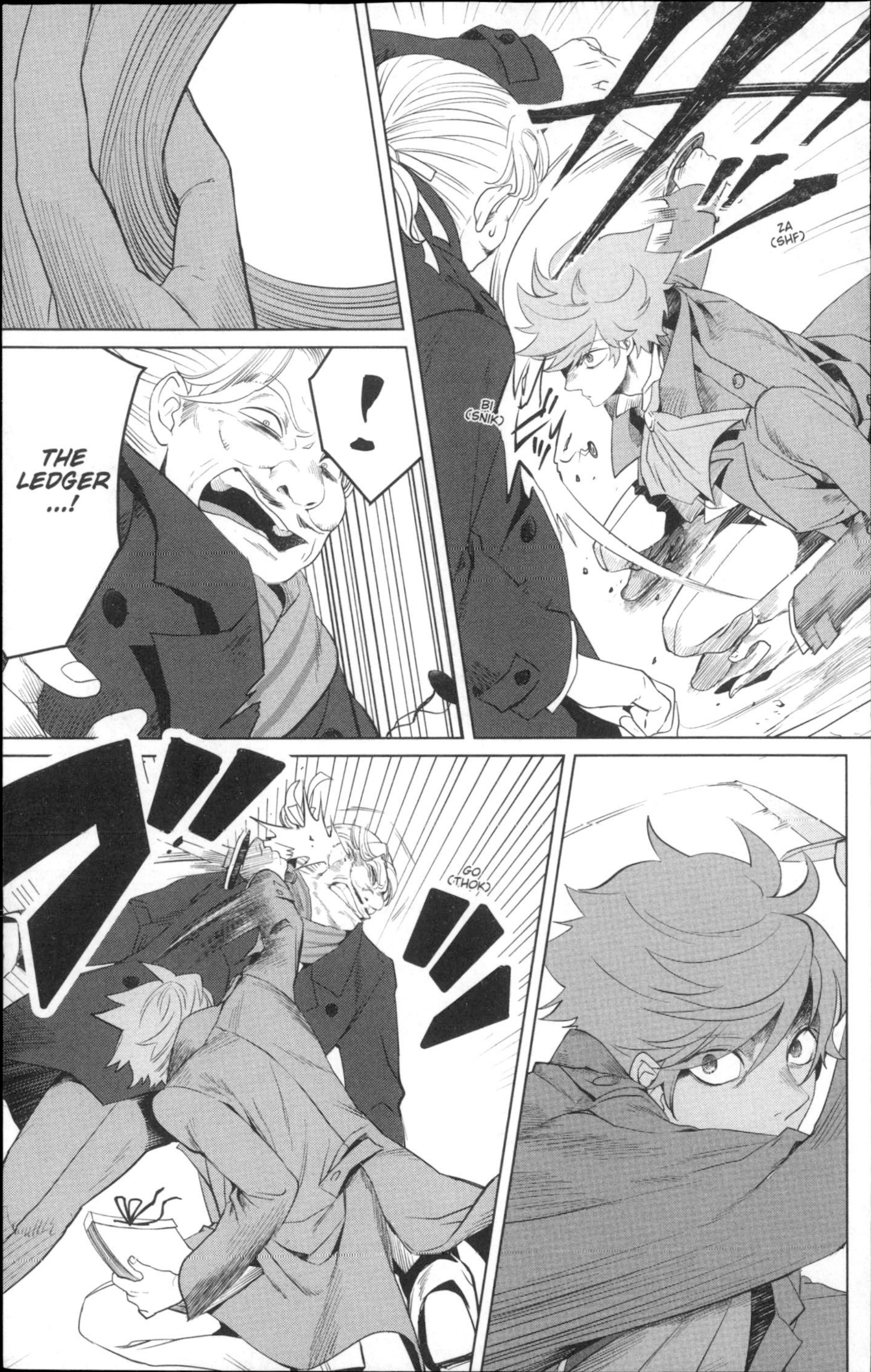
ZA
(SHF)
BI
(SNIK)
!
THE LEDGER ...!
GO
(THOK)

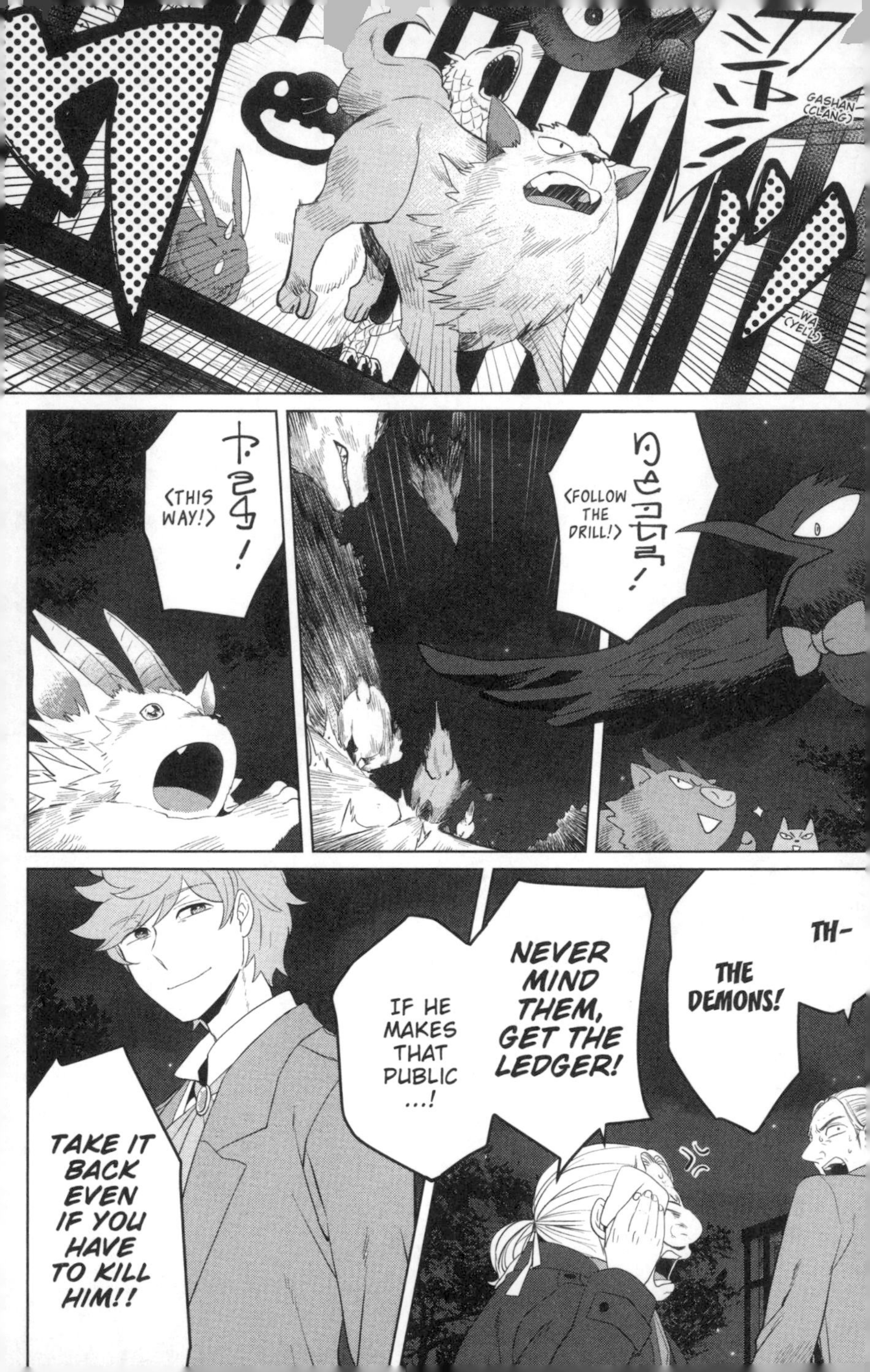
GASHAN (CLANG)
WA (YELL)
<FOLLOW THE DRILL!>
<THIS WAY!>
TH- THE DEMONS!
NEVER MIND THEM, GET THE LEDGER!
IF HE MAKES THAT PUBLIC ...!
TAKE IT BACK EVEN IF YOU HAVE TO KILL HIM!!

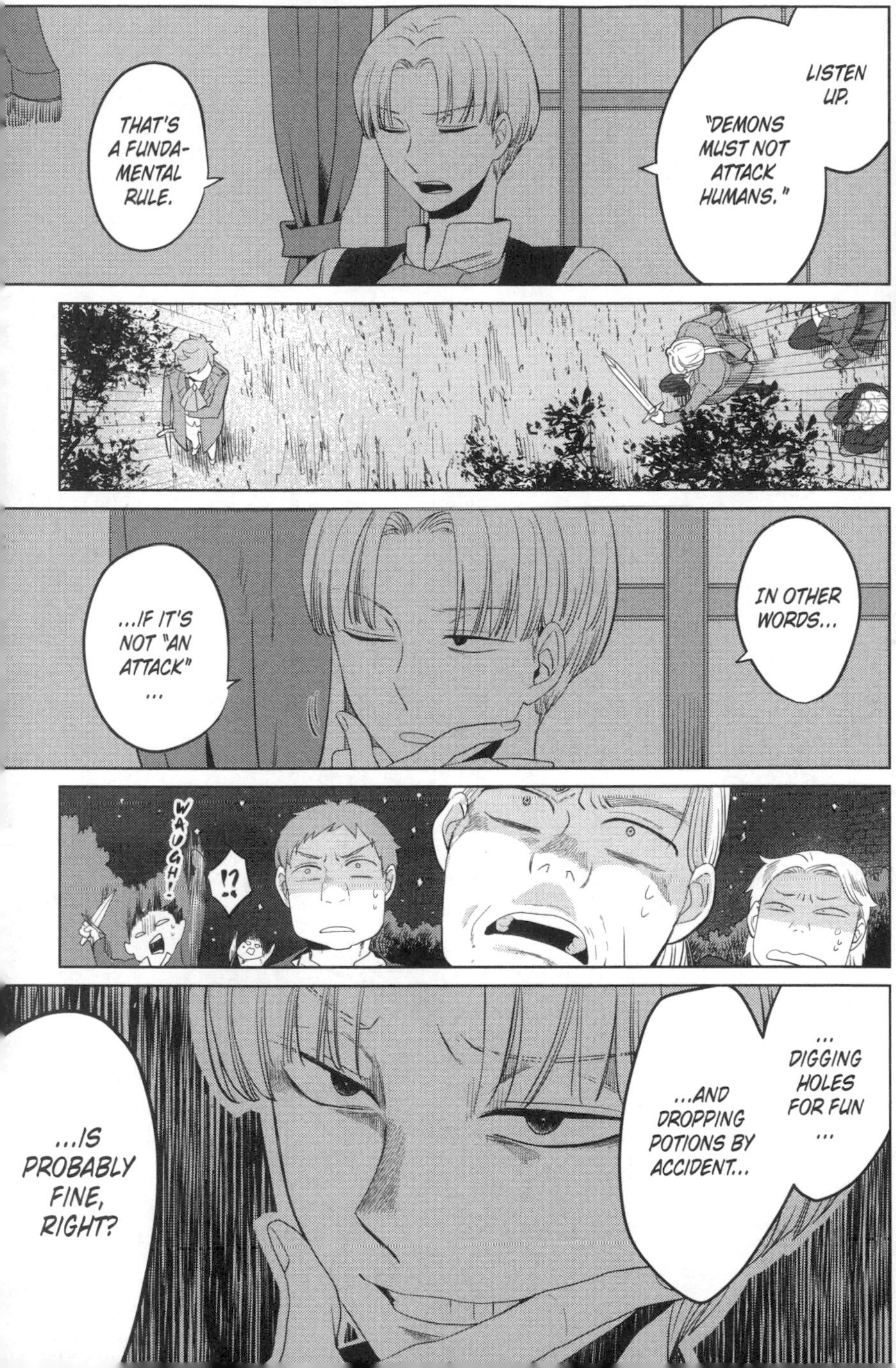
LISTEN UP.
"DEMONS MUST NOT ATTACK HUMANS."
THAT'S A FUNDA-MENTAL RULE.
IN OTHER WORDS...
...IF IT'S NOT "AN ATTACK" ...
!?
WAUGH!
... DIGGING HOLES FOR FUN ...
...AND DROPPING POTIONS BY ACCIDENT...
...IS PROBABLY FINE, RIGHT?

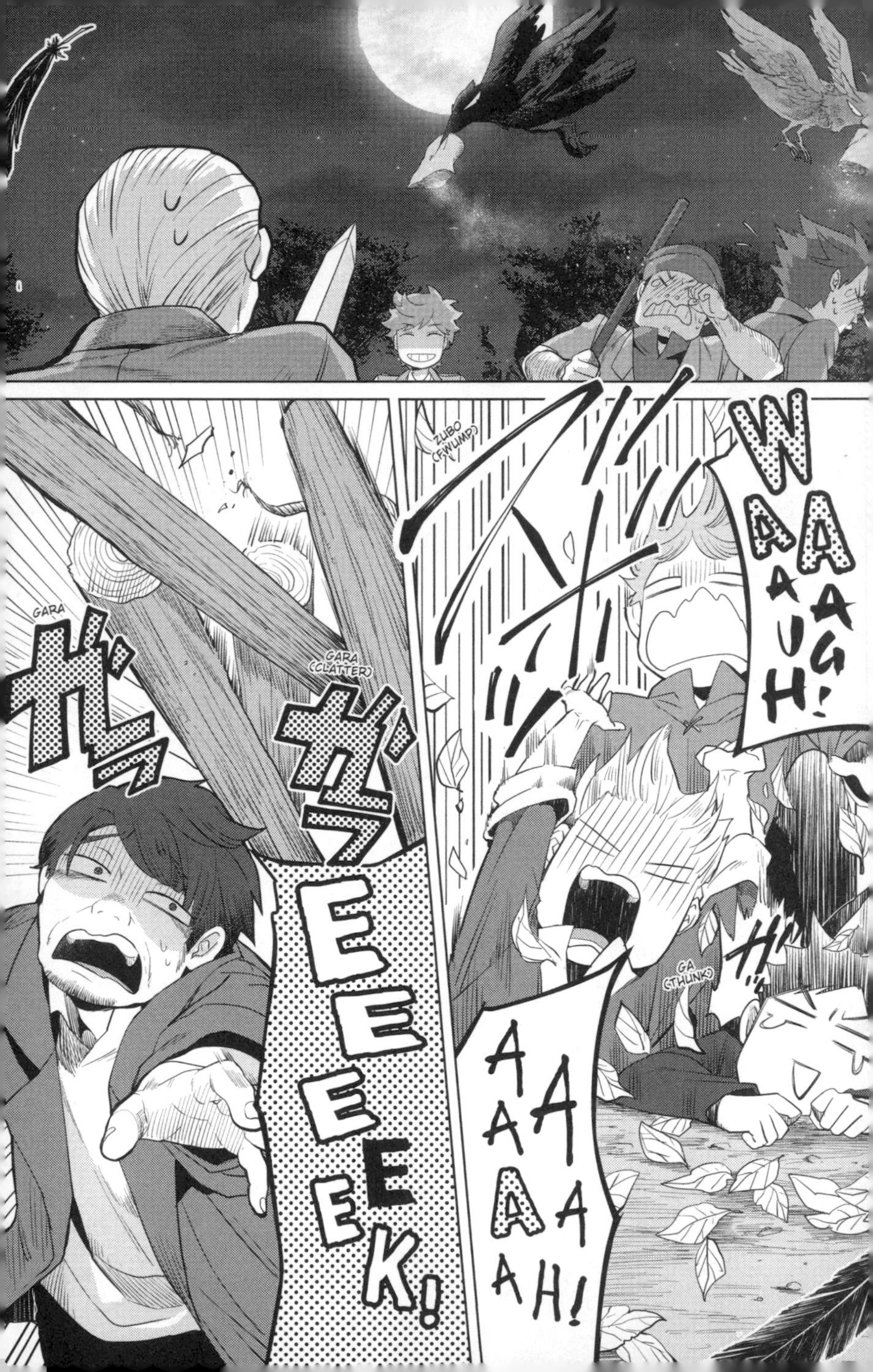
ZUBO (FWUMP)
WAAAAUGH!
GA (THUNK)
H!
AAAAAAAH!
GARA (CLATTER)
ガラ
GARA
ガラッ
EEEEEK!

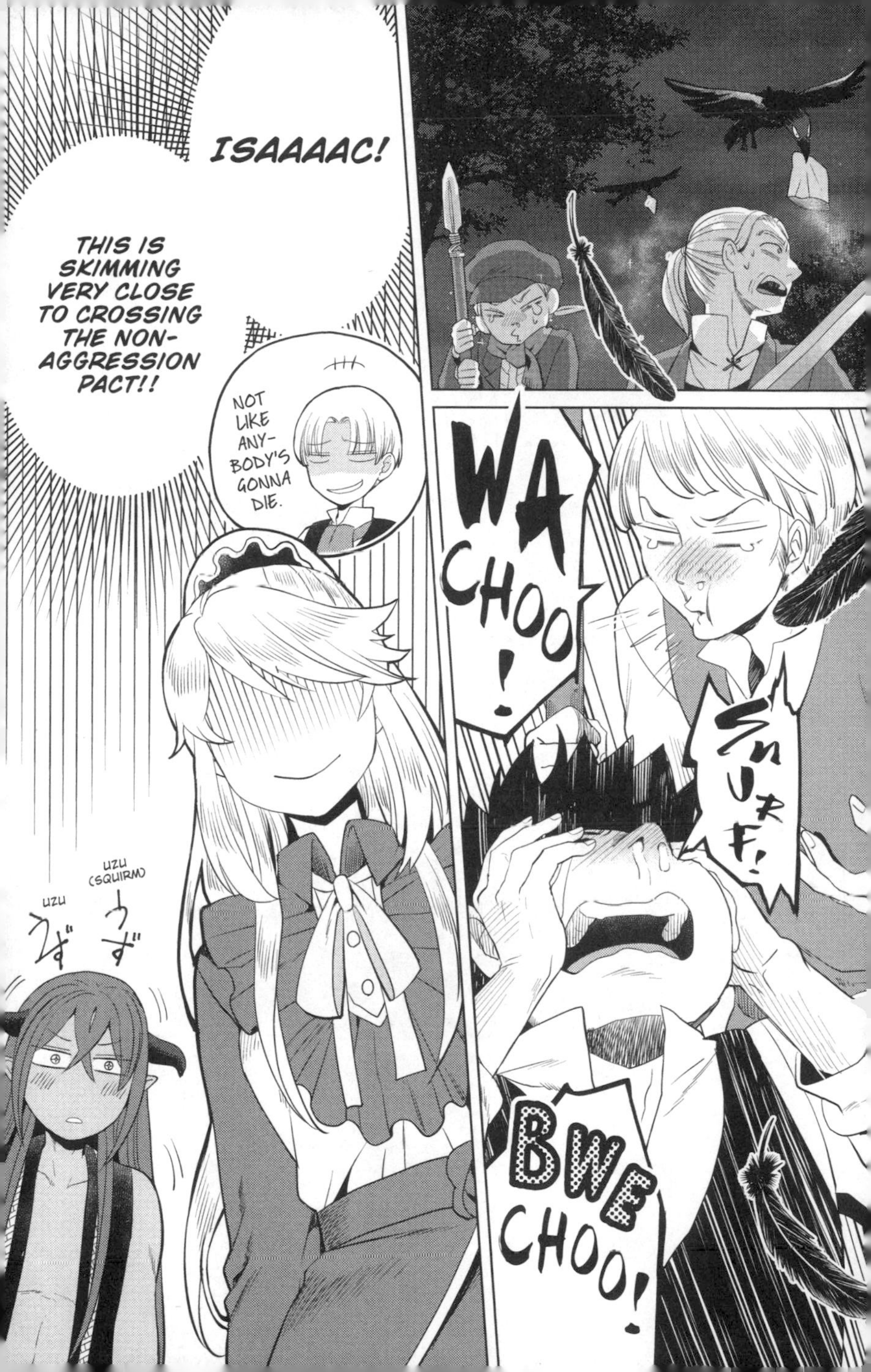
WA CHOO!
SNURF!
BWE CHOO!
ISAAAAC!
THIS IS SKIMMING VERY CLOSE TO CROSSING THE NON-AGGRESSION PACT!!
NOT LIKE ANY-BODY'S GONNA DIE.
UZU (SQUIRM)
UZU
うず うず

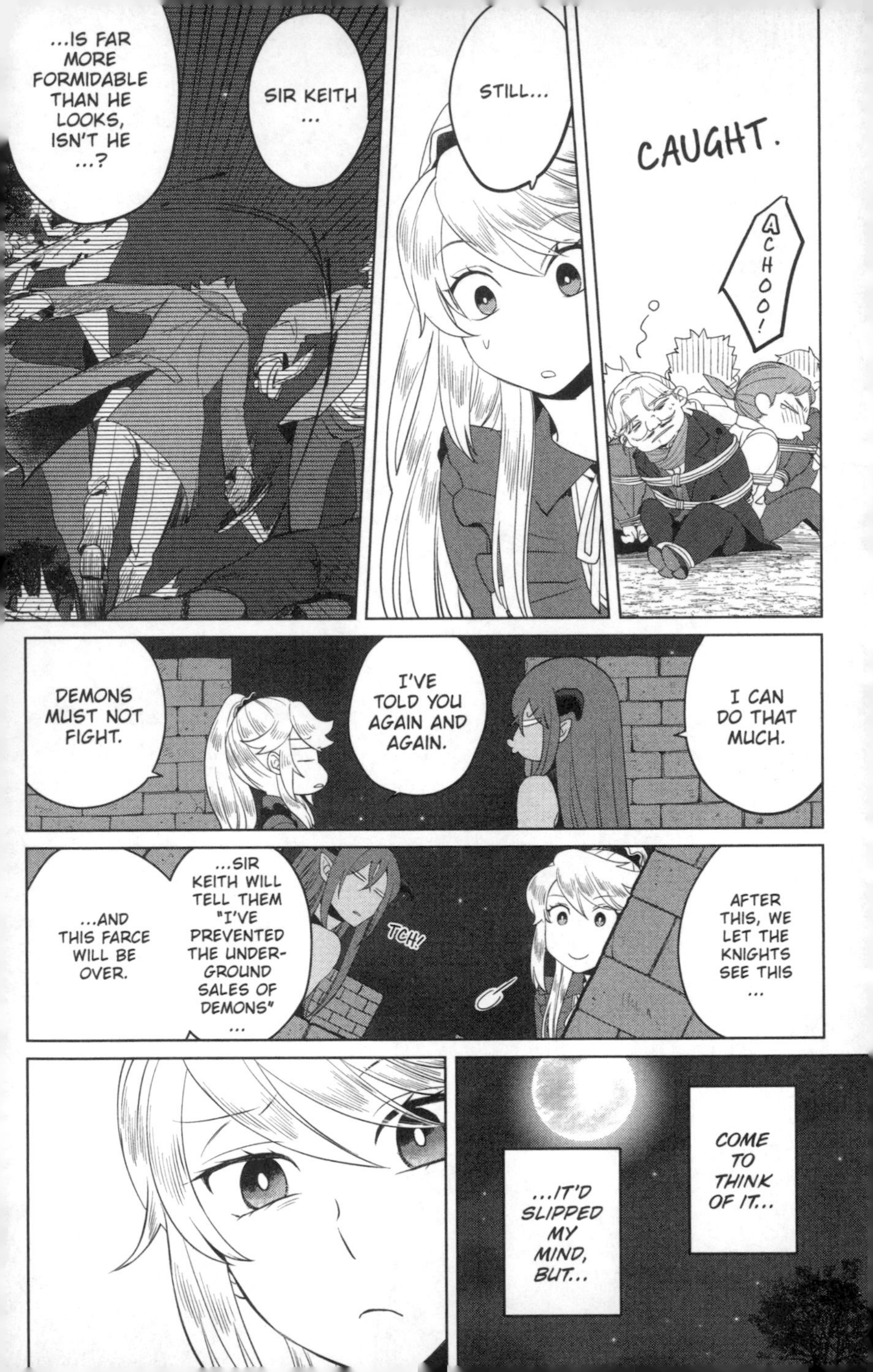
CAUGHT.
ACHOO!
STILL...
SIR KEITH ...
...IS FAR MORE FORMIDABLE THAN HE LOOKS, ISN'T HE ...?
I CAN DO THAT MUCH.
I'VE TOLD YOU AGAIN AND AGAIN.
DEMONS MUST NOT FIGHT.
AFTER THIS, WE LET THE KNIGHTS SEE THIS ...
TCH!
...SIR KEITH WILL TELL THEM "I'VE PREVENTED THE UNDER-GROUND SALES OF DEMONS" ...
...AND THIS FARCE WILL BE OVER.
COME TO THINK OF IT...
...IT'D SLIPPED MY MIND, BUT...

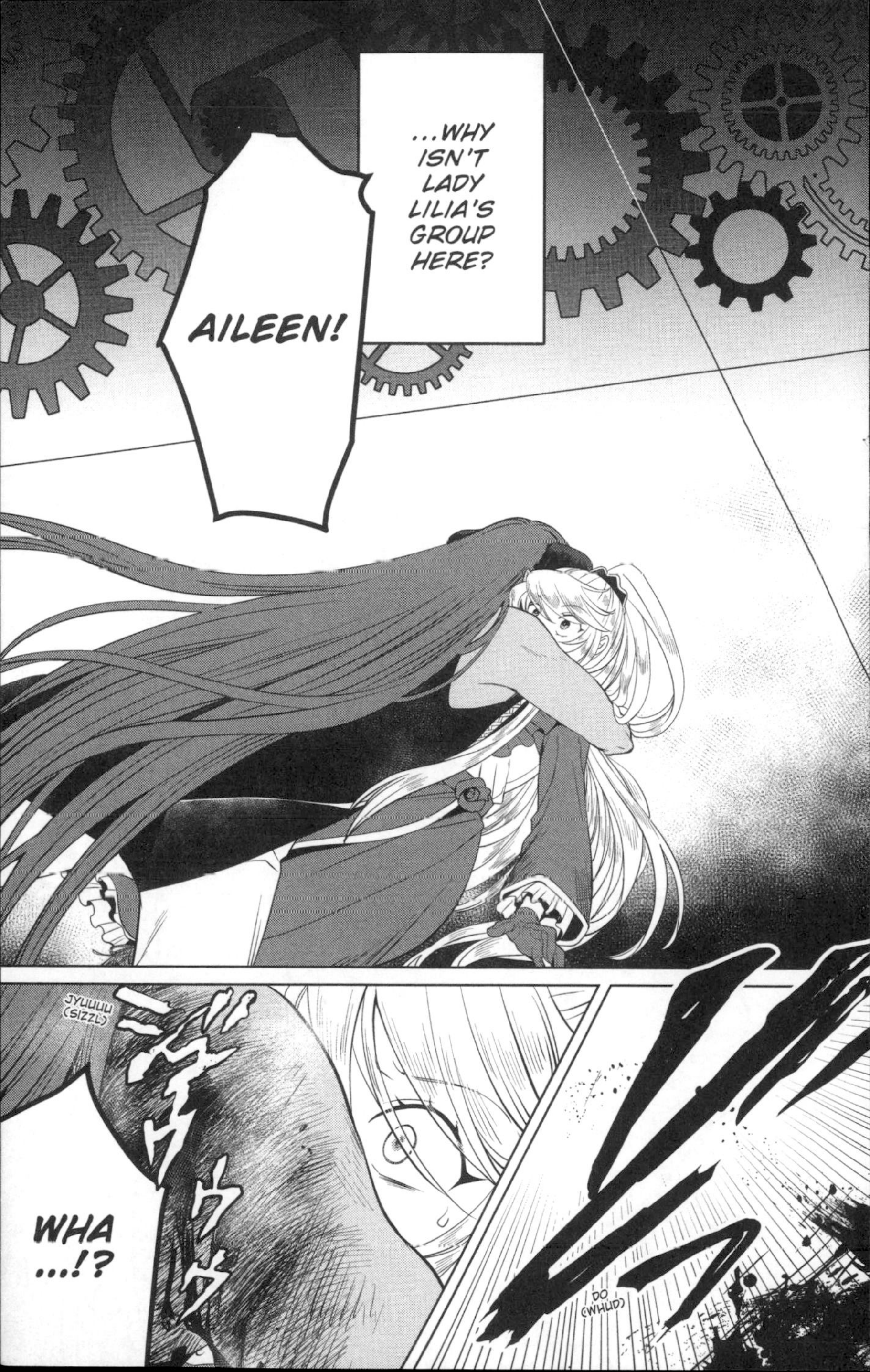
...WHY ISN'T LADY LILIA'S GROUP HERE?
AILEEN!
DO (WHUD)
JYUUUU (SIZZL)
WHA ...!?

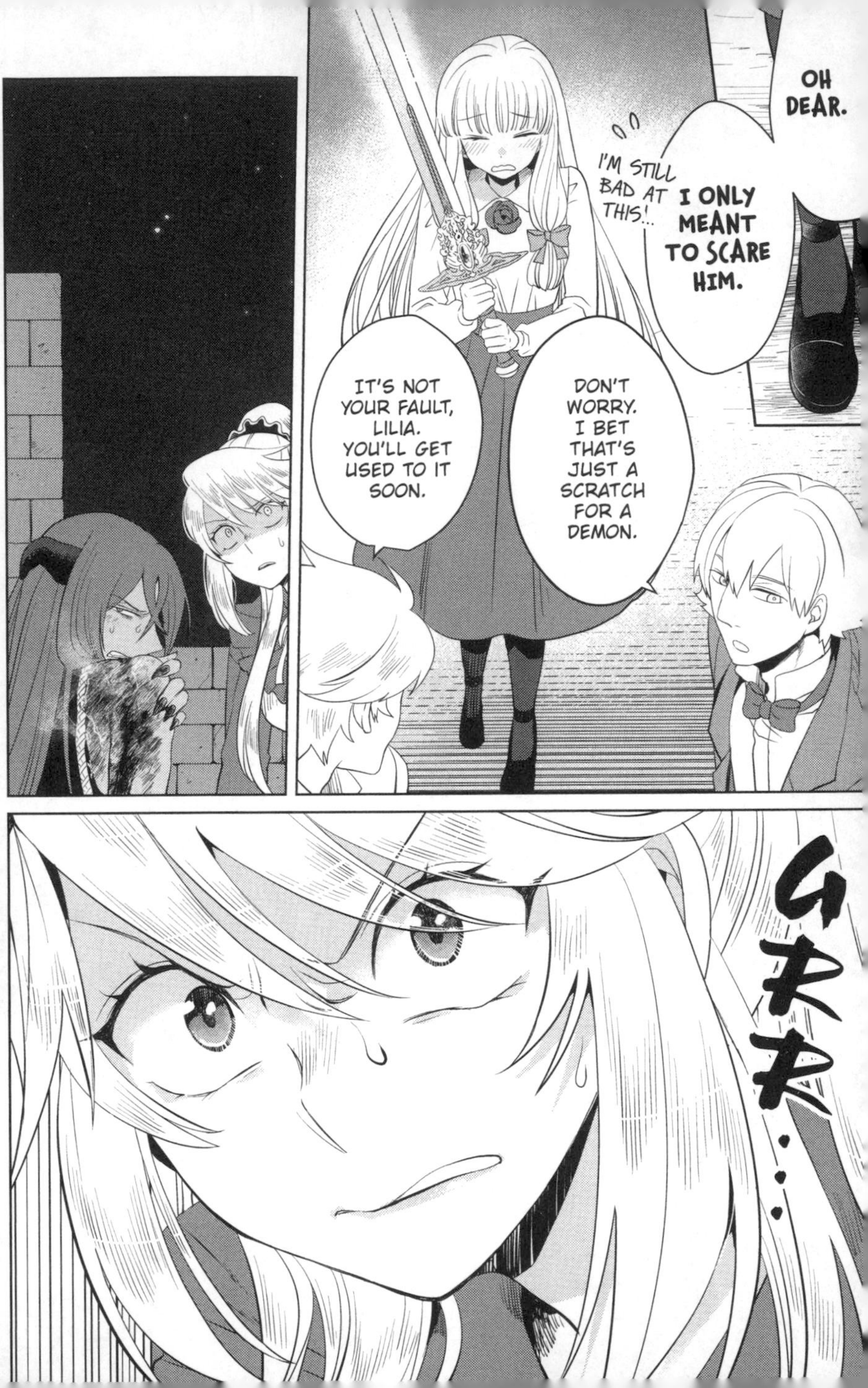
OH DEAR.
I ONLY MEANT TO SCARE HIM.
I'M STILL BAD AT THIS!...
DON'T WORRY. I BET THAT'S JUST A SCRATCH FOR A DEMON.
IT'S NOT YOUR FAULT, LILIA. YOU'LL GET USED TO IT SOON.
GRR...

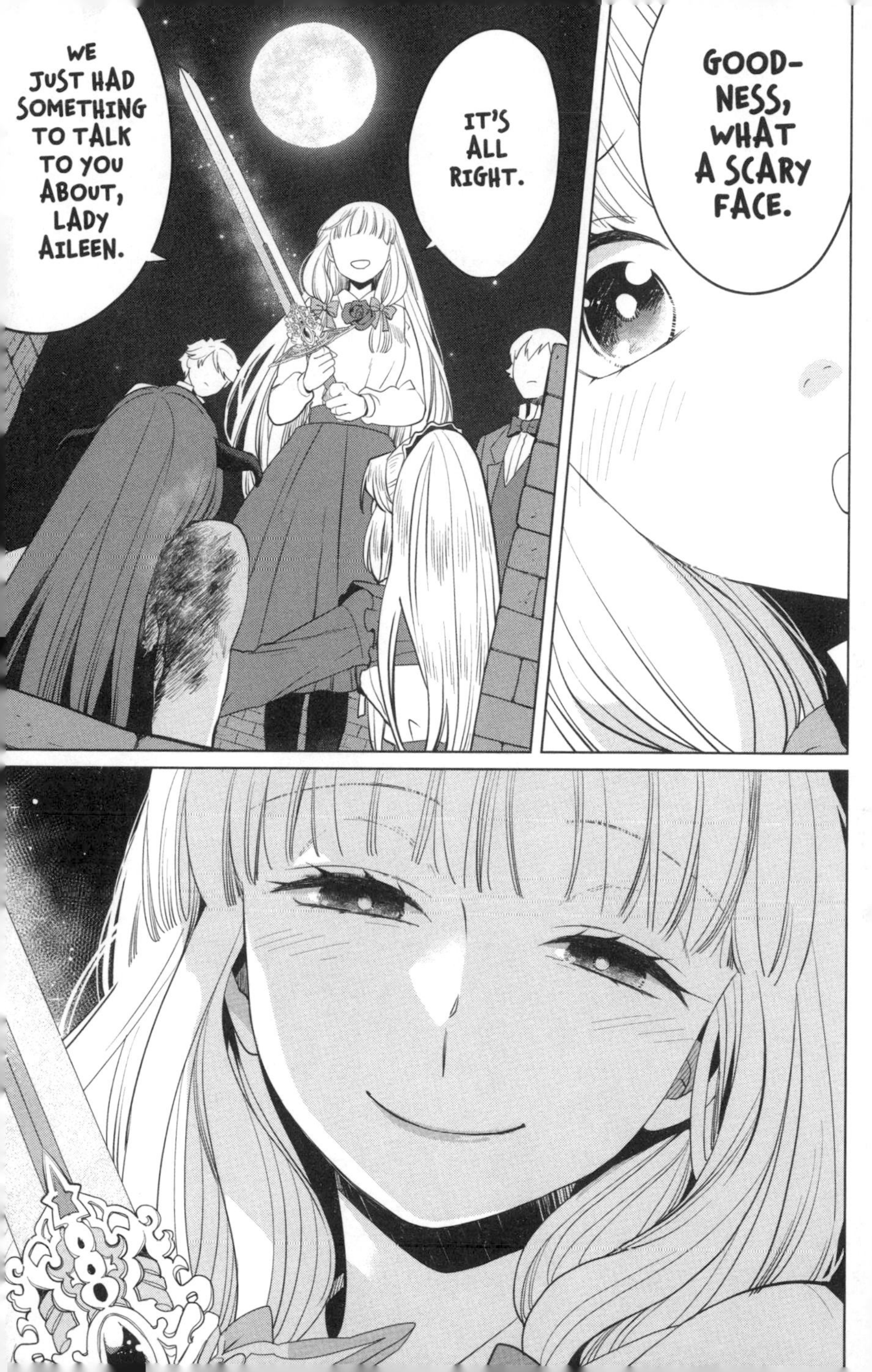
GOOD-NESS, WHAT A SCARY FACE.
IT'S ALL RIGHT.
WE JUST HAD SOMETHING TO TALK TO YOU ABOUT, LADY AILEEN.

Chapter 11

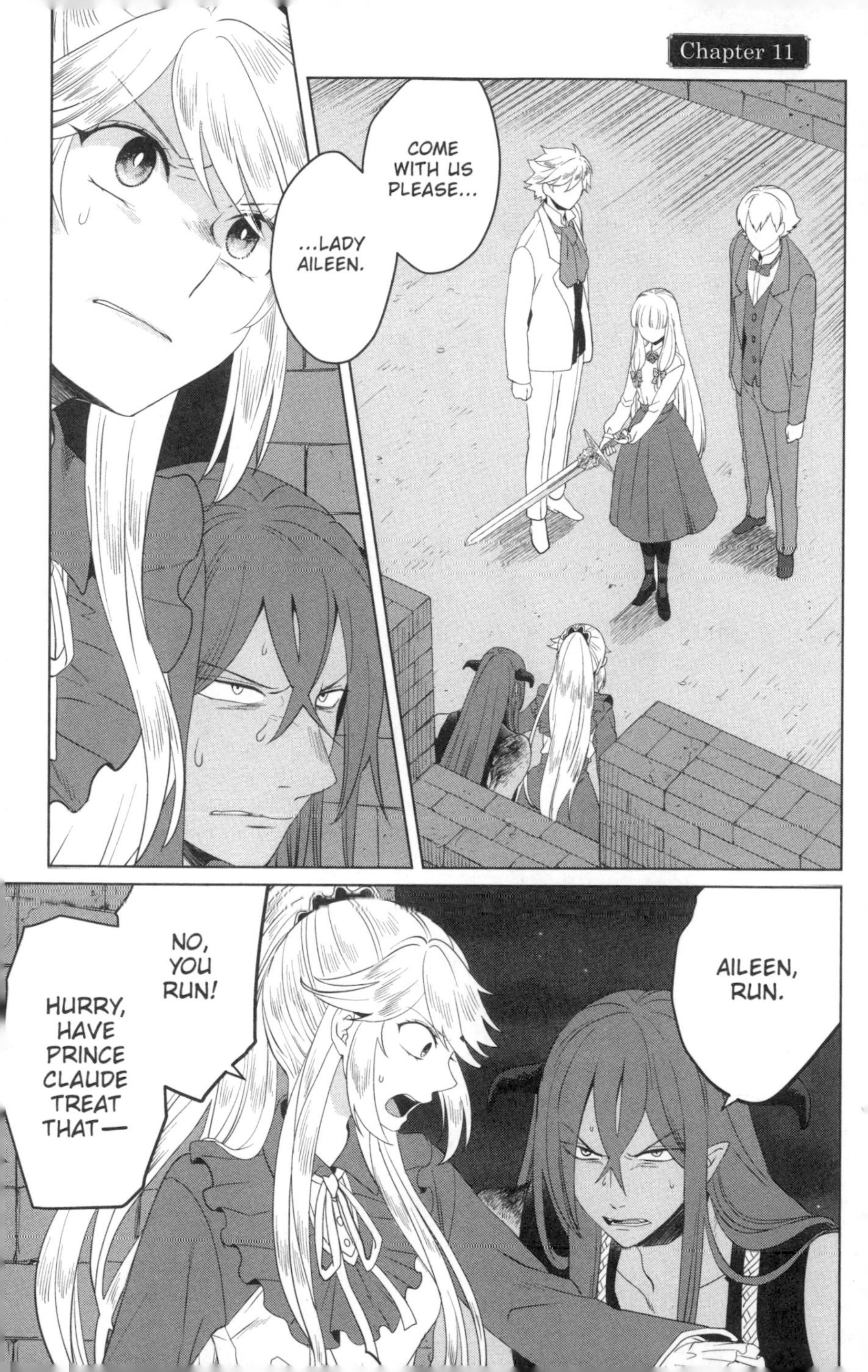
COME WITH US PLEASE...
...LADY AILEEN.
AILEEN, RUN.
NO, YOU RUN!
HURRY, HAVE PRINCE CLAUDE TREAT THAT—

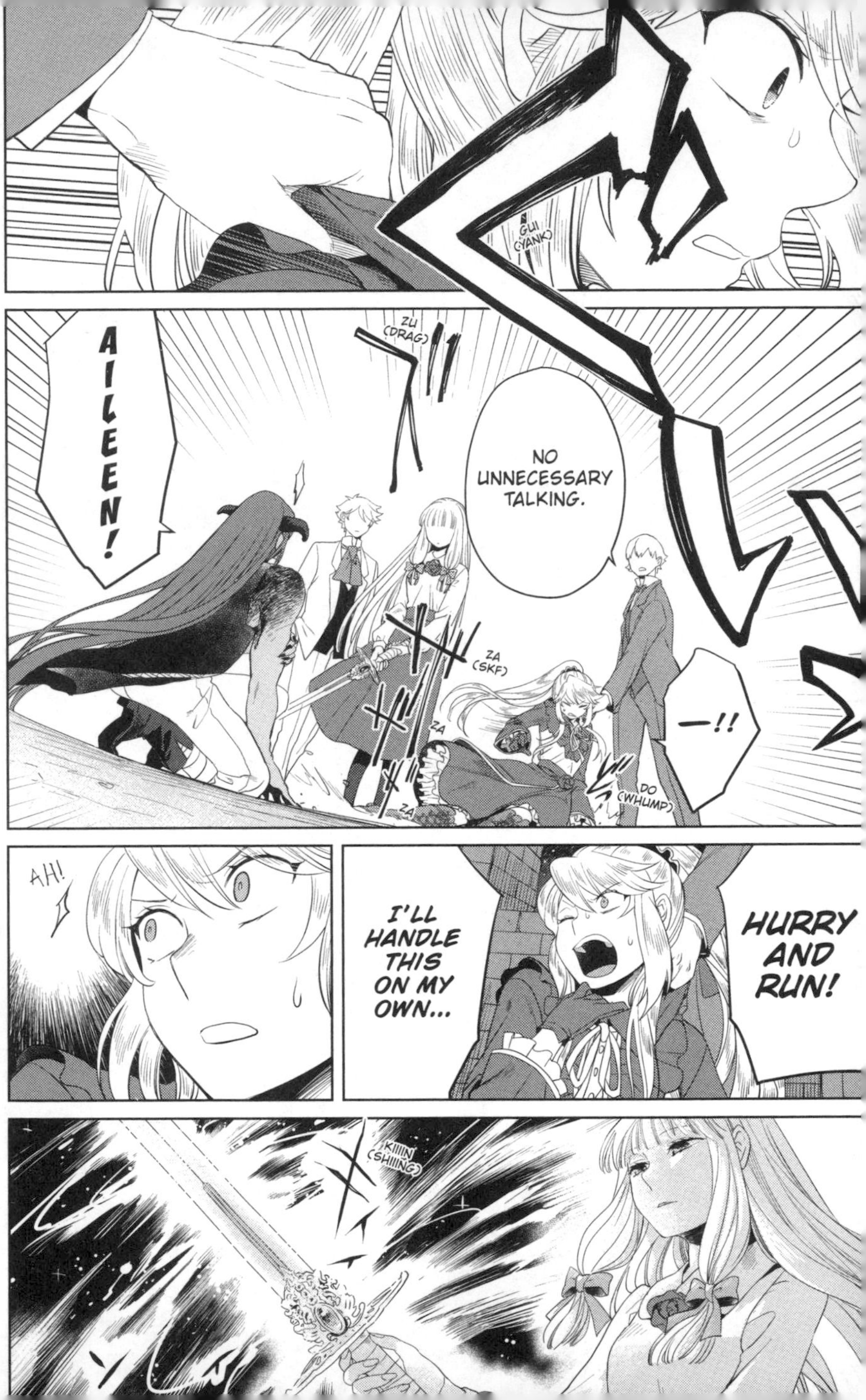
GUI (YANK)
—!!
DO (WHUMP)
ZA
ZA
ZA (SKF)
NO UNNECESSARY TALKING.
ZU (DRAG)
AILEEN!
HURRY AND RUN!
I'LL HANDLE THIS ON MY OWN...
AH!
KIIIN (SHIIING)

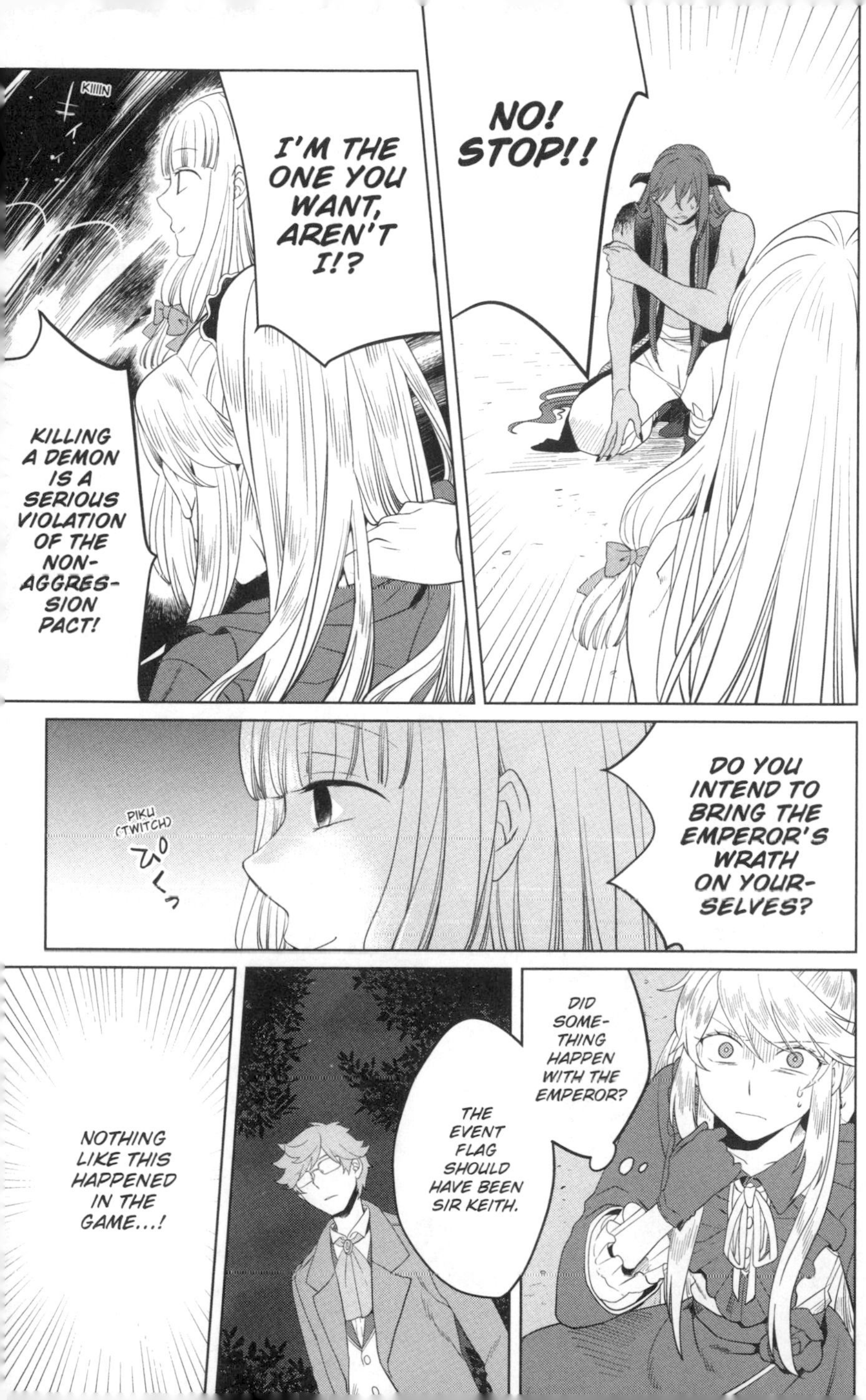
NO! STOP!!
I'M THE ONE YOU WANT, AREN'T I!?
KIIIN
KILLING A DEMON IS A SERIOUS VIOLATION OF THE NON-AGGRESSION PACT!
DO YOU INTEND TO BRING THE EMPEROR'S WRATH ON YOURSELVES?
PIKU (TWITCH)
DID SOMETHING HAPPEN WITH THE EMPEROR?
THE EVENT FLAG SHOULD HAVE BEEN SIR KEITH.
NOTHING LIKE THIS HAPPENED IN THE GAME...!

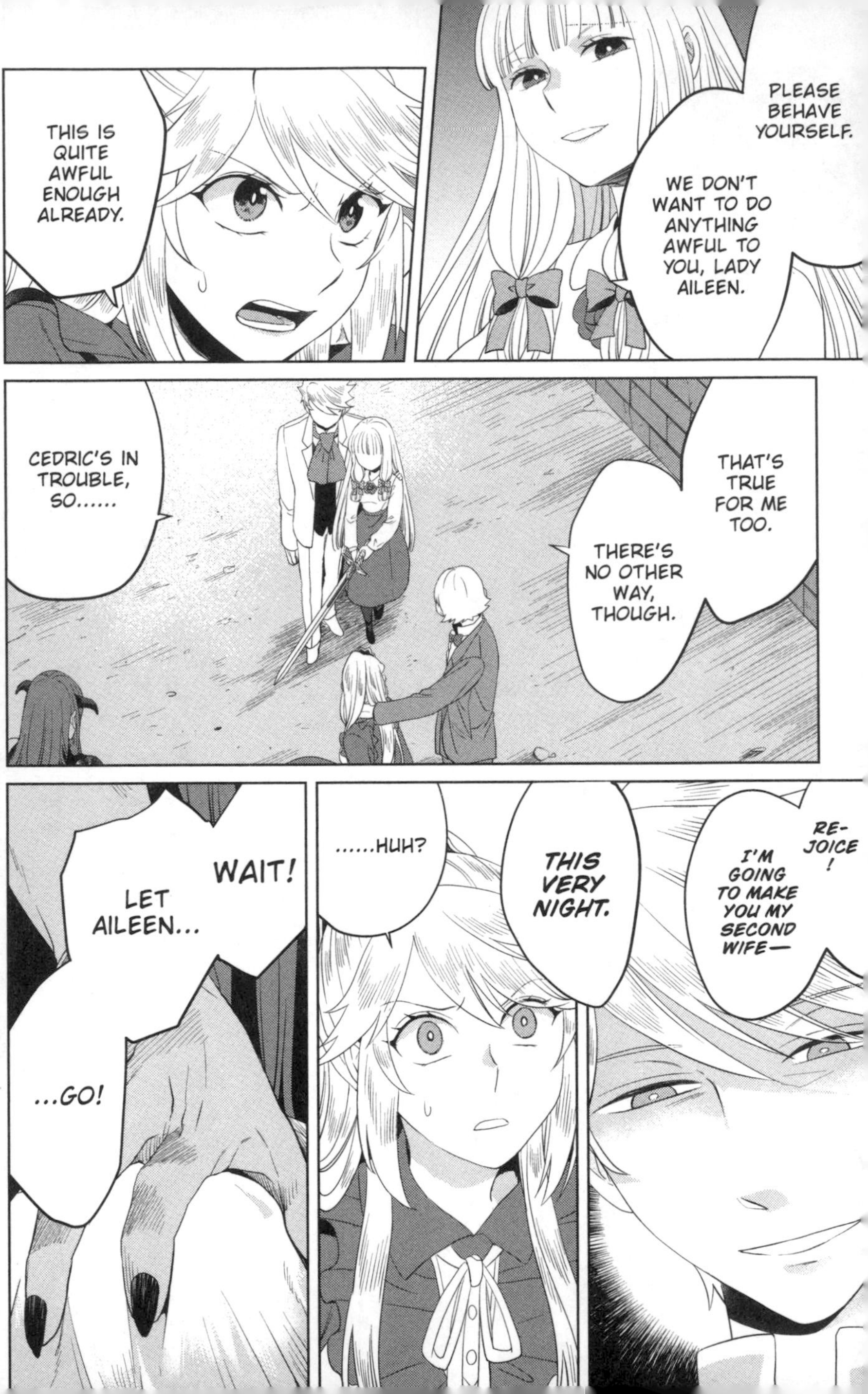
PLEASE BEHAVE YOURSELF.
WE DON'T WANT TO DO ANYTHING AWFUL TO YOU, LADY AILEEN.
THIS IS QUITE AWFUL ENOUGH ALREADY.
THAT'S TRUE FOR ME TOO.
THERE'S NO OTHER WAY, THOUGH.
CEDRIC'S IN TROUBLE, SO......
RE-JOICE!
I'M GOING TO MAKE YOU MY SECOND WIFE—
THIS VERY NIGHT.
......HUH?
WAIT!
LET AILEEN...
...GO!

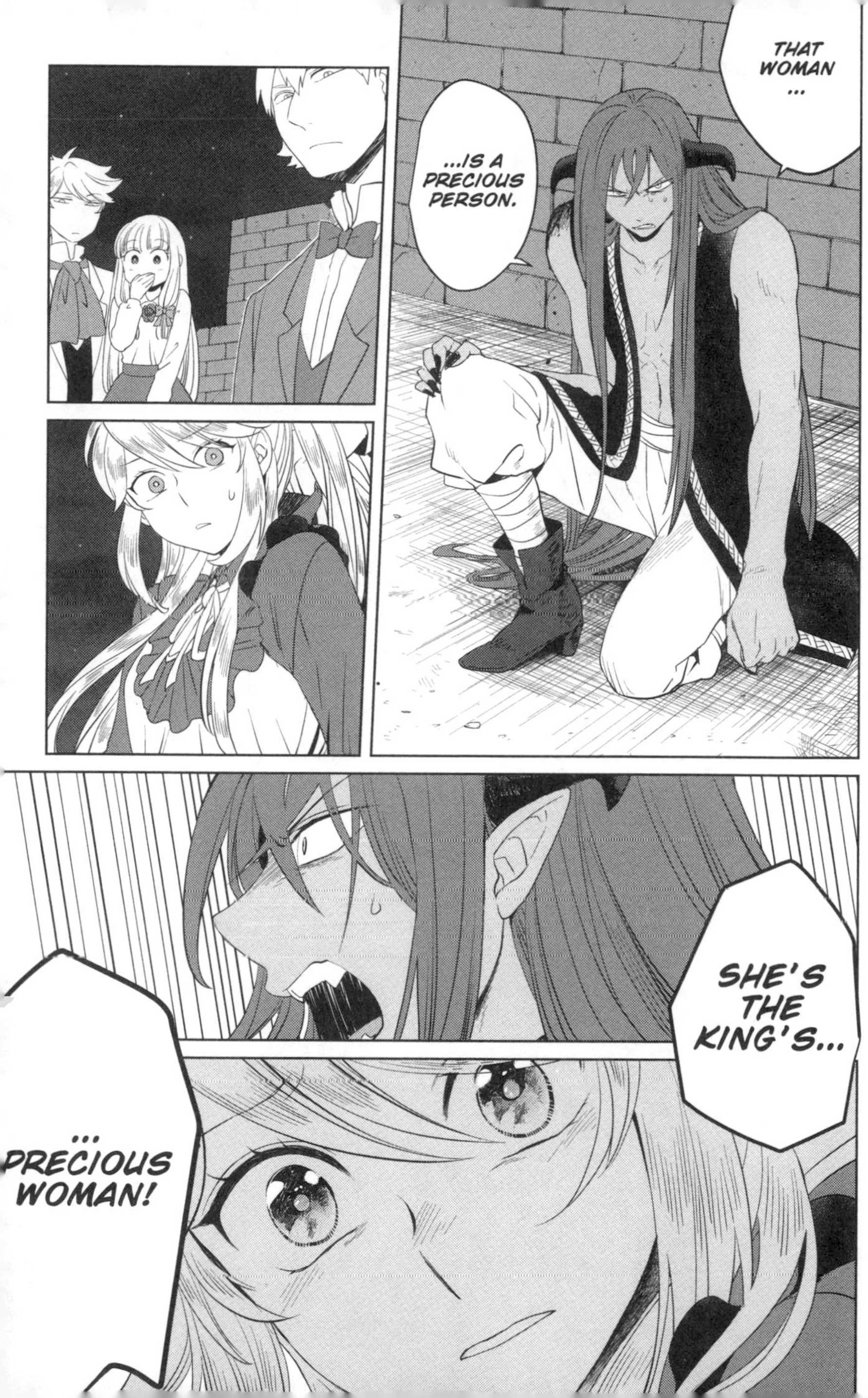
THAT WOMAN ...
...IS A PRECIOUS PERSON.
SHE'S THE KING'S...
...PRECIOUS WOMAN!

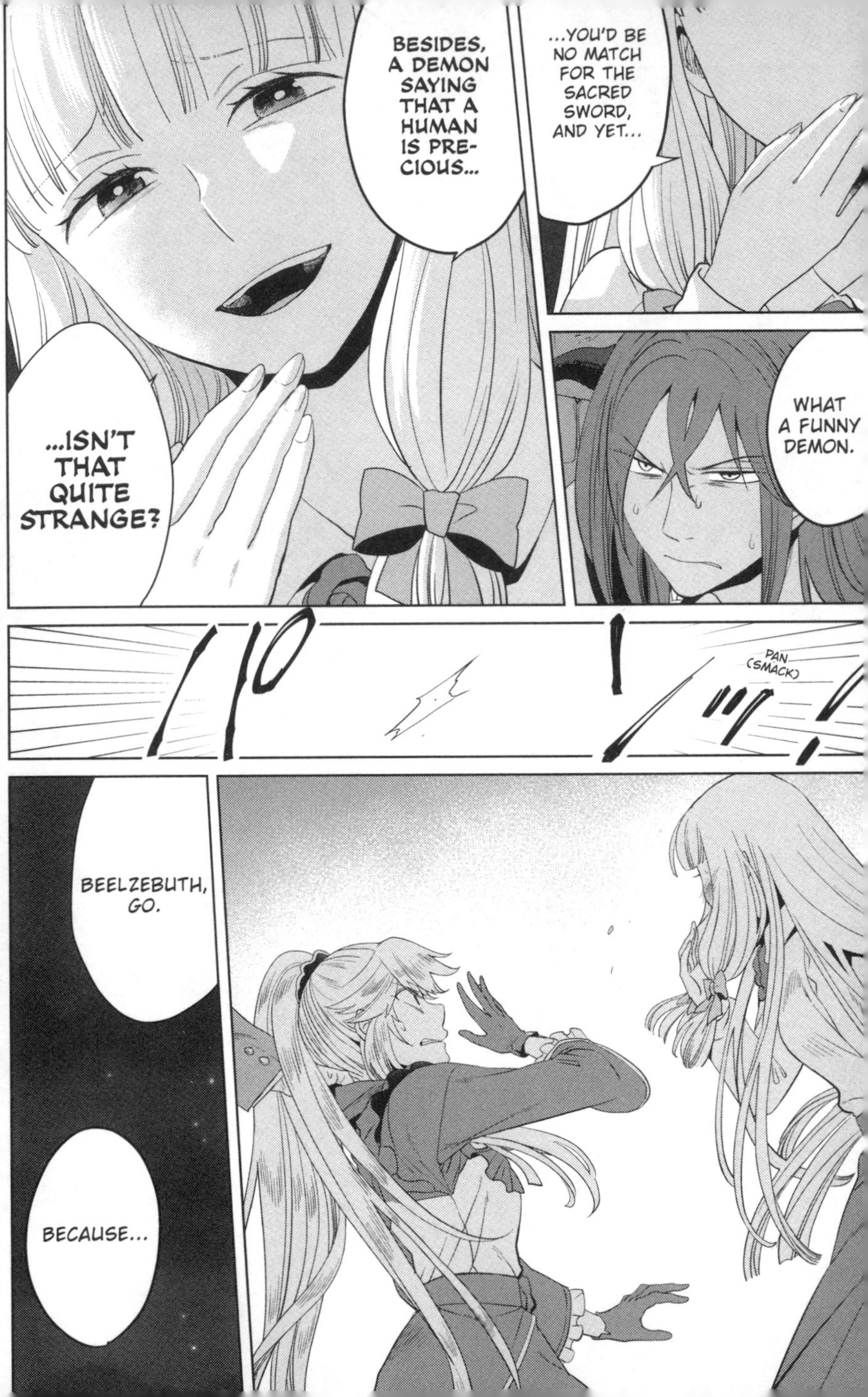
...YOU'D BE NO MATCH FOR THE SACRED SWORD, AND YET...
WHAT A FUNNY DEMON.
BESIDES, A DEMON SAYING THAT A HUMAN IS PRE-CIOUS...
...ISN'T THAT QUITE STRANGE?
PAN (SMACK)
BEELZEBUTH, GO.
BECAUSE...

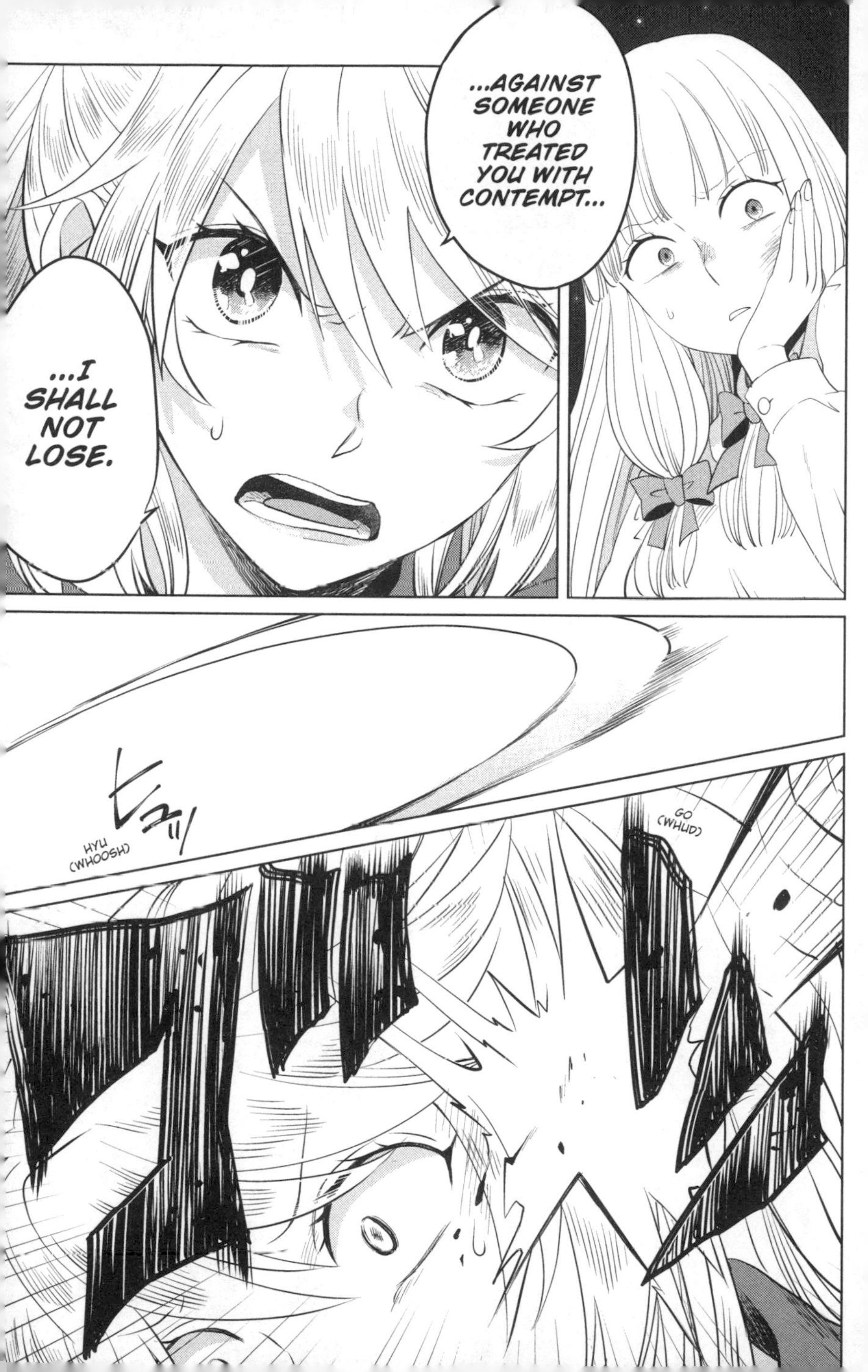
...AGAINST SOMEONE WHO TREATED YOU WITH CONTEMPT...
...I SHALL NOT LOSE.
HYU (WHOOSH)
GO (WHUD)

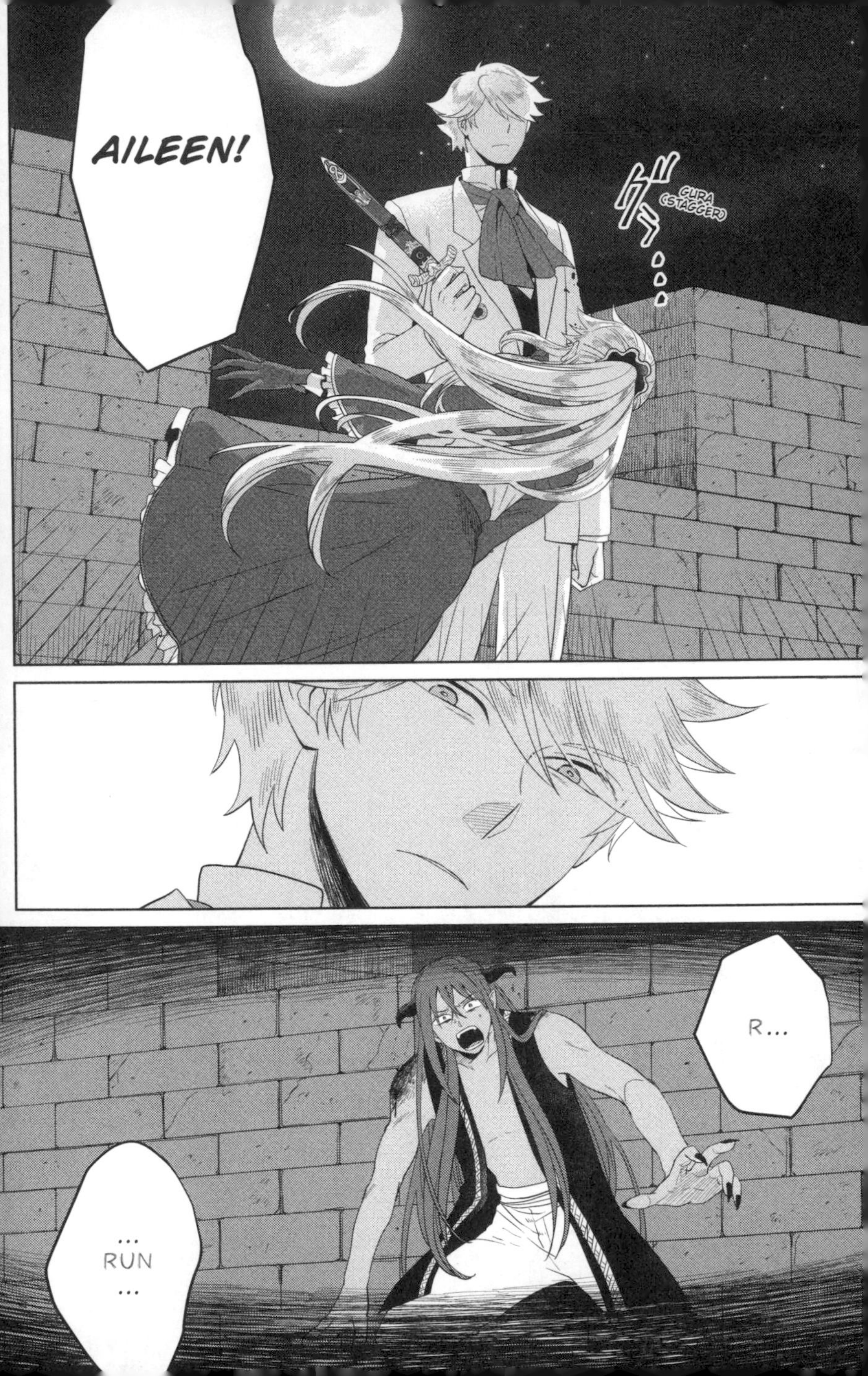
AILEEN!
GURA (STAGGER)
R...
... RUN ...

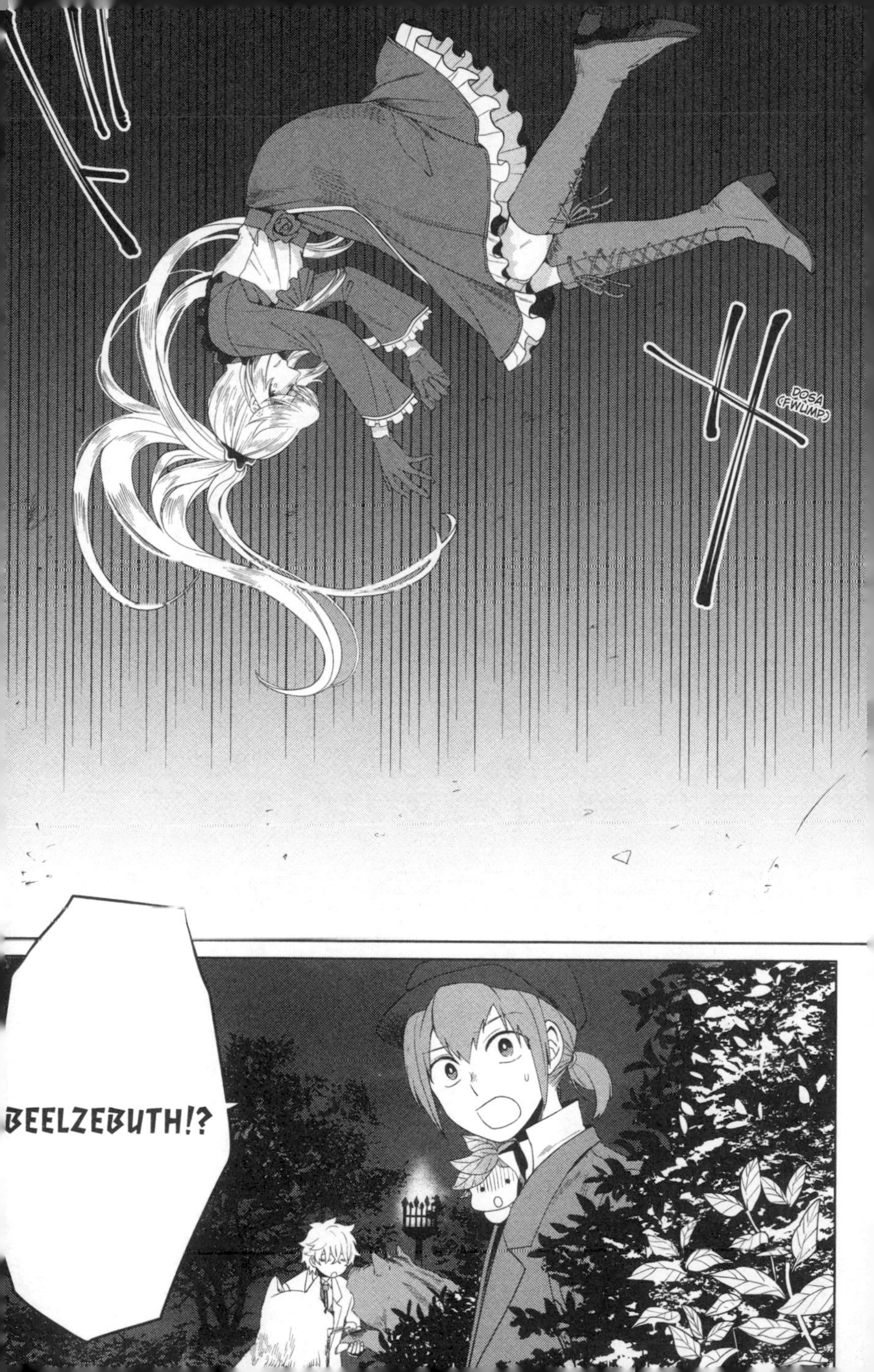
DOSA (FWUMP)
BEELZEBUTH!?

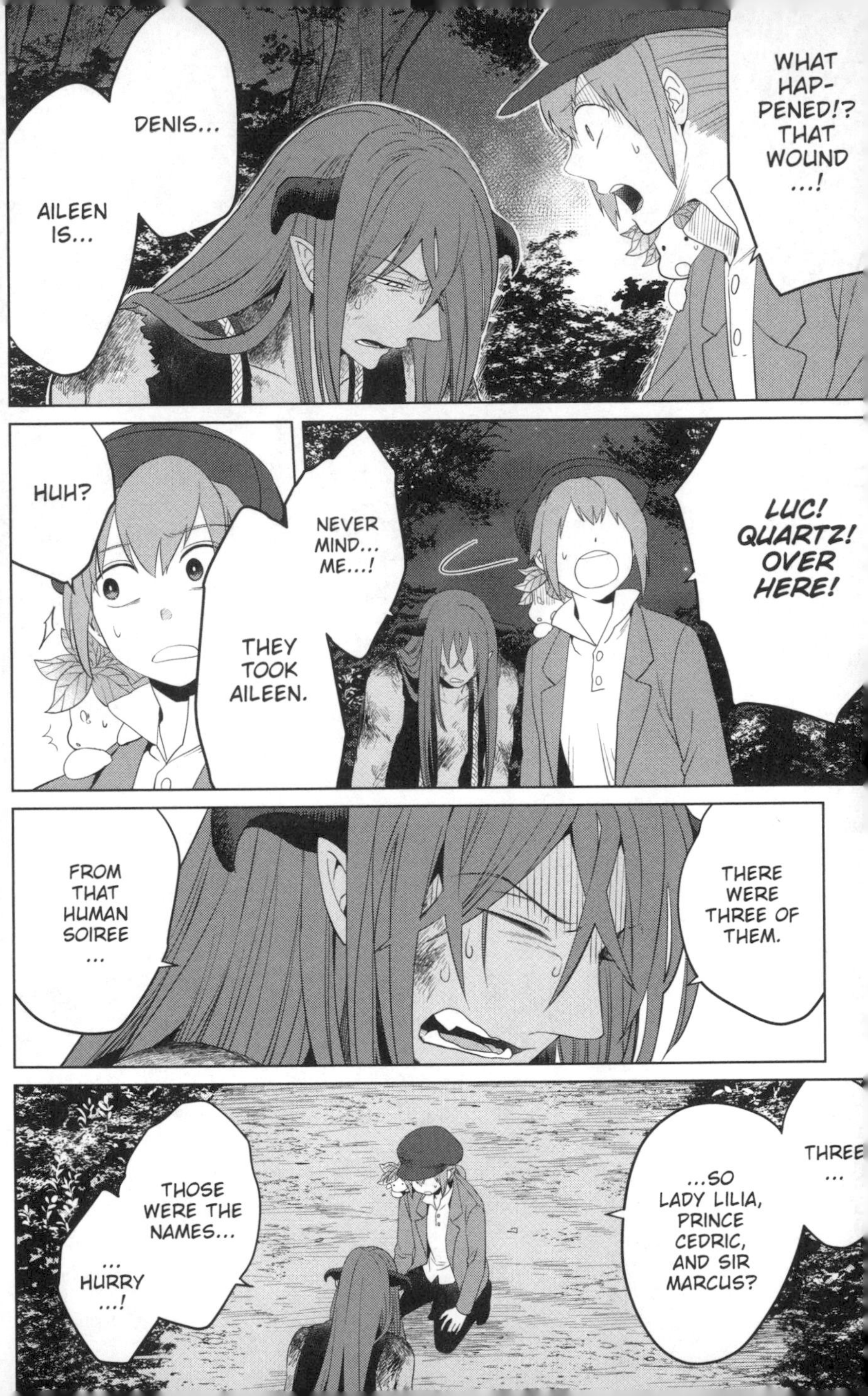
WHAT HAP-PENED!? THAT WOUND ...!
DENIS...
AILEEN IS...
LUC! QUARTZ! OVER HERE!
NEVER MIND... ME...!
THEY TOOK AILEEN.
HUH?
THERE WERE THREE OF THEM.
FROM THAT HUMAN SOIREE ...
THREE ...
...SO LADY LILIA, PRINCE CEDRIC, AND SIR MARCUS?
THOSE WERE THE NAMES...
... HURRY ...!

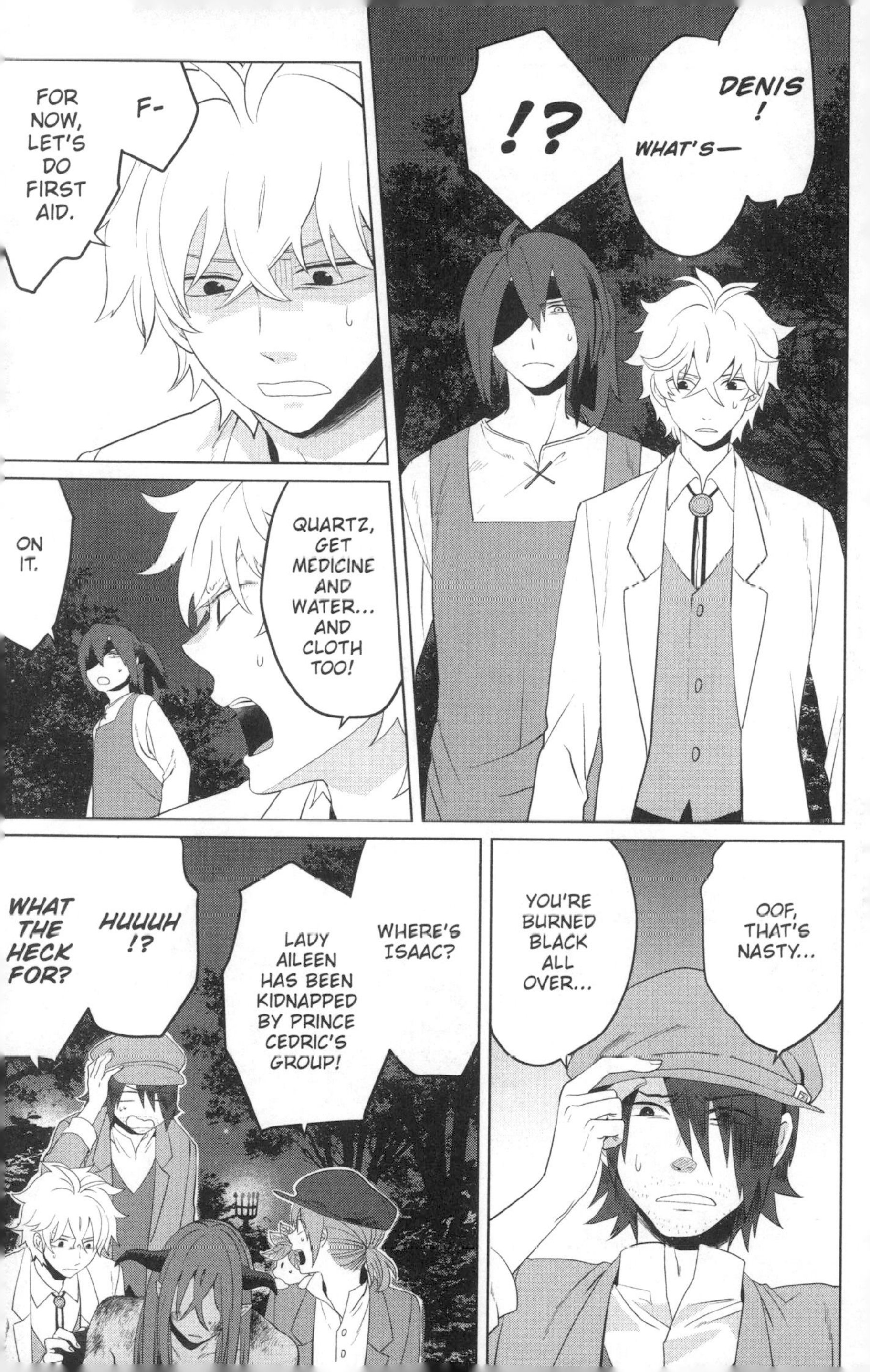
DENIS! WHAT'S—
!?
F-
FOR NOW, LET'S DO FIRST AID.
QUARTZ, GET MEDICINE AND WATER... AND CLOTH TOO!
ON IT.
OOF, THAT'S NASTY...
YOU'RE BURNED BLACK ALL OVER...
WHERE'S ISAAC?
LADY AILEEN HAS BEEN KIDNAPPED BY PRINCE CEDRIC'S GROUP!
HUUUH!?
WHAT THE HECK FOR?

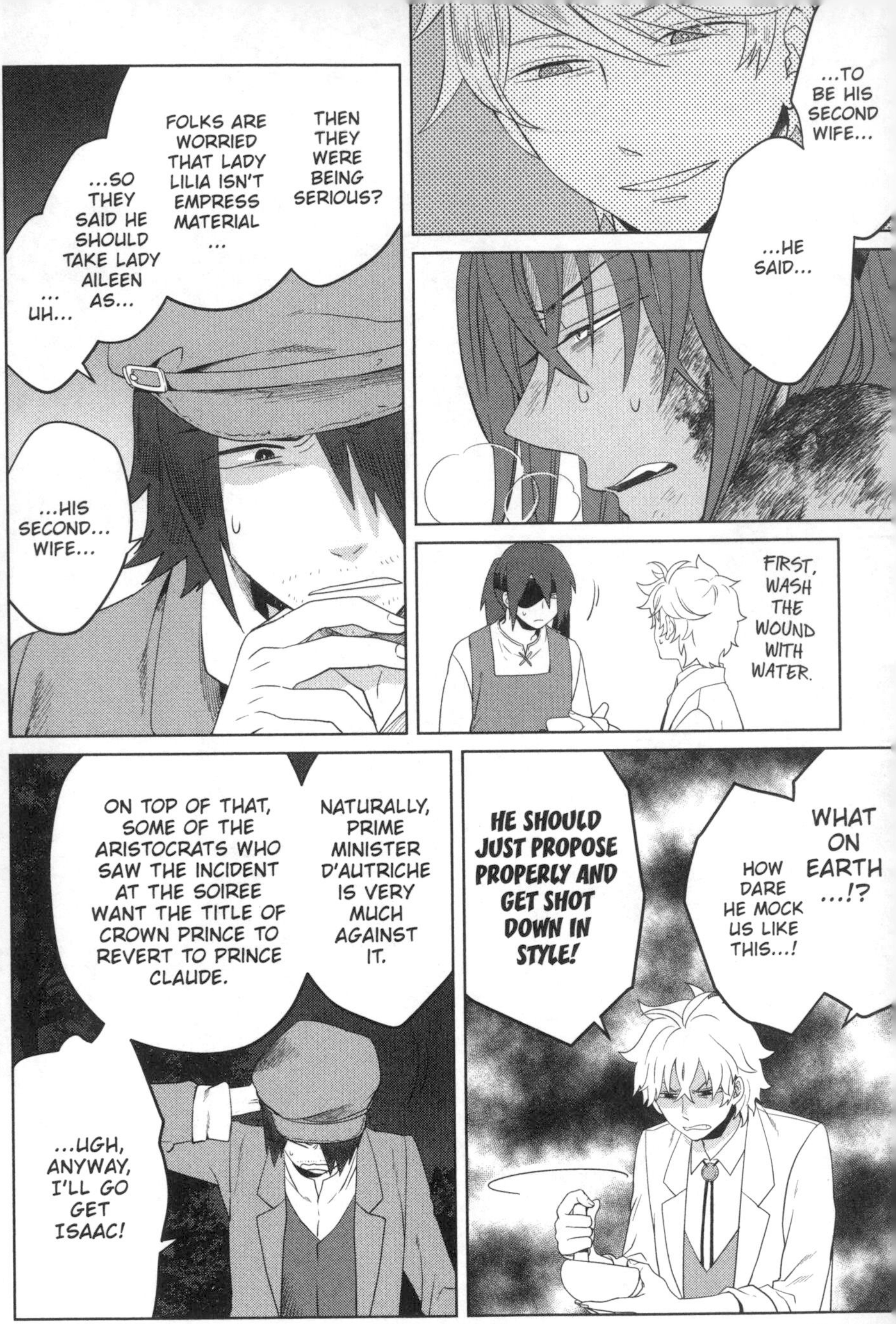
...TO BE HIS SECOND WIFE...
...HE SAID...
FIRST, WASH THE WOUND WITH WATER.
THEN THEY WERE BEING SERIOUS?
FOLKS ARE WORRIED THAT LADY LILIA ISN'T EMPRESS MATERIAL ...
...SO THEY SAID HE SHOULD TAKE LADY AILEEN AS... ... UH...
...HIS SECOND... WIFE...
WHAT ON EARTH ...!?
HOW DARE HE MOCK US LIKE THIS...!
HE SHOULD JUST PROPOSE PROPERLY AND GET SHOT DOWN IN STYLE!
NATURALLY, PRIME MINISTER D'AUTRICHE IS VERY MUCH AGAINST IT.
ON TOP OF THAT, SOME OF THE ARISTOCRATS WHO SAW THE INCIDENT AT THE SOIREE WANT THE TITLE OF CROWN PRINCE TO REVERT TO PRINCE CLAUDE.
...UGH, ANYWAY, I'LL GO GET ISAAC!

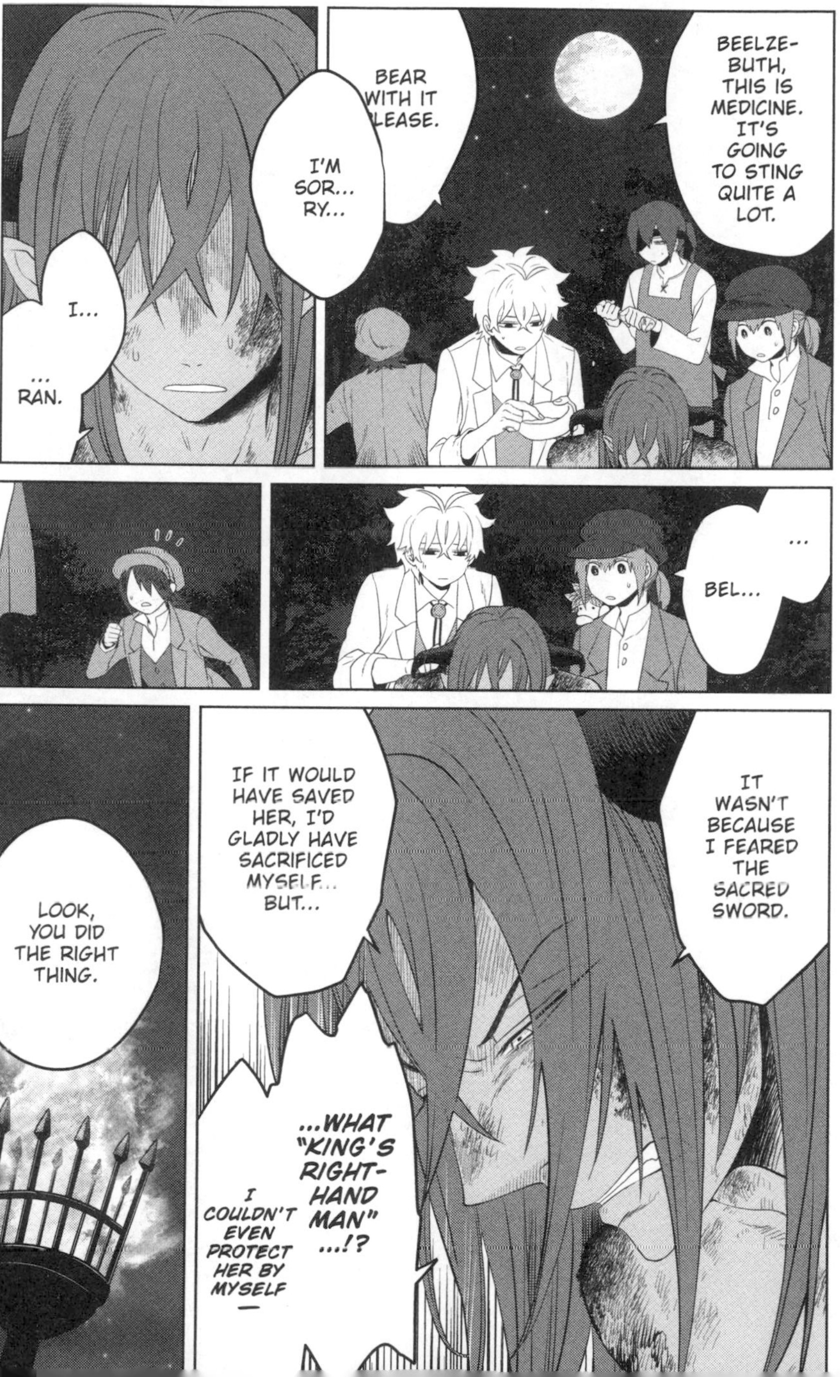
BEELZEBUTH, THIS IS MEDICINE. IT'S GOING TO STING QUITE A LOT.
BEAR WITH IT LEASE.
I'M SOR... RY...
I...
... RAN.
...
BEL...
IT WASN'T BECAUSE I FEARED THE SACRED SWORD.
IF IT WOULD HAVE SAVED HER, I'D GLADLY HAVE SACRIFICED MYSELF... BUT...
...WHAT "KING'S RIGHT-HAND MAN" ...!?
I COULDN'T EVEN PROTECT HER BY MYSELF—
LOOK, YOU DID THE RIGHT THING.

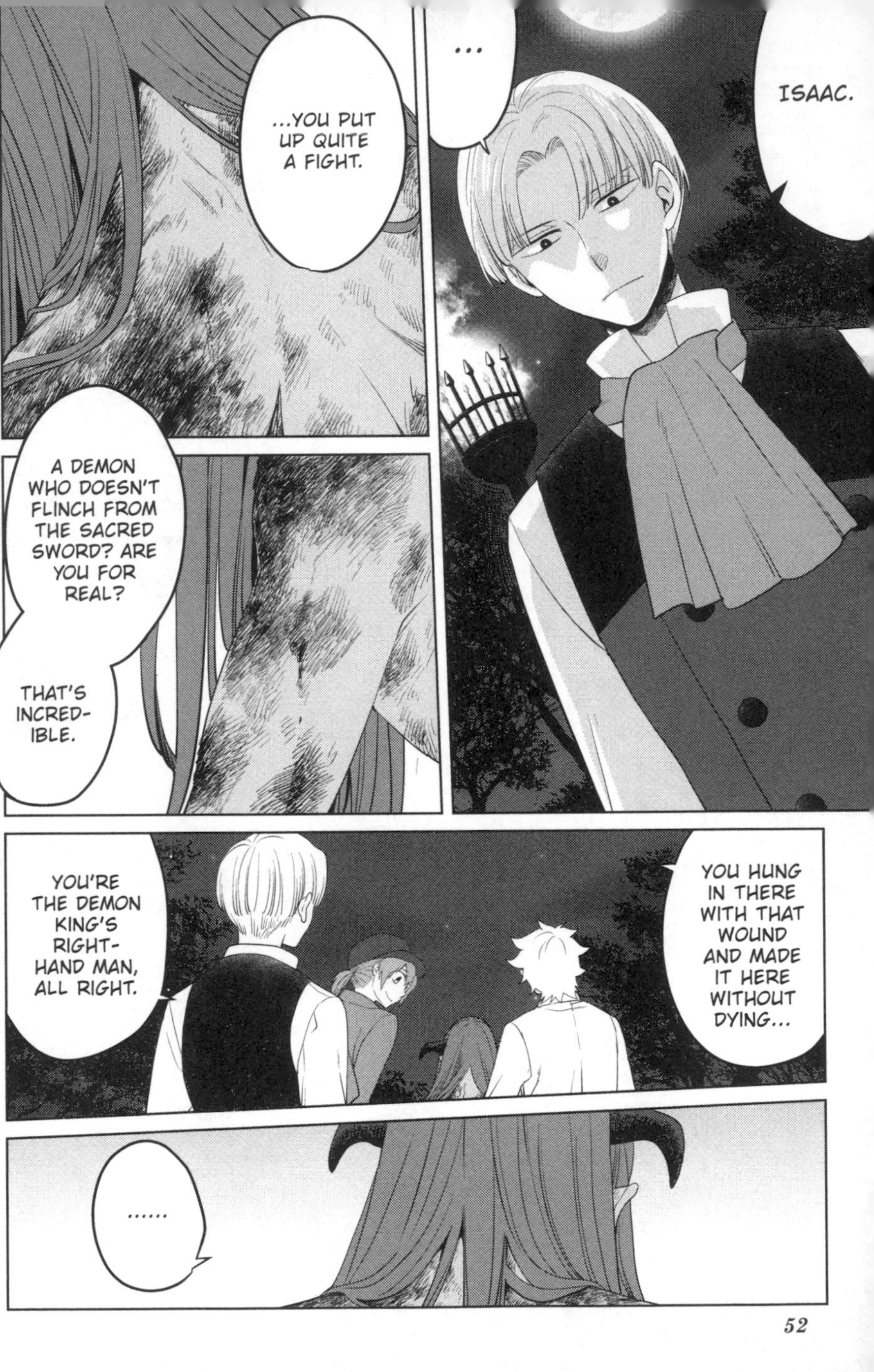
ISAAC.
...
...YOU PUT UP QUITE A FIGHT.
A DEMON WHO DOESN'T FLINCH FROM THE SACRED SWORD? ARE YOU FOR REAL?
THAT'S INCRED-IBLE.
YOU HUNG IN THERE WITH THAT WOUND AND MADE IT HERE WITHOUT DYING...
YOU'RE THE DEMON KING'S RIGHT-HAND MAN, ALL RIGHT.
......

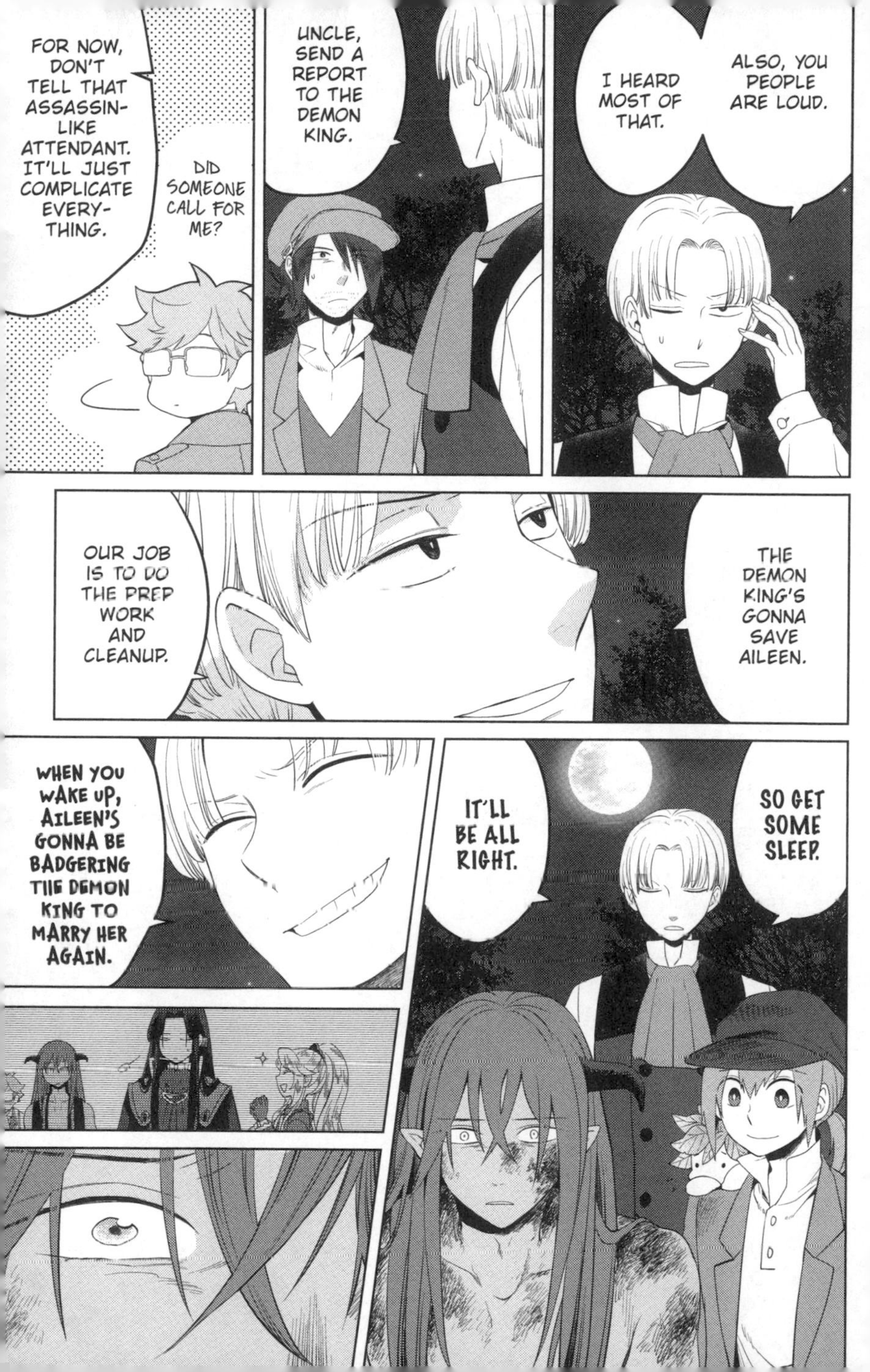
ALSO, YOU PEOPLE ARE LOUD.
I HEARD MOST OF THAT.
UNCLE, SEND A REPORT TO THE DEMON KING.
FOR NOW, DON'T TELL THAT ASSASSIN-LIKE ATTENDANT. IT'LL JUST COMPLICATE EVERYTHING.
DID SOMEONE CALL FOR ME?
THE DEMON KING'S GONNA SAVE AILEEN.
OUR JOB IS TO DO THE PREP WORK AND CLEANUP.
SO GET SOME SLEEP.
IT'LL BE ALL RIGHT.
WHEN YOU WAKE UP, AILEEN'S GONNA BE BADGERING THE DEMON KING TO MARRY HER AGAIN.

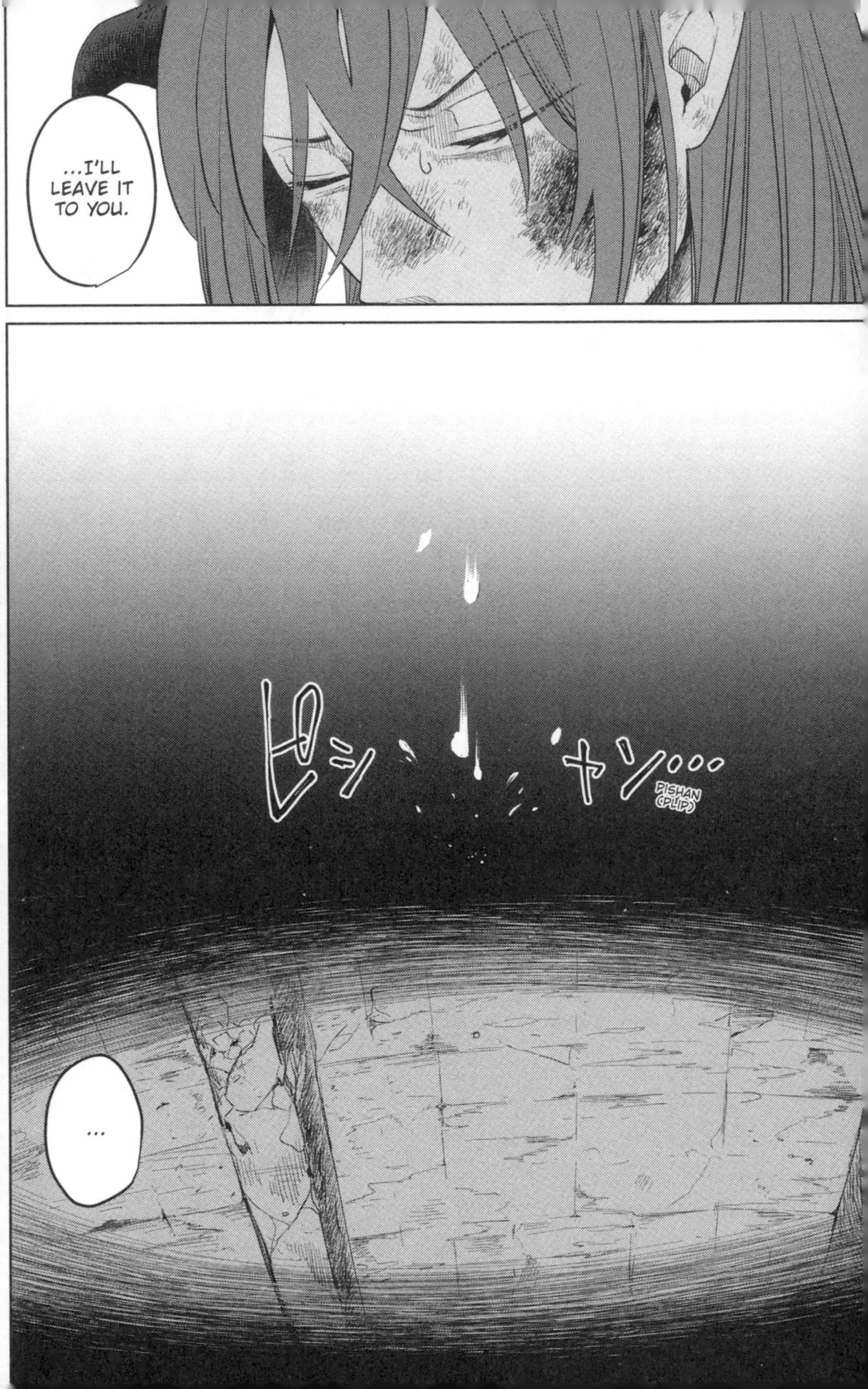
...I'LL LEAVE IT TO YOU.
ピシャン
PISHAN (PLIP)
...

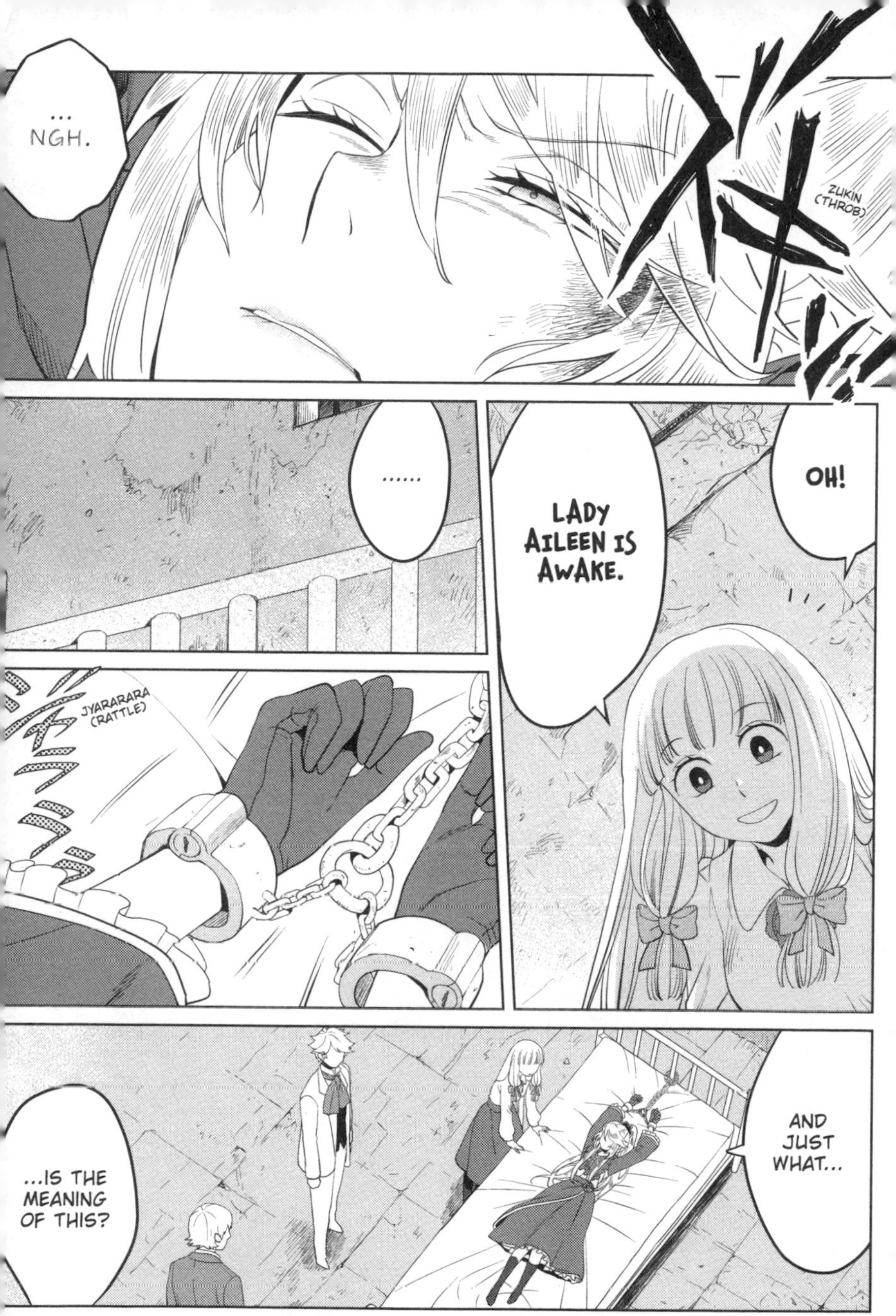
ZUKIN (THROB)
... NGH.
OH!
LADY AILEEN IS AWAKE.
......
JYARARARA (RATTLE)
AND JUST WHAT...
...IS THE MEANING OF THIS?

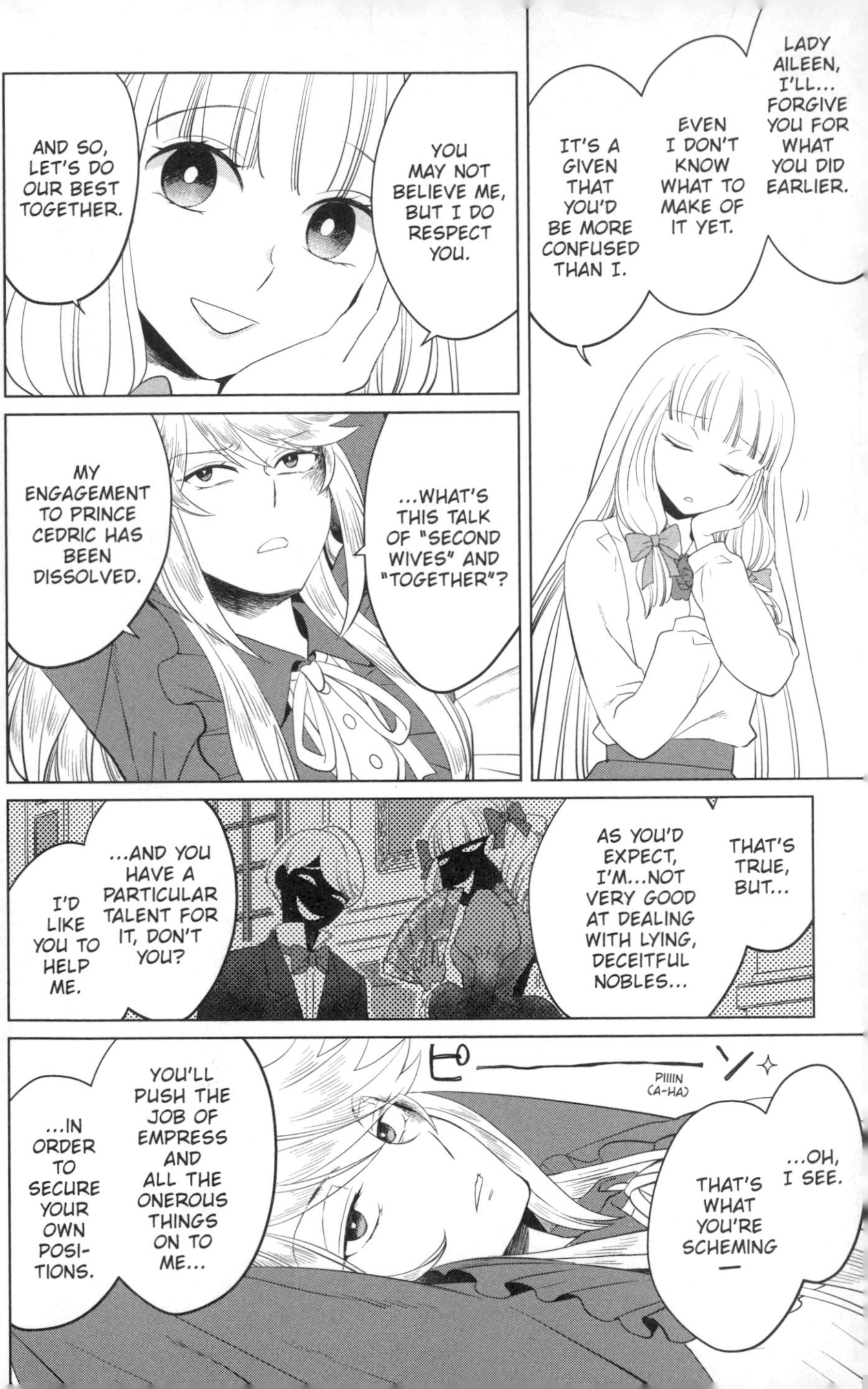
LADY AILEEN, I'LL... FORGIVE YOU FOR WHAT YOU DID EARLIER.
EVEN I DON'T KNOW WHAT TO MAKE OF IT YET.
IT'S A GIVEN THAT YOU'D BE MORE CONFUSED THAN I.
YOU MAY NOT BELIEVE ME, BUT I DO RESPECT YOU.
AND SO, LET'S DO OUR BEST TOGETHER.
...WHAT'S THIS TALK OF "SECOND WIVES" AND "TOGETHER"?
MY ENGAGEMENT TO PRINCE CEDRIC HAS BEEN DISSOLVED.
THAT'S TRUE, BUT...
AS YOU'D EXPECT, I'M...NOT VERY GOOD AT DEALING WITH LYING, DECEITFUL NOBLES...
...AND YOU HAVE A PARTICULAR TALENT FOR IT, DON'T YOU?
I'D LIKE YOU TO HELP ME.
ピーン
PIIIN (A-HA)
...OH, I SEE.
THAT'S WHAT YOU'RE SCHEMING—
YOU'LL PUSH THE JOB OF EMPRESS AND ALL THE ONEROUS THINGS ON TO ME...
...IN ORDER TO SECURE YOUR OWN POSI-TIONS.

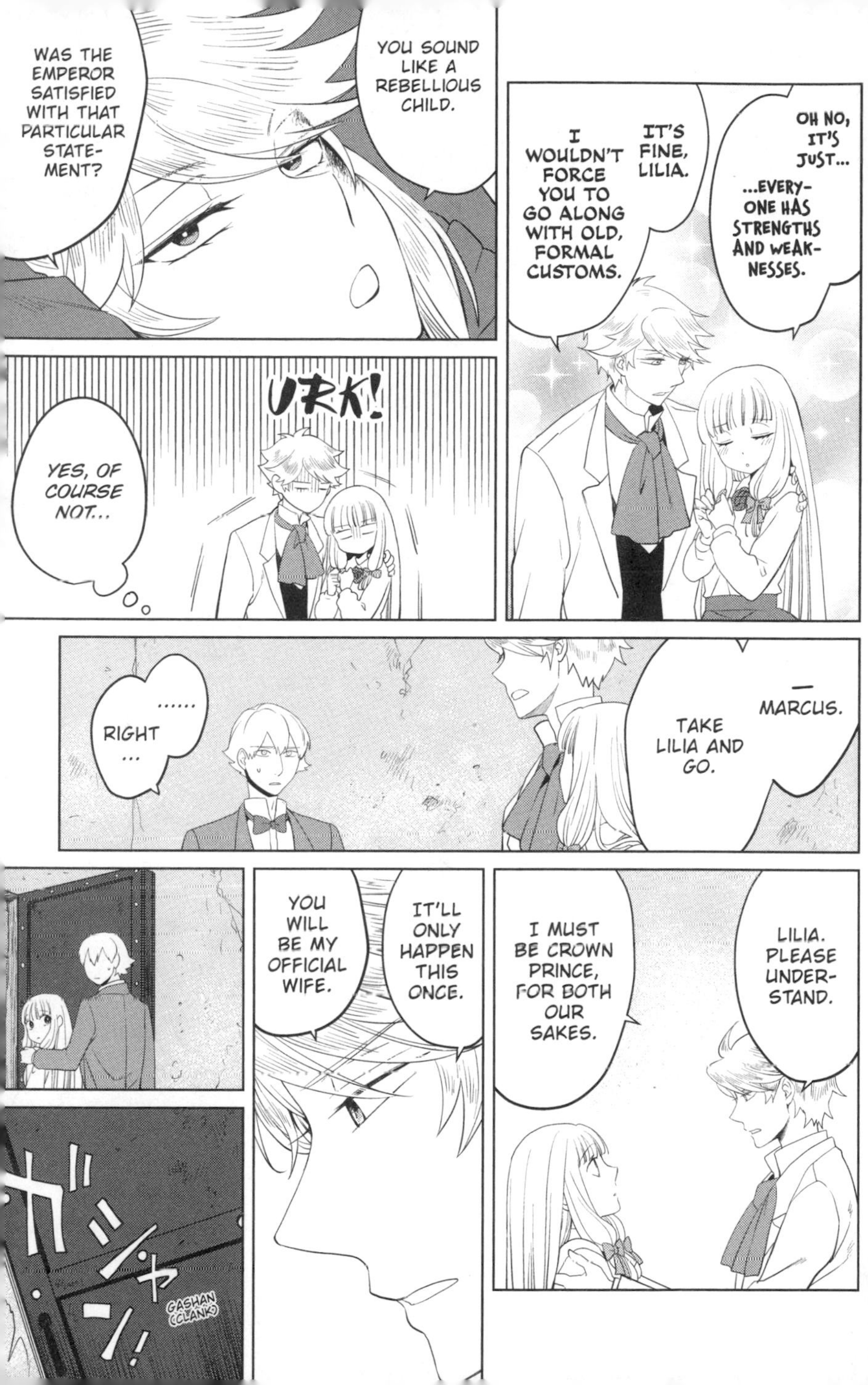
OH NO, IT'S JUST...
...EVERYONE HAS STRENGTHS AND WEAKNESSES.
IT'S FINE, LILIA.
I WOULDN'T FORCE YOU TO GO ALONG WITH OLD, FORMAL CUSTOMS.
YOU SOUND LIKE A REBELLIOUS CHILD.
WAS THE EMPEROR SATISFIED WITH THAT PARTICULAR STATEMENT?
URK!
YES, OF COURSE NOT...
—MARCUS.
TAKE LILIA AND GO.
......RIGHT...
LILIA. PLEASE UNDERSTAND.
I MUST BE CROWN PRINCE, FOR BOTH OUR SAKES.
IT'LL ONLY HAPPEN THIS ONCE.
YOU WILL BE MY OFFICIAL WIFE.
ガシャーン!
GASHAN (CLANK)

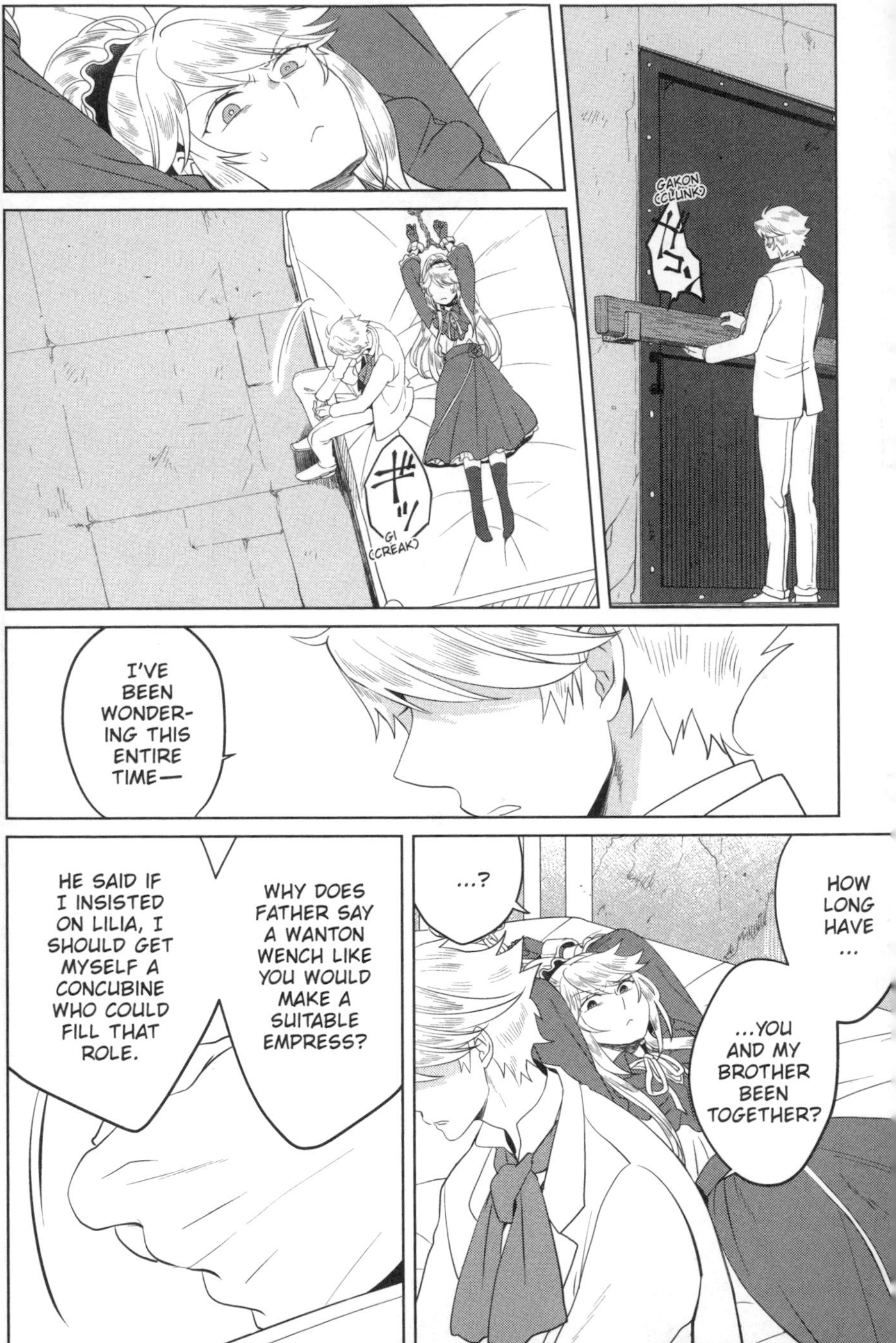
GAKON (CLUNK)
GI (CREAK)
I'VE BEEN WONDERING THIS ENTIRE TIME—
...?
HOW LONG HAVE ...
...YOU AND MY BROTHER BEEN TOGETHER?
WHY DOES FATHER SAY A WANTON WENCH LIKE YOU WOULD MAKE A SUITABLE EMPRESS?
HE SAID IF I INSISTED ON LILIA, I SHOULD GET MYSELF A CONCUBINE WHO COULD FILL THAT ROLE.

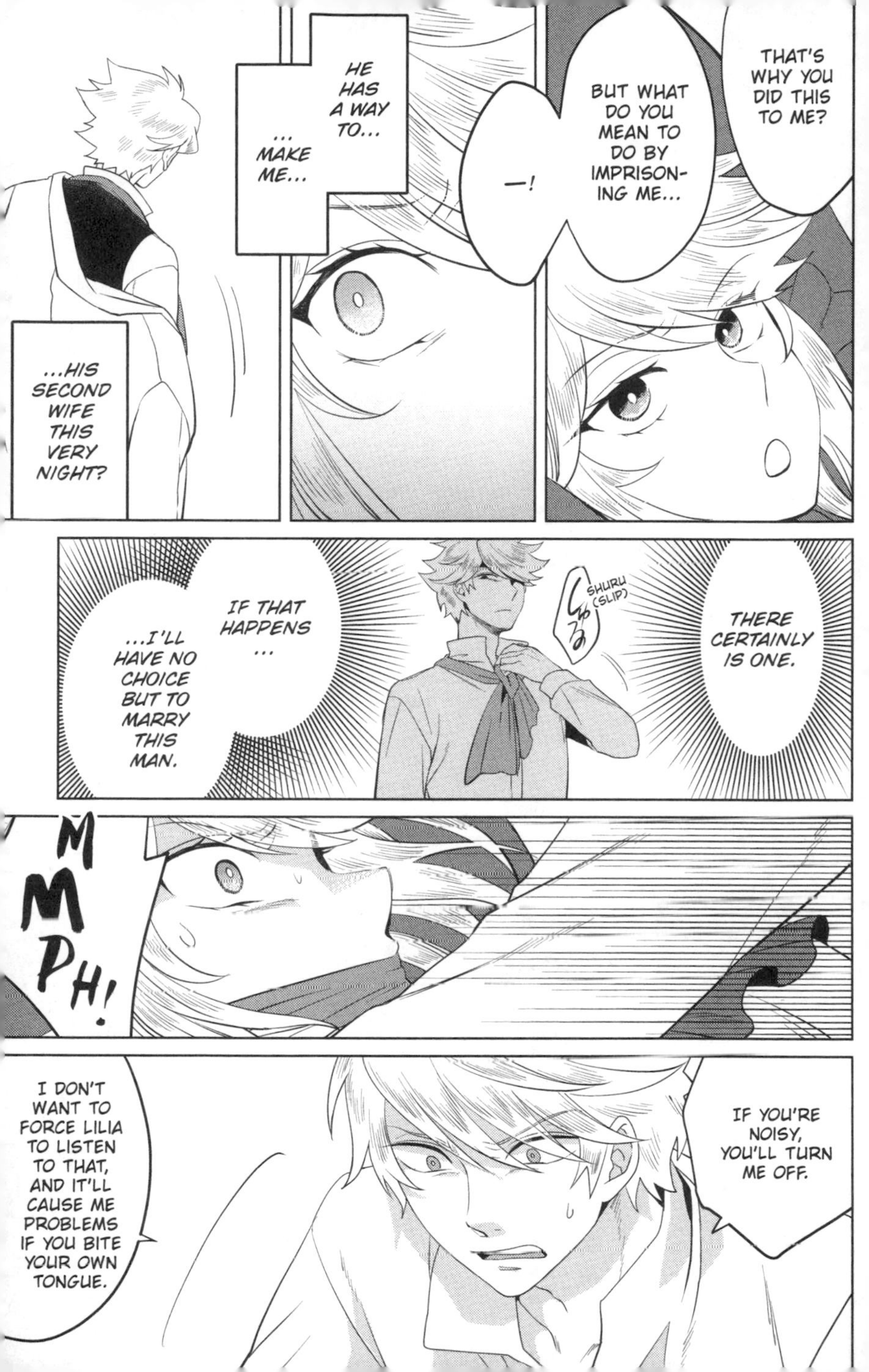
THAT'S WHY YOU DID THIS TO ME?
BUT WHAT DO YOU MEAN TO DO BY IMPRISONING ME...
—!
HE HAS A WAY TO...
...MAKE ME...
...HIS SECOND WIFE THIS VERY NIGHT?
THERE CERTAINLY IS ONE.
SHURU (SLIP)
IF THAT HAPPENS...
...I'LL HAVE NO CHOICE BUT TO MARRY THIS MAN.
MMPH!
IF YOU'RE NOISY, YOU'LL TURN ME OFF.
I DON'T WANT TO FORCE LILIA TO LISTEN TO THAT, AND IT'LL CAUSE ME PROBLEMS IF YOU BITE YOUR OWN TONGUE.

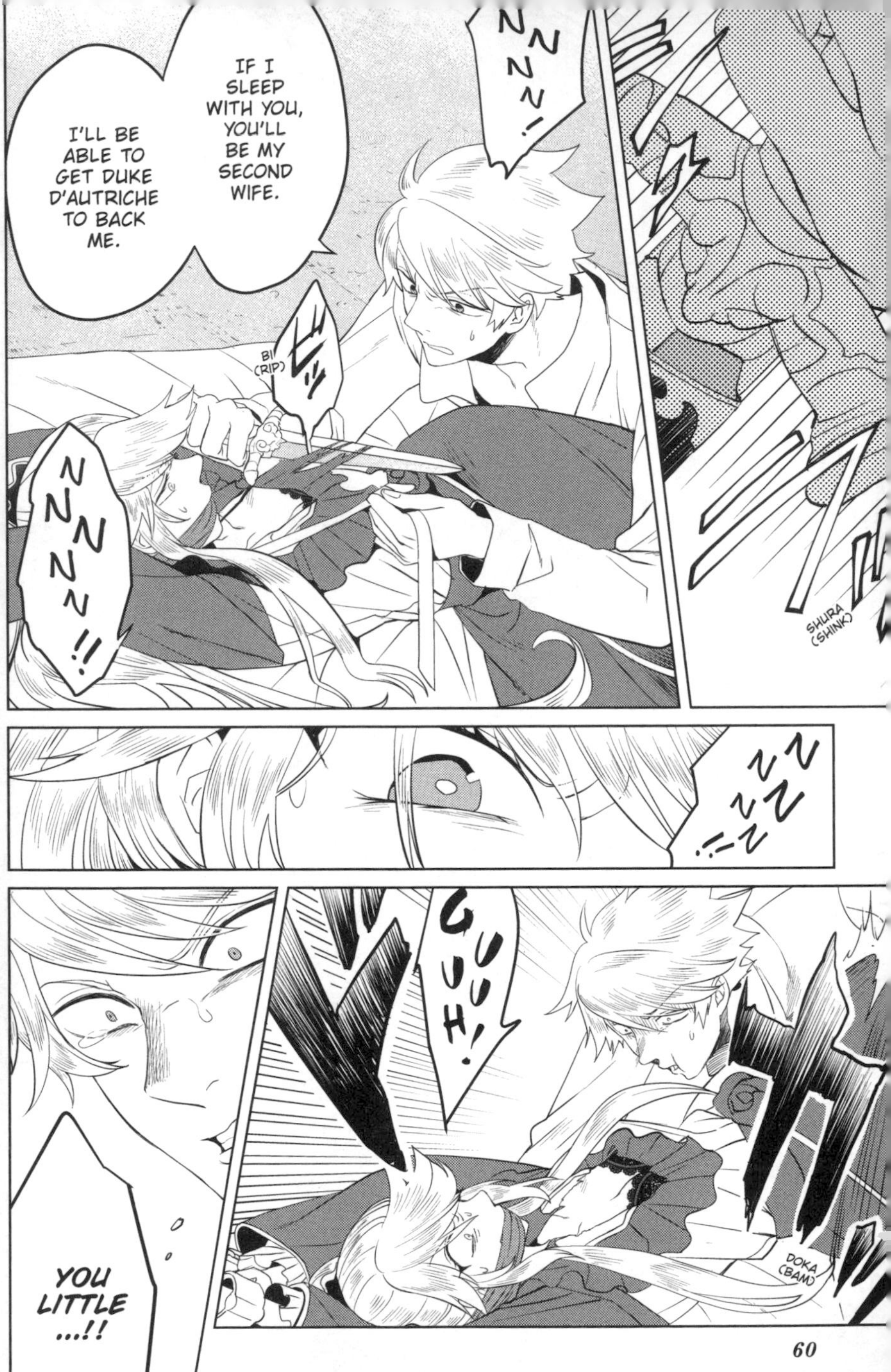
NNNN!
SHURA (SHINK)
IF I SLEEP WITH YOU, YOU'LL BE MY SECOND WIFE.
I'LL BE ABLE TO GET DUKE D'AUTRICHE TO BACK ME.
BI (RIP)
NNNNN!!
NNNNN!!
GUUUH!
DOKA (BAM)
YOU LITTLE ...!!

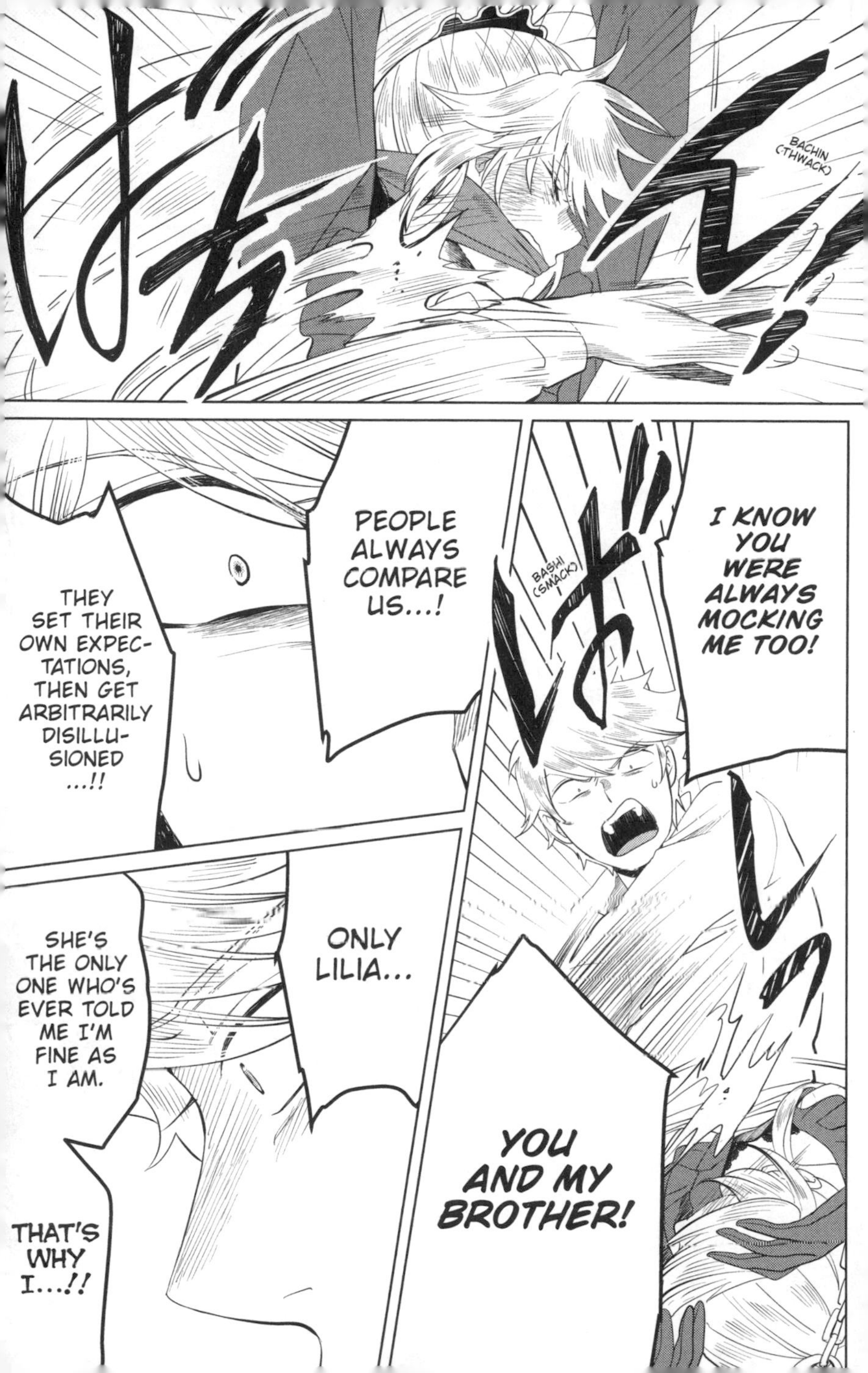
BACHIN (THWACK)
I KNOW YOU WERE ALWAYS MOCKING ME TOO!
BASHI (SMACK)
YOU AND MY BROTHER!
PEOPLE ALWAYS COMPARE US...!
THEY SET THEIR OWN EXPECTATIONS, THEN GET ARBITRARILY DISILLUSIONED...!!
ONLY LILIA...
SHE'S THE ONLY ONE WHO'S EVER TOLD ME I'M FINE AS I AM.
THAT'S WHY I...!!

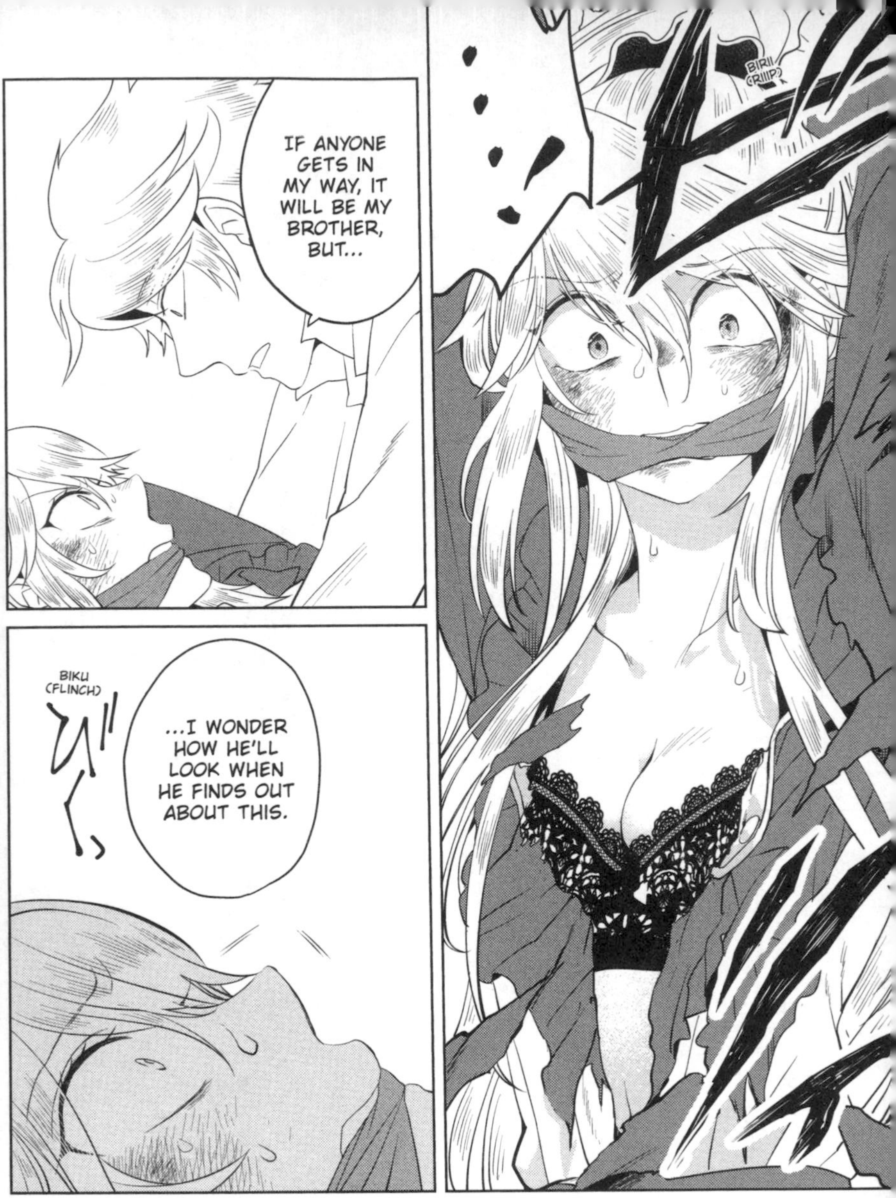
BIRII (RIIIP)
!
IF ANYONE GETS IN MY WAY, IT WILL BE MY BROTHER, BUT...
BIKU (FLINCH)
...I WONDER HOW HE'LL LOOK WHEN HE FINDS OUT ABOUT THIS.

—IF PRINCE CLAUDE...FINDS OUT...?

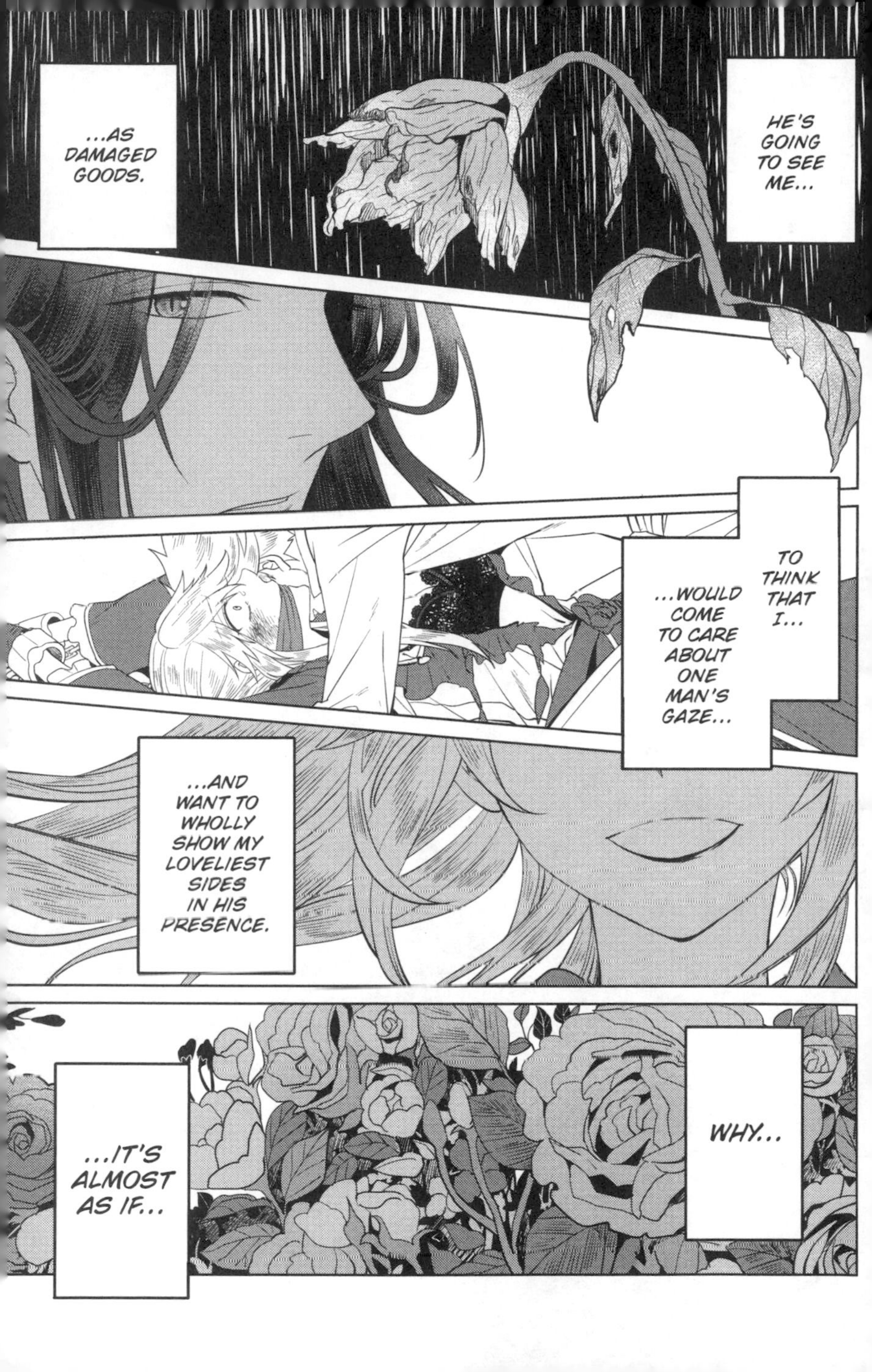
HE'S GOING TO SEE ME...
...AS DAMAGED GOODS.
TO THINK THAT I...
...WOULD COME TO CARE ABOUT ONE MAN'S GAZE...
...AND WANT TO WHOLLY SHOW MY LOVELIEST SIDES IN HIS PRESENCE.
WHY...
...IT'S ALMOST AS IF...

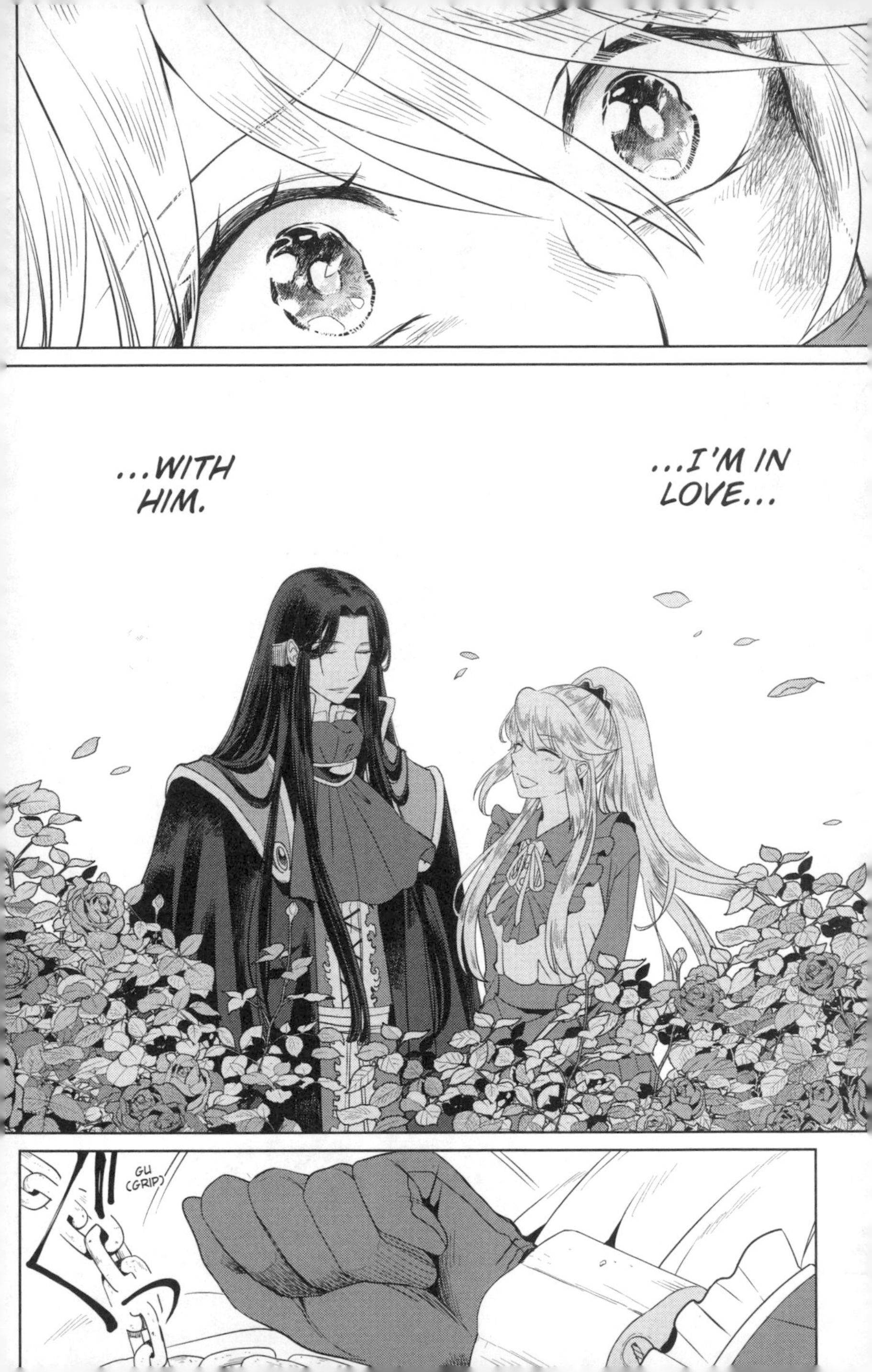
...I'M IN LOVE...
...WITH HIM.
GU (GRIP)

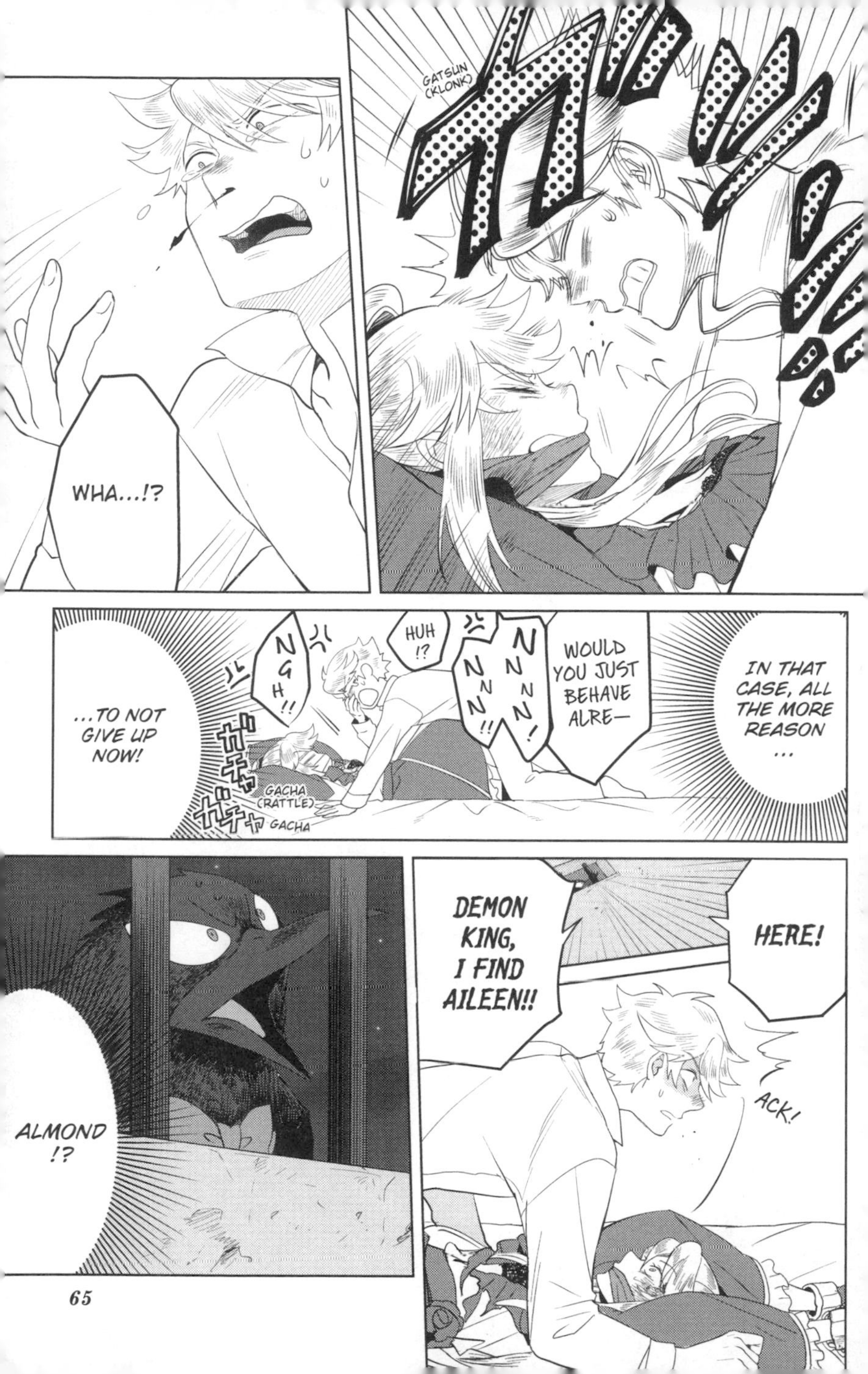
GATSUN (KLONK)
WHA...!?
IN THAT CASE, ALL THE MORE REASON...
WOULD YOU JUST BEHAVE ALRE—
NNNNN!
NNNN!!
HUH!?
NGH!!
GACHA (RATTLE)
GACHA
...TO NOT GIVE UP NOW!
HERE!
DEMON KING, I FIND AILEEN!!
ACK!
ALMOND!?

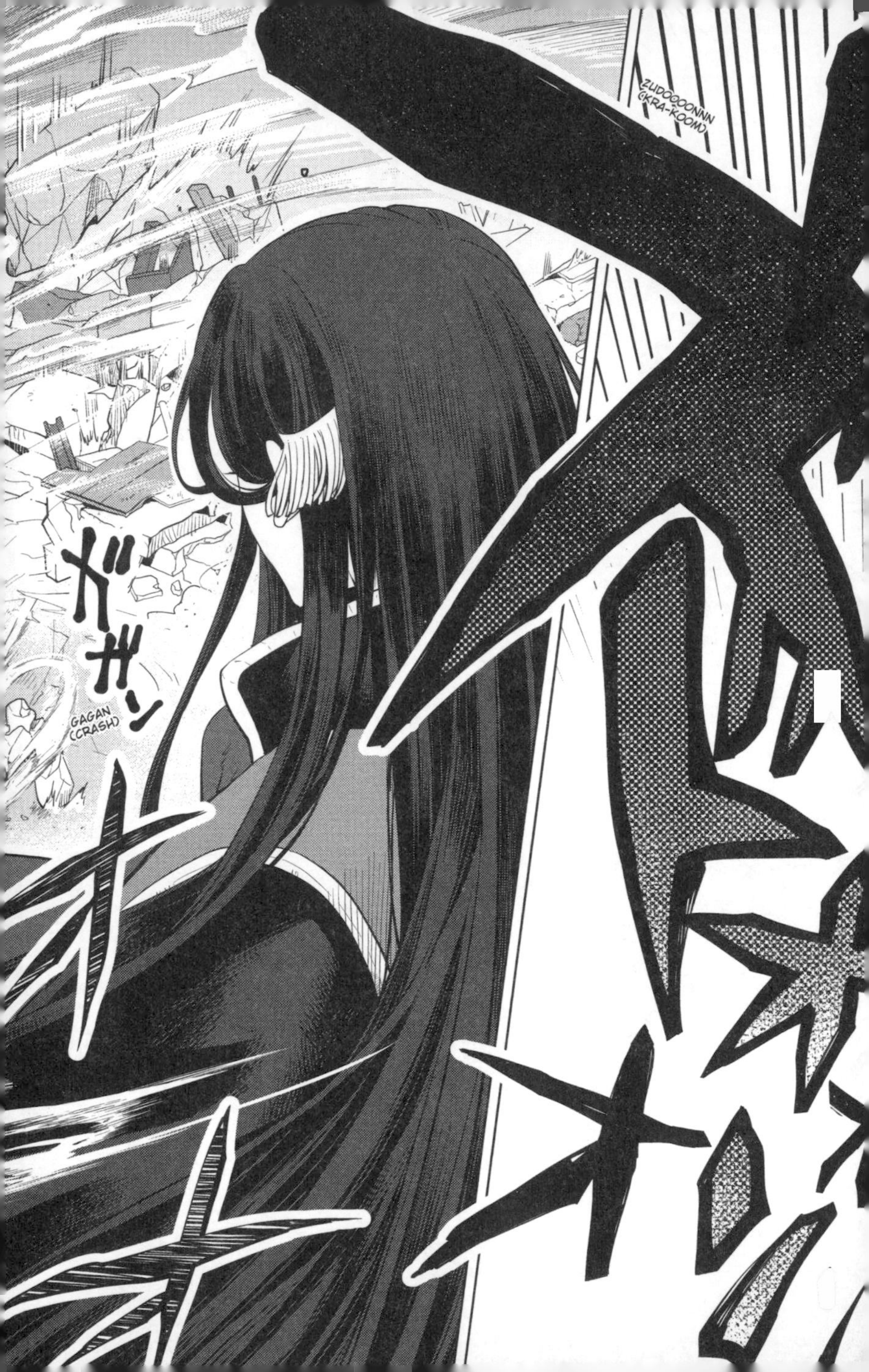
ZUDOOOONNN
(KRA-KOOM)
ガガン
GAGAN
(CRASH)

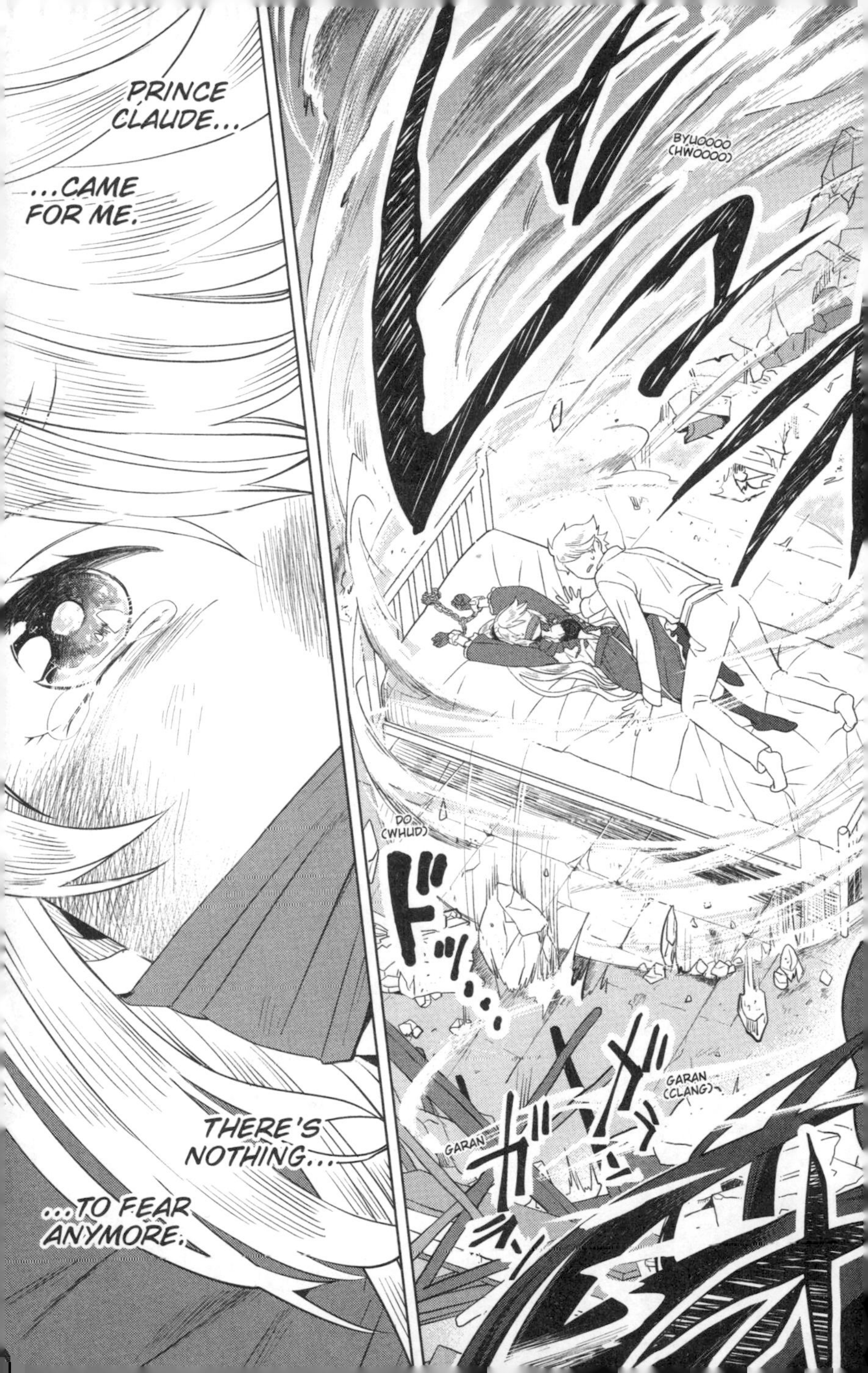
BYUOOOO
(HWOOOO)
DO
(WHUD)
GARAN
(CLANG)
GARAN
PRINCE CLAUDE...
...CAME FOR ME.
THERE'S NOTHING...
...TO FEAR ANYMORE.

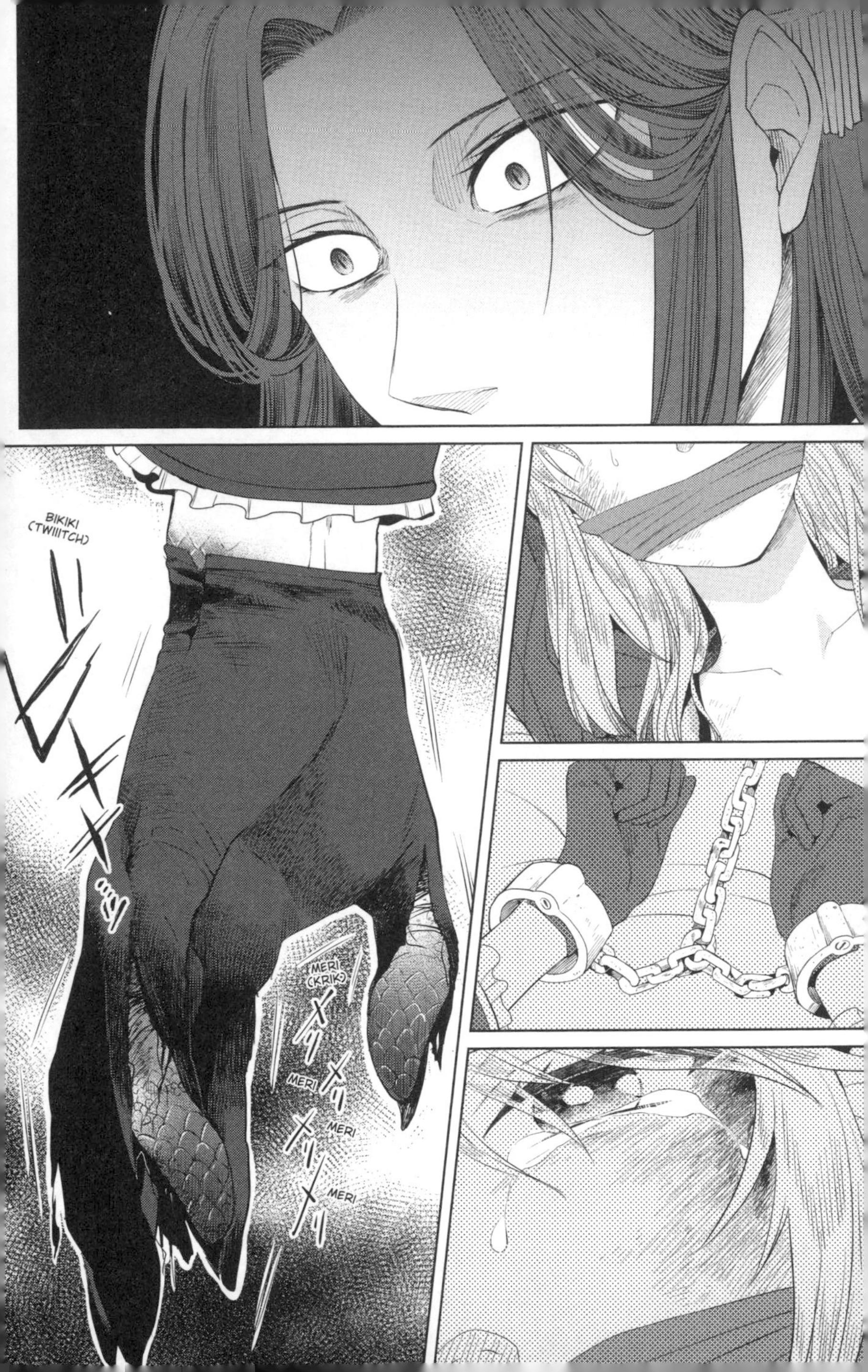
BIKIKI
(TWIIITCH)
MERI
(KRIK)
MERI
MERI
MERI

I'm the **VILLAINESS**, So I'm
the
Taming the **Final Boss**

I'm the VILLAINESS, So I'm Taming the Final Boss

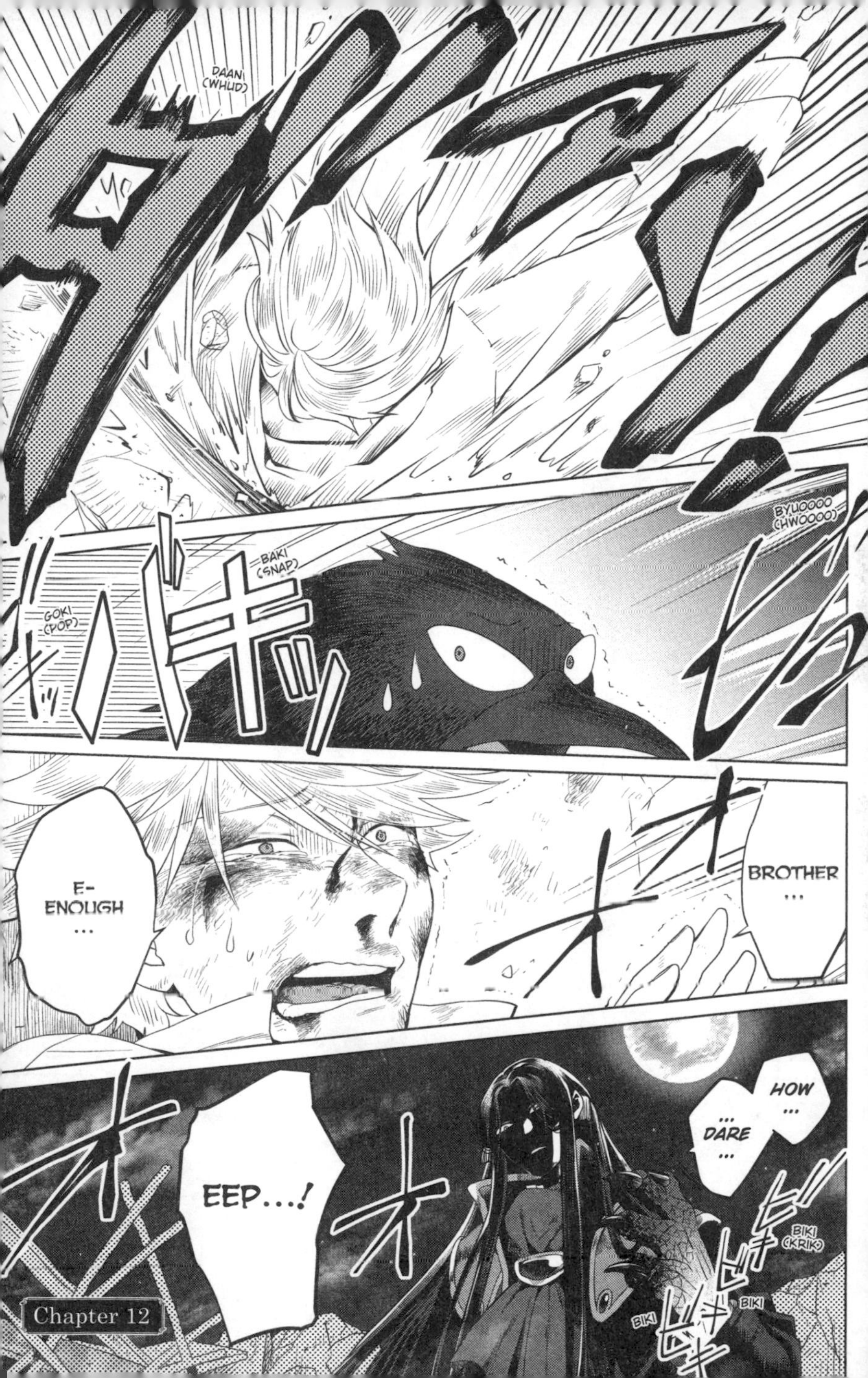
DAAN (WHUD)
BYUOOOO (HWOOOO)
BAKI (SNAP)
GOKI (POP)
BROTHER ...
E-ENOUGH ...
HOW ... ... DARE ...
BIKI (KRIK)
BIKI
BIKI
EEP...!
Chapter 12

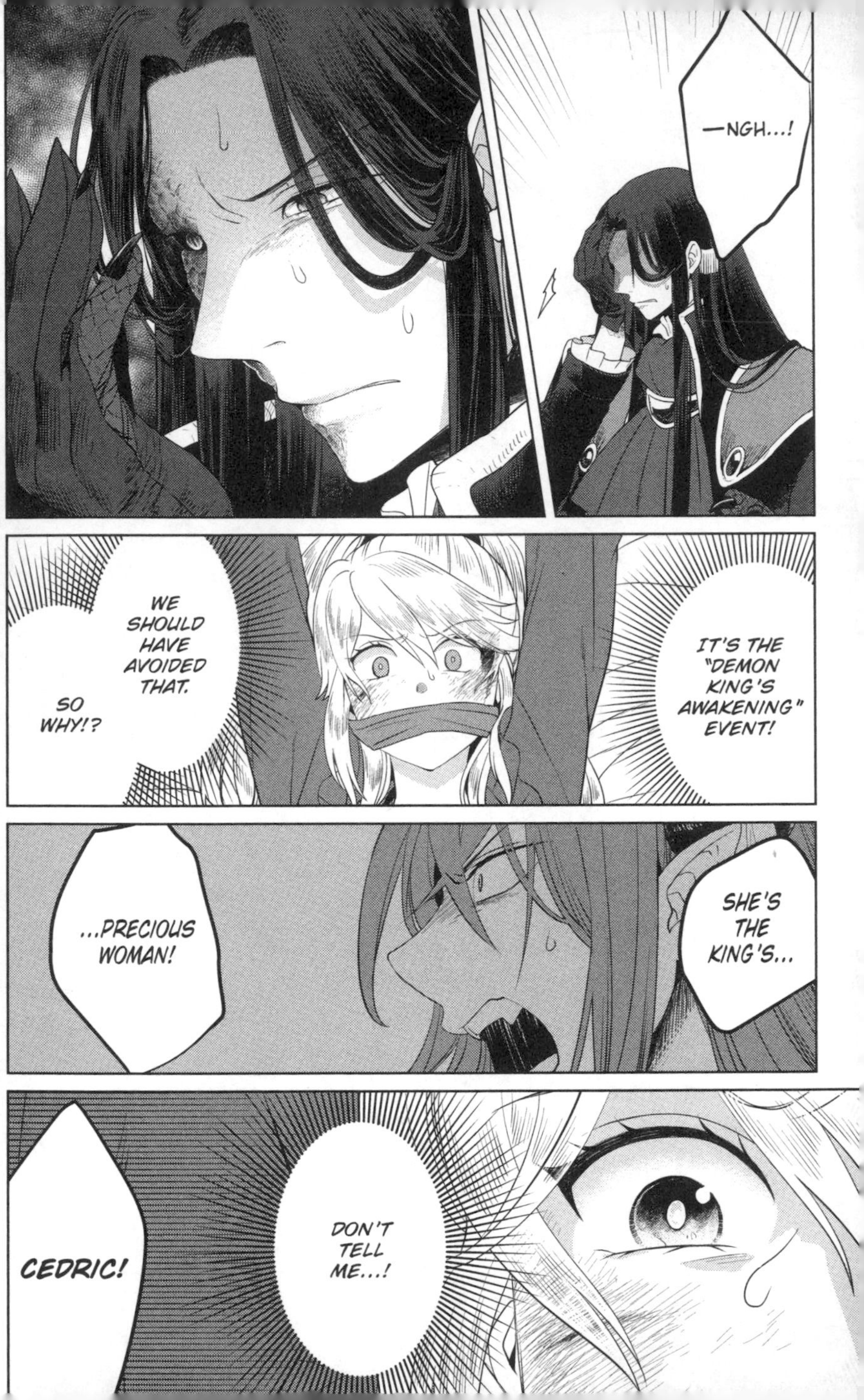
—NGH...!
IT'S THE "DEMON KING'S AWAKENING" EVENT!
WE SHOULD HAVE AVOIDED THAT.
SO WHY!?
SHE'S THE KING'S...
...PRECIOUS WOMAN!
DON'T TELL ME...!
CEDRIC!

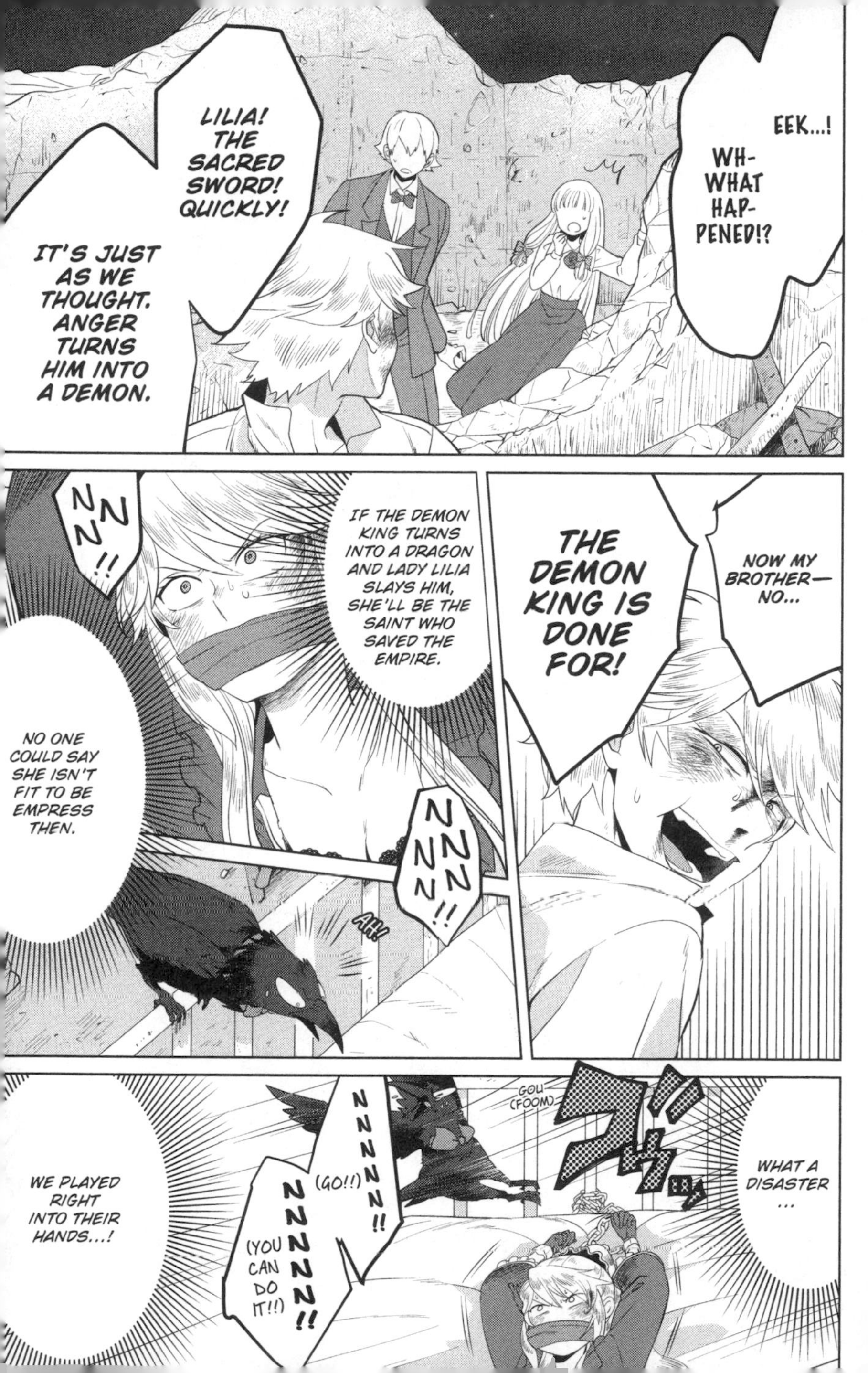
EEK...!
WH-WHAT HAP-PENED!?
LILIA! THE SACRED SWORD! QUICKLY!
IT'S JUST AS WE THOUGHT. ANGER TURNS HIM INTO A DEMON.
NOW MY BROTHER—NO...
THE DEMON KING IS DONE FOR!
IF THE DEMON KING TURNS INTO A DRAGON AND LADY LILIA SLAYS HIM, SHE'LL BE THE SAINT WHO SAVED THE EMPIRE.
NNN!!
NO ONE COULD SAY SHE ISN'T FIT TO BE EMPRESS THEN.
NNNNN!!
AH!
WHAT A DISASTER...
GOU (FOOM)
NNNNN!!
(GO!!)
NNNNN!!
(YOU CAN DO IT!!)
WE PLAYED RIGHT INTO THEIR HANDS...!

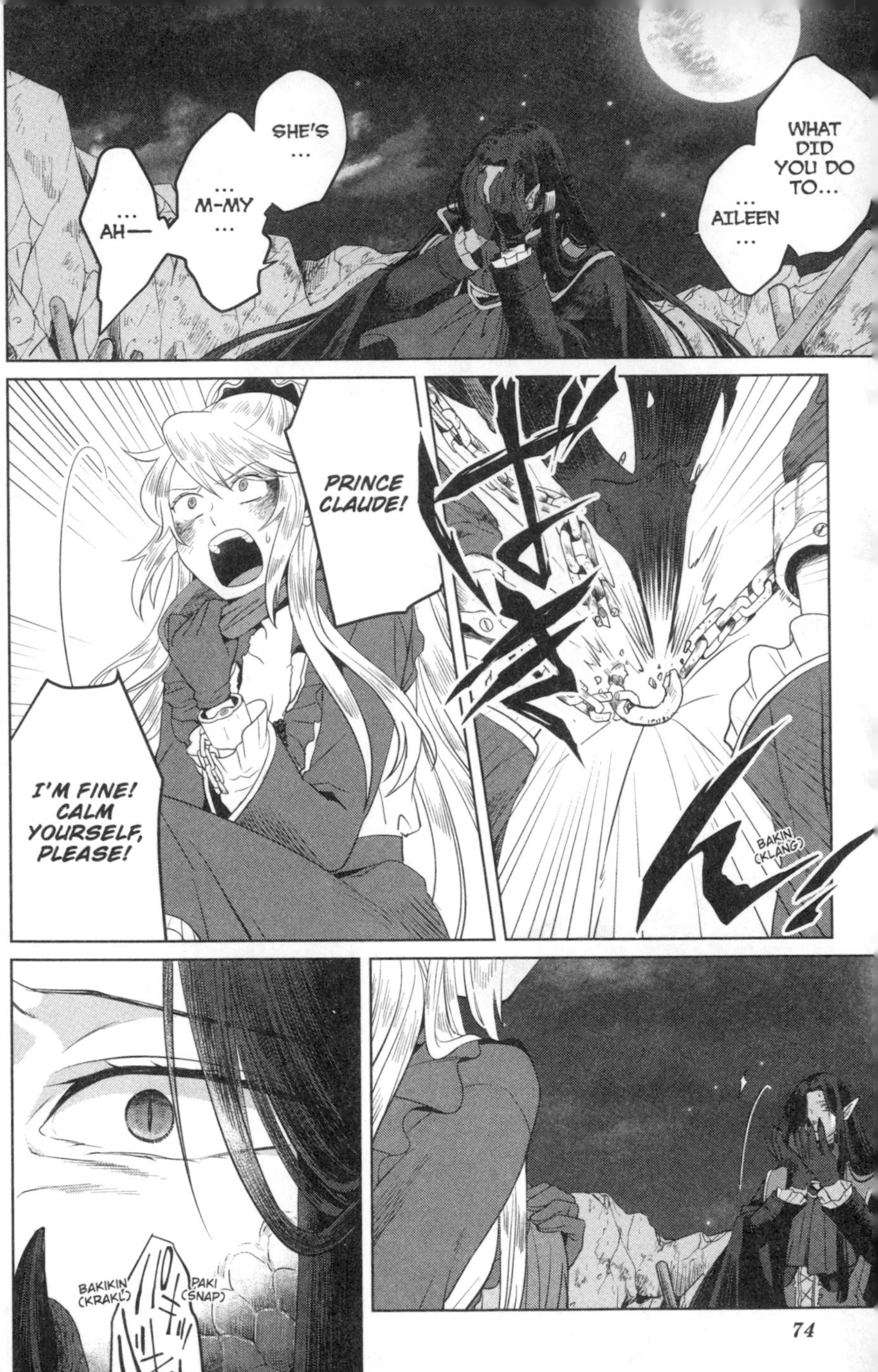
WHAT DID YOU DO TO… …AILEEN…
SHE'S …
… M-MY …
… AH—
BAKIN (KLANG)
PRINCE CLAUDE!
I'M FINE! CALM YOURSELF, PLEASE!
PAKI (SNAP)
BAKIKIN (KRAKL)

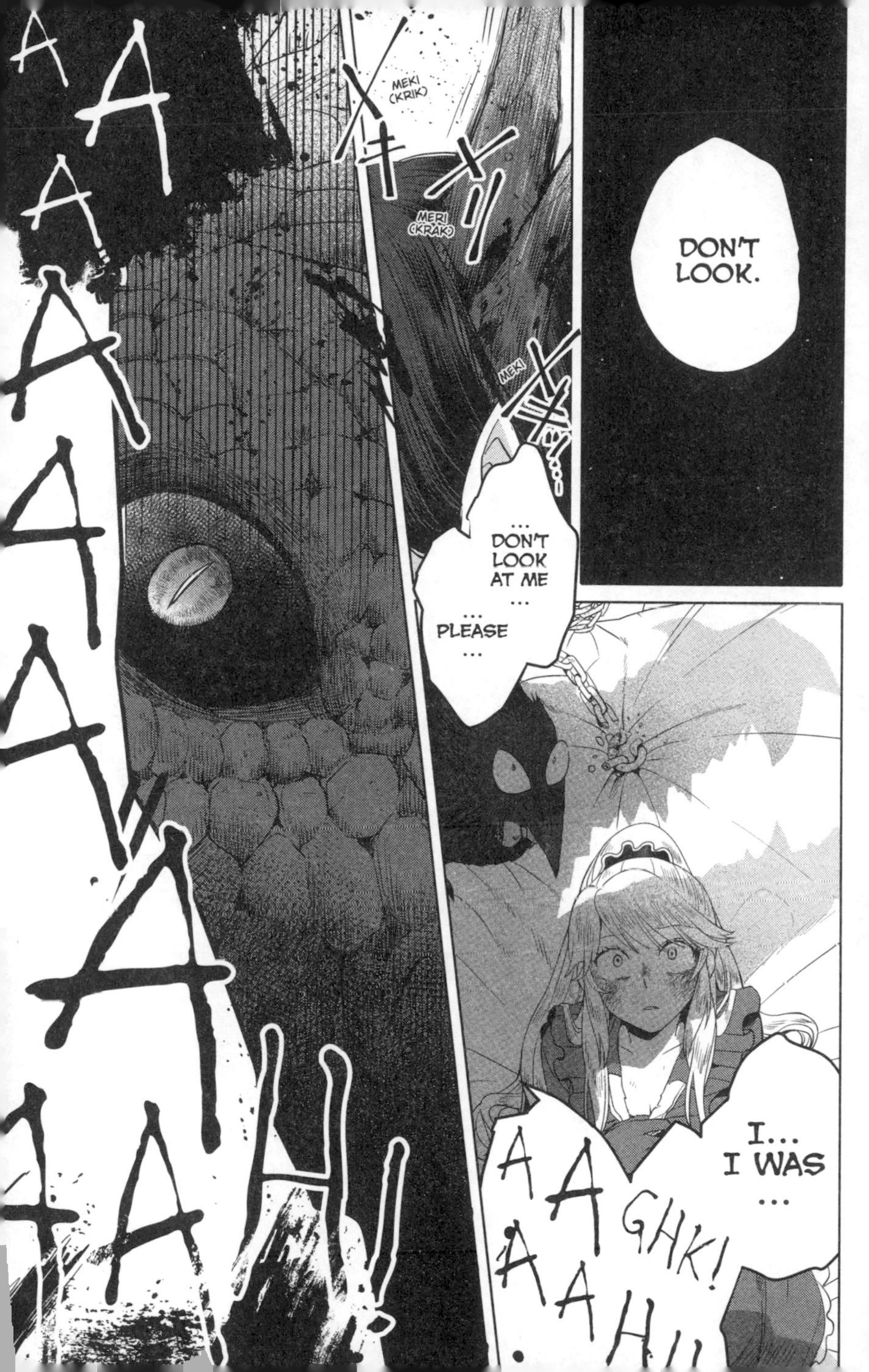
DON'T LOOK.
MEKI (KRIK)
MERI (KRAK)
MEKI
... DON'T LOOK AT ME ... ... PLEASE ...
I... I WAS ...
AAGHK! AAH!!
AAAAAAAAAAAH!!

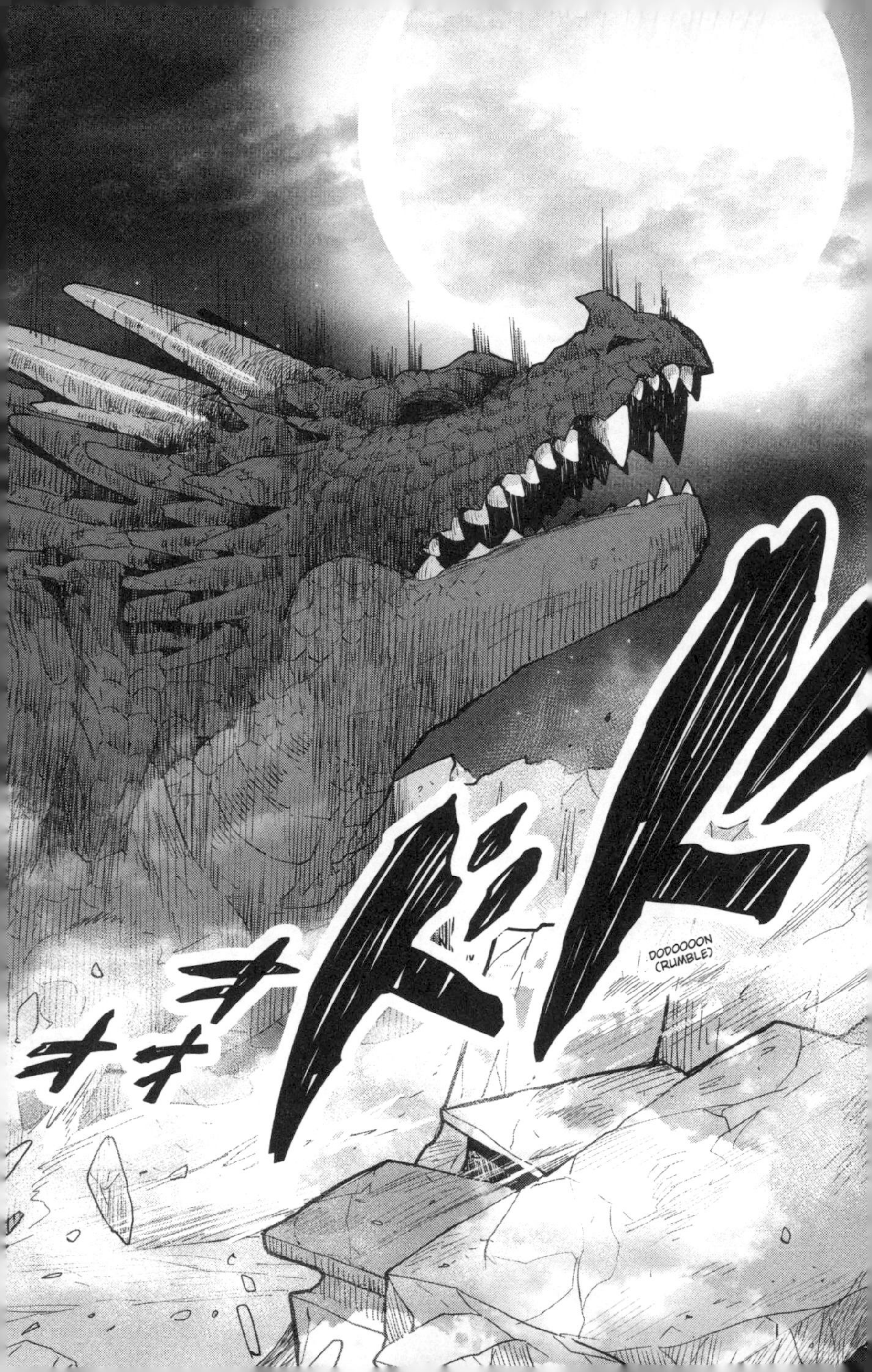
DODOOOON
(RUMBLE)

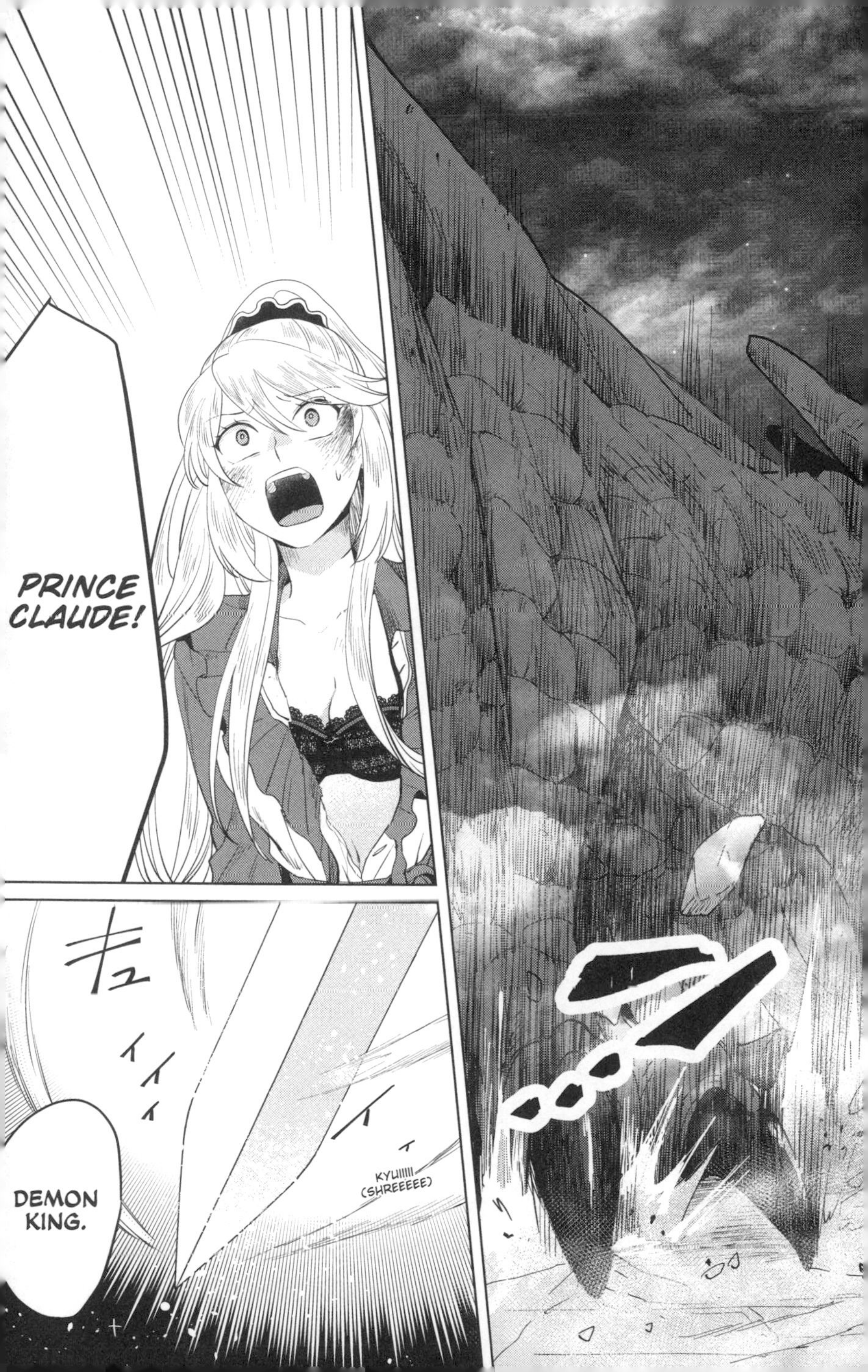
PRINCE CLAUDE!
KYUIIII (SHREEEEE)
DEMON KING.

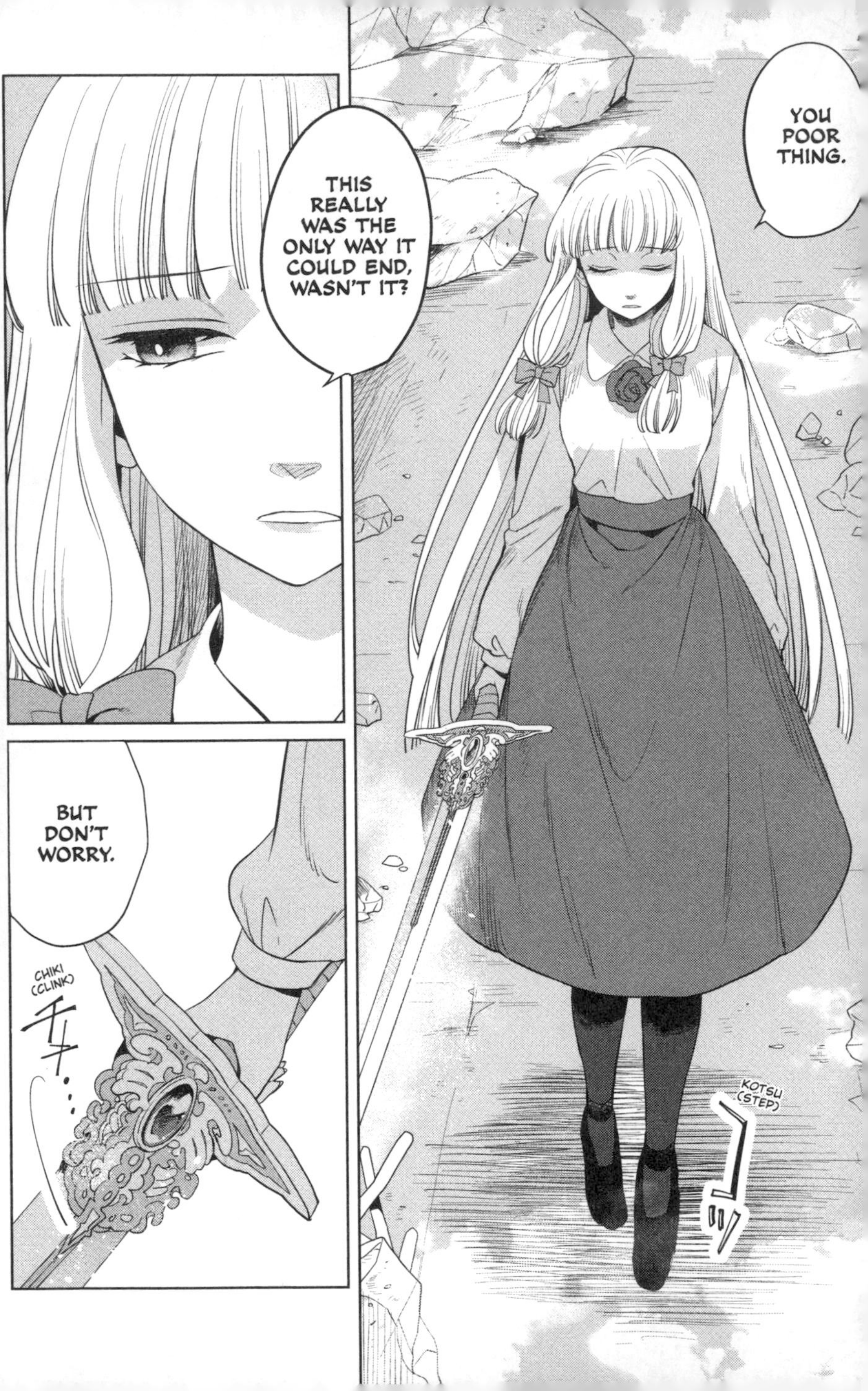
YOU POOR THING.
KOTSU (STEP)
THIS REALLY WAS THE ONLY WAY IT COULD END, WASN'T IT?
BUT DON'T WORRY.
CHIKI (CLINK)

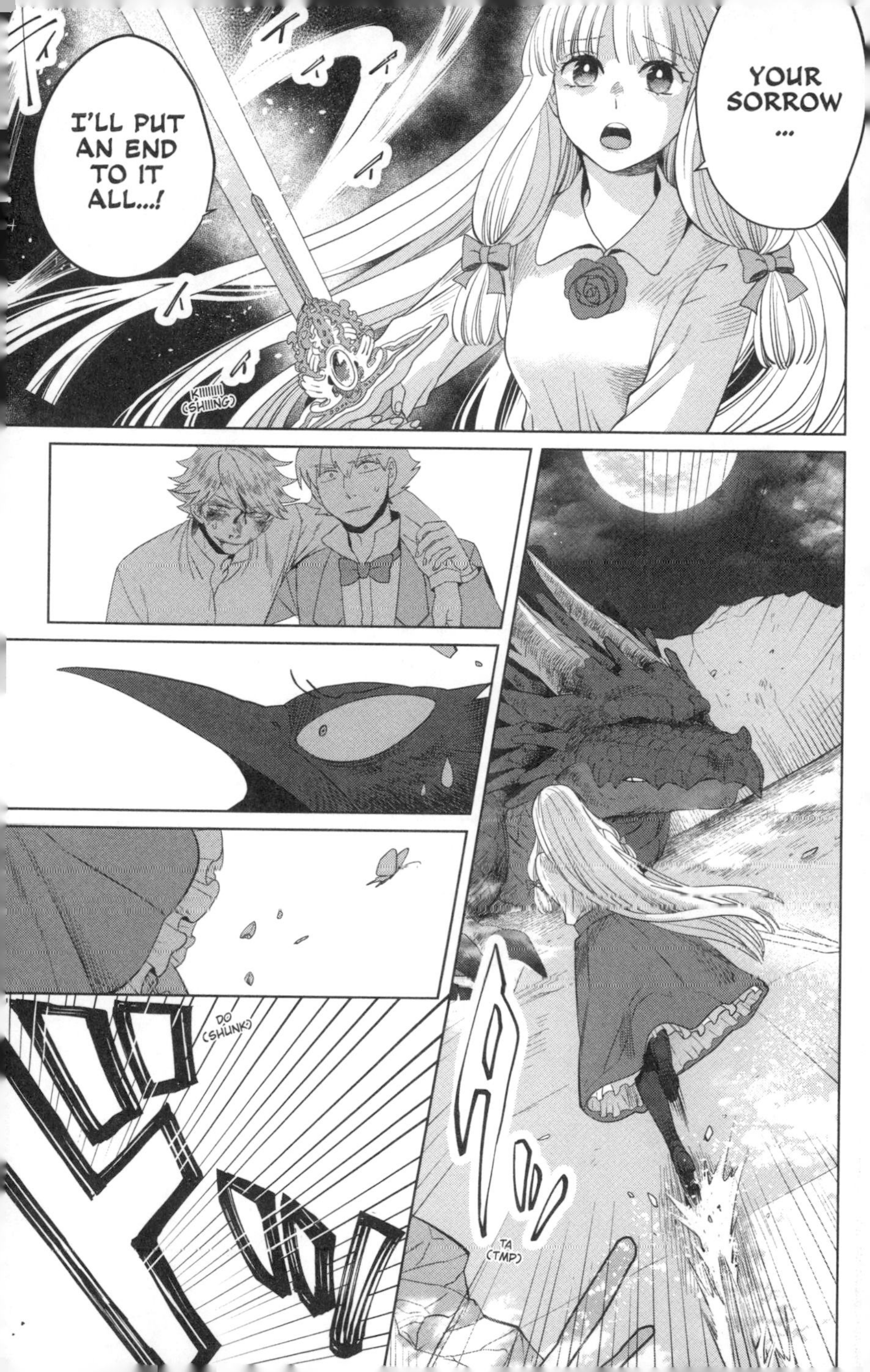
YOUR SORROW ...
I'LL PUT AN END TO IT ALL...!
KIIIIIIII (SHIIING)
TA (TMP)
DO (SHUNK)

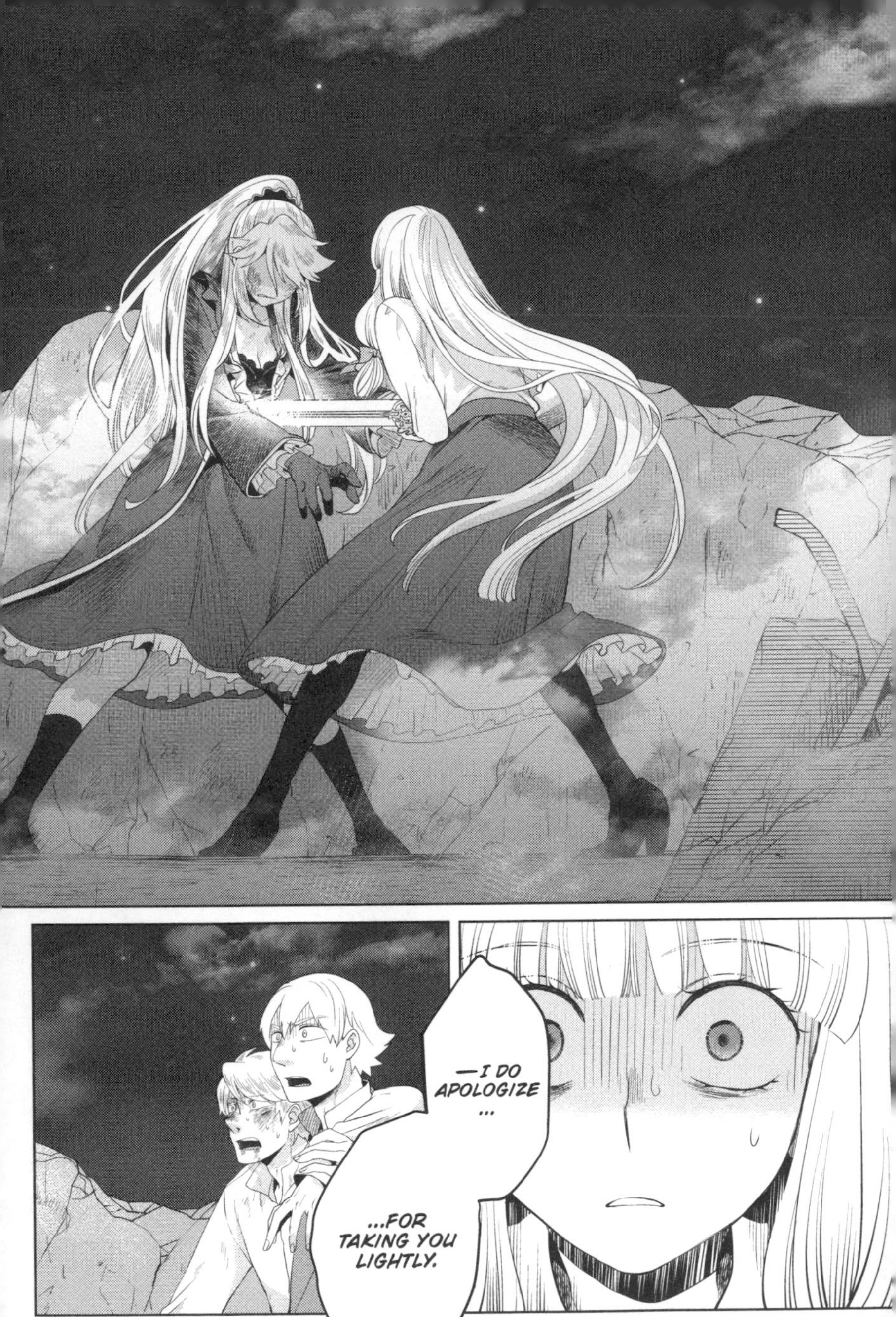
—I DO APOLOGIZE ...
...FOR TAKING YOU LIGHTLY.

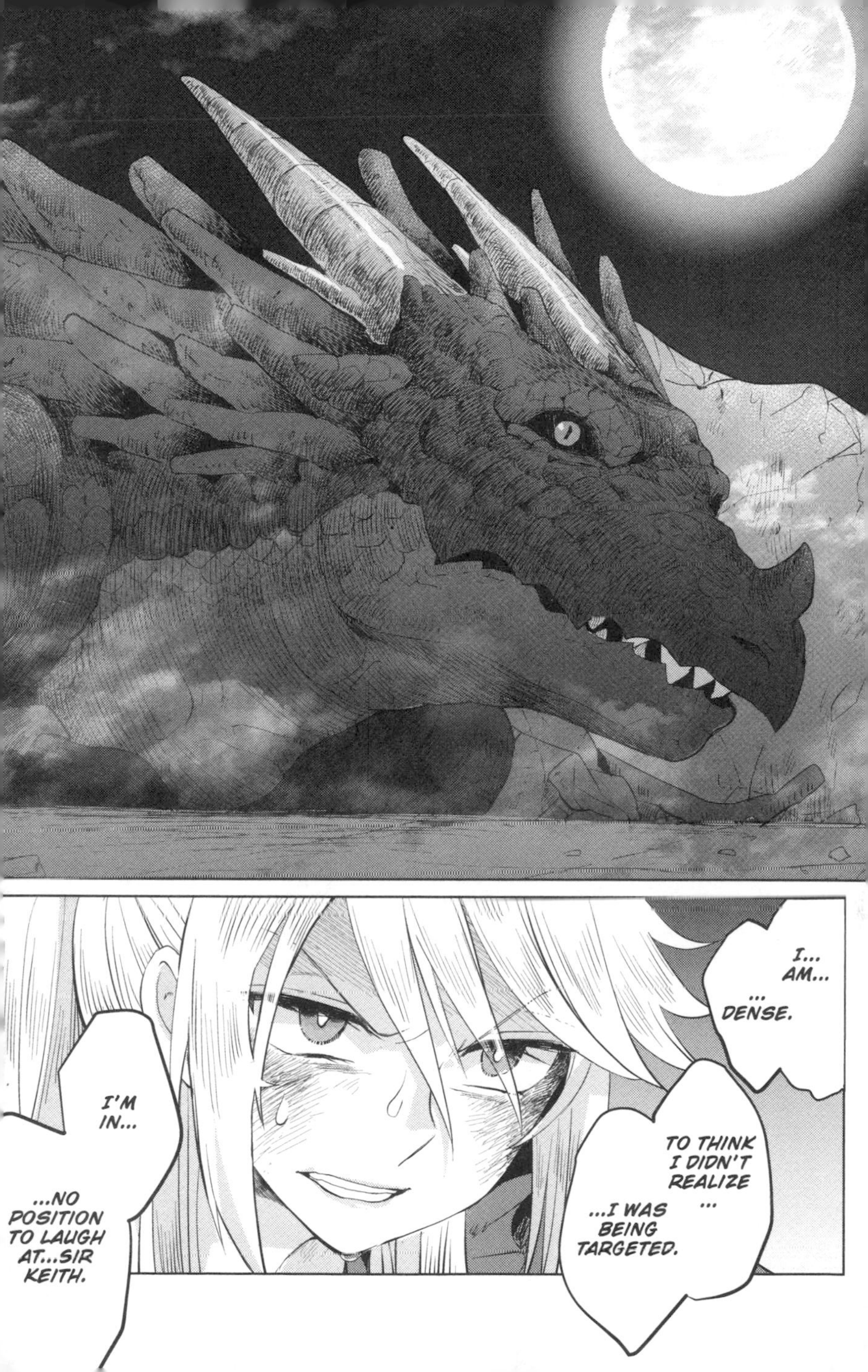
I... AM...
...DENSE.
TO THINK I DIDN'T REALIZE ...
...I WAS BEING TARGETED.
I'M IN...
...NO POSITION TO LAUGH AT...SIR KEITH.

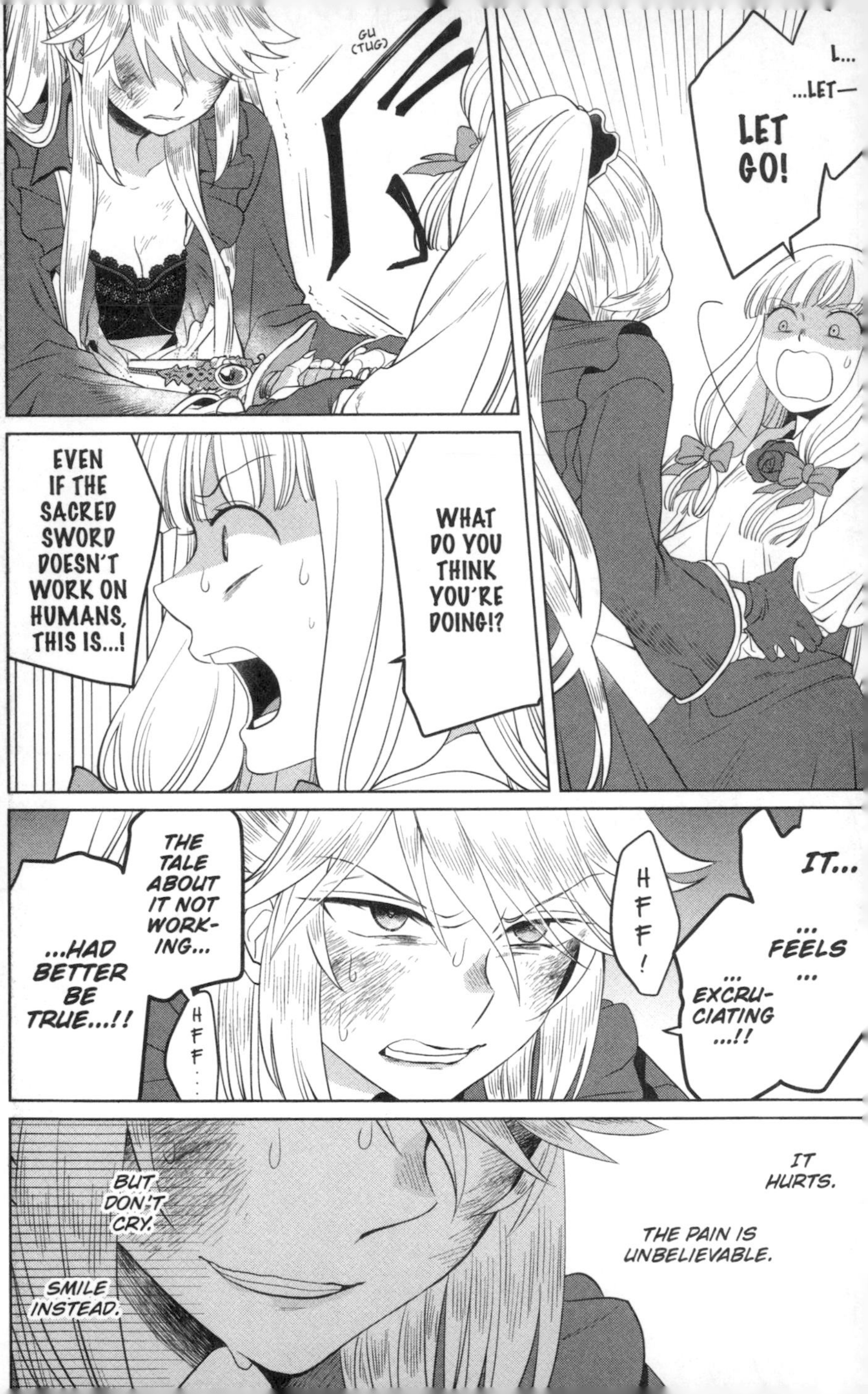
L...
...LET—
LET GO!
GU (TUG)
WHAT DO YOU THINK YOU'RE DOING!?
EVEN IF THE SACRED SWORD DOESN'T WORK ON HUMANS, THIS IS...!
IT... ...FEELS... ...EXCRUCIATING...!!
HFF!
THE TALE ABOUT IT NOT WORKING...
HFF...
...HAD BETTER BE TRUE...!!
IT HURTS.
THE PAIN IS UNBELIEVABLE.
BUT DON'T CRY.
SMILE INSTEAD.

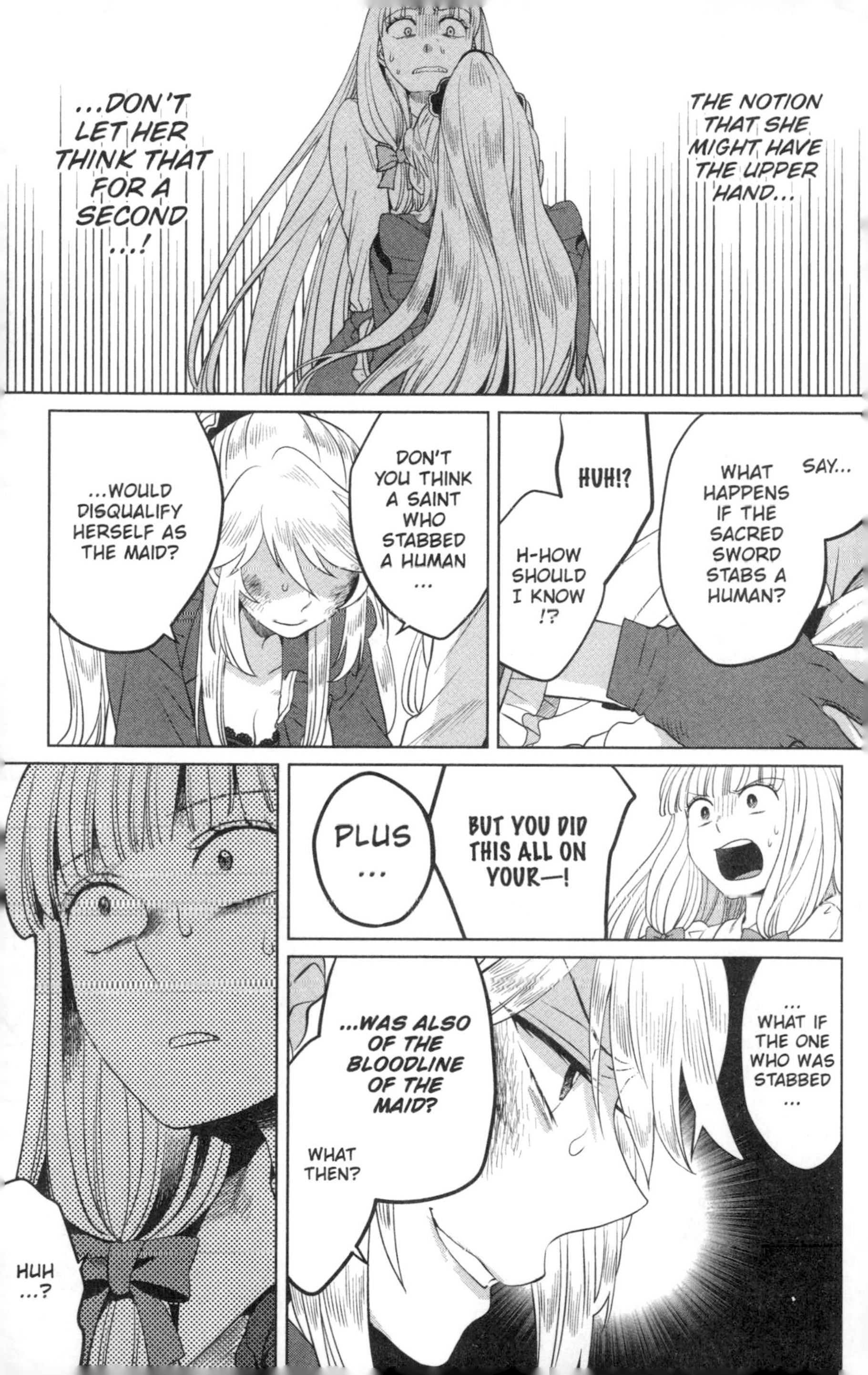
THE NOTION THAT SHE MIGHT HAVE THE UPPER HAND...
...DON'T LET HER THINK THAT FOR A SECOND...!
SAY...
WHAT HAPPENS IF THE SACRED SWORD STABS A HUMAN?
HUH!?
H-HOW SHOULD I KNOW!?
DON'T YOU THINK A SAINT WHO STABBED A HUMAN...
...WOULD DISQUALIFY HERSELF AS THE MAID?
BUT YOU DID THIS ALL ON YOUR—!
PLUS...
...WHAT IF THE ONE WHO WAS STABBED...
...WAS ALSO OF THE BLOODLINE OF THE MAID?
WHAT THEN?
HUH...?

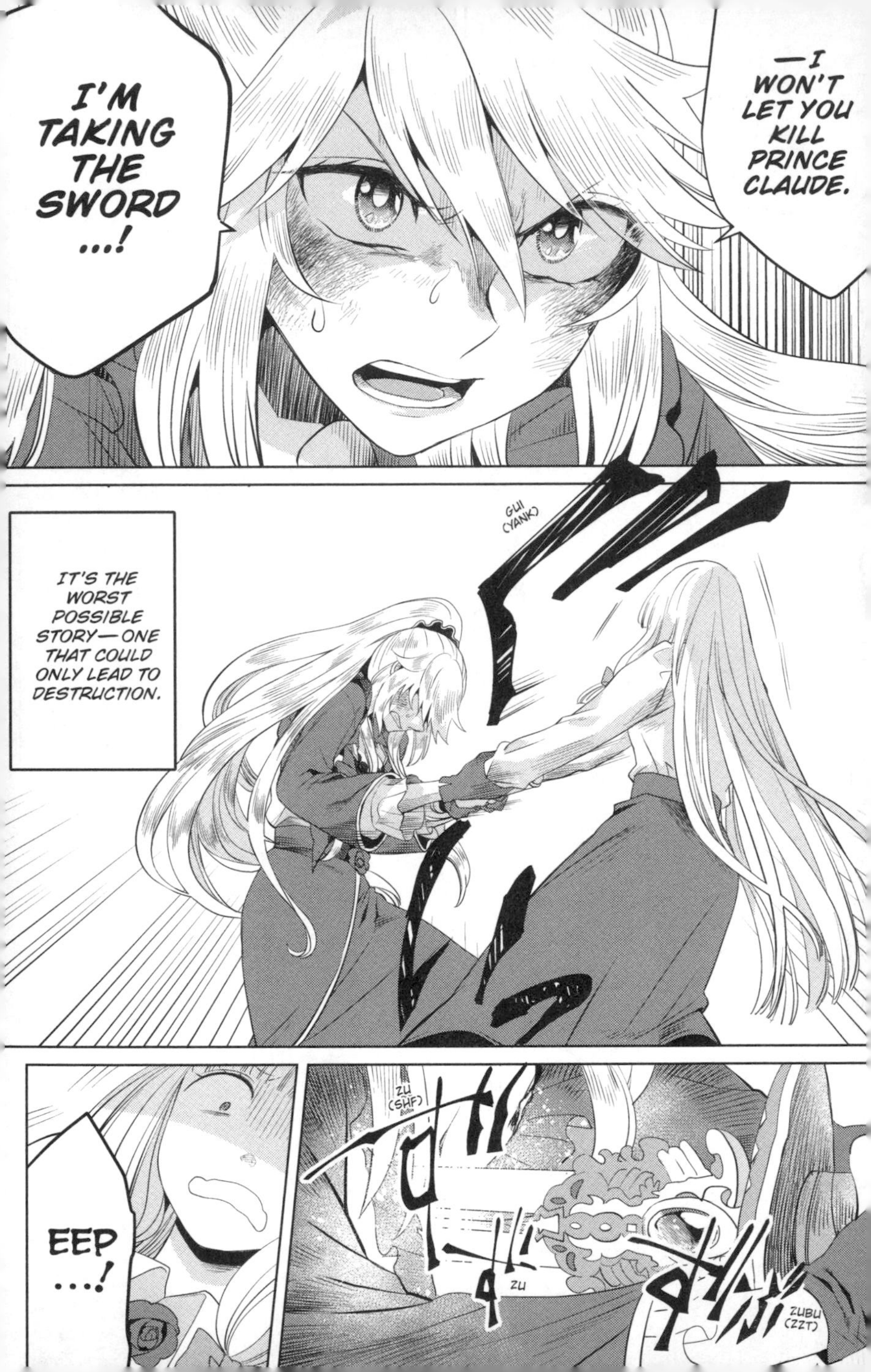
—I WON'T LET YOU KILL PRINCE CLAUDE.
I'M TAKING THE SWORD ...!
GUI (YANK)
IT'S THE WORST POSSIBLE STORY—ONE THAT COULD ONLY LEAD TO DESTRUCTION.
ZU (SHF)
ZU
ZUBU (ZZT)
EEP ...!

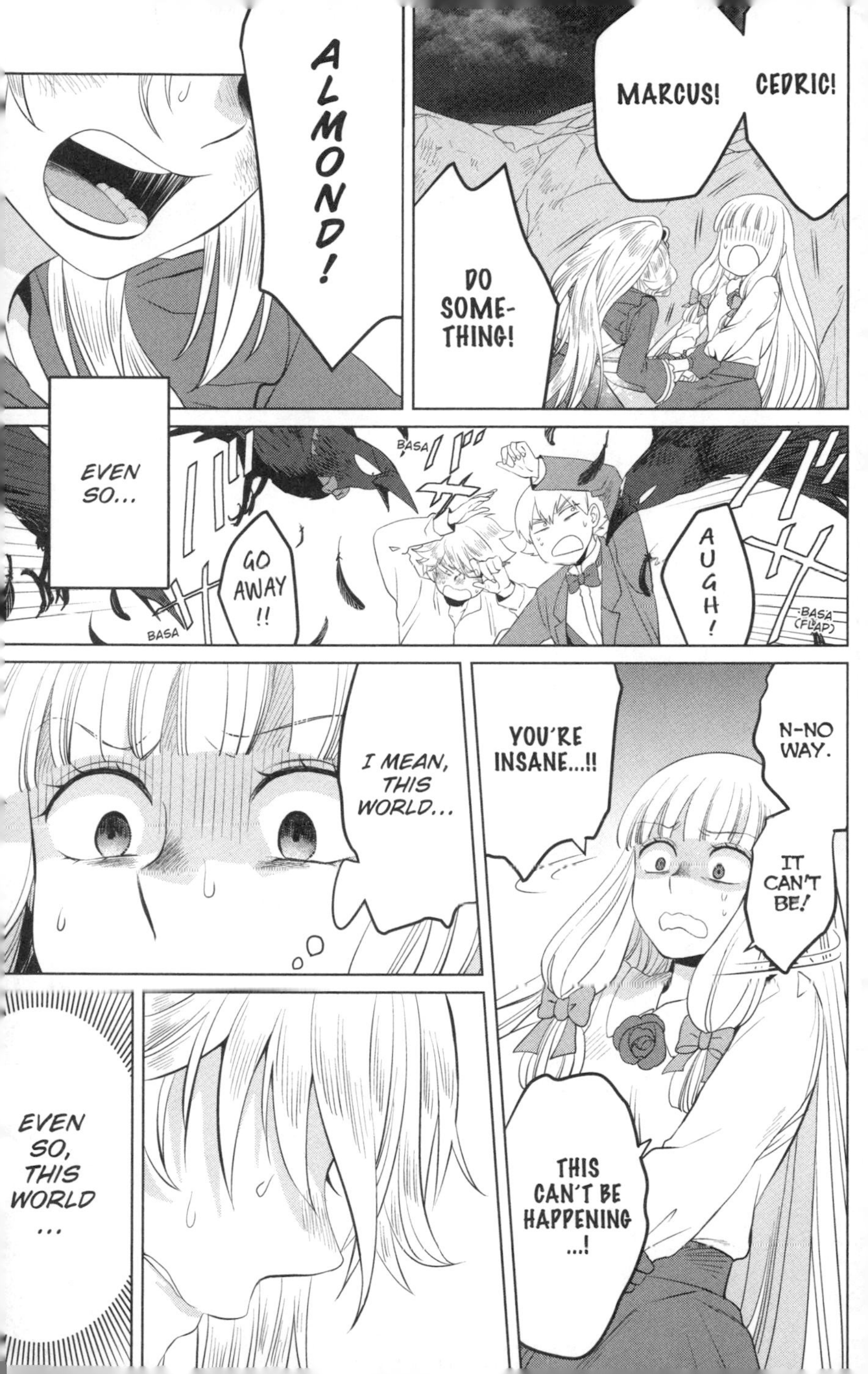
CEDRIC!
MARCUS!
DO SOMETHING!
ALMOND!
BASA
AUGH!
BASA (FLAP)
GO AWAY!!
EVEN SO...
BASA
N-NO WAY.
YOU'RE INSANE...!!
IT CAN'T BE!
THIS CAN'T BE HAPPENING...!
I MEAN, THIS WORLD...
EVEN SO, THIS WORLD...

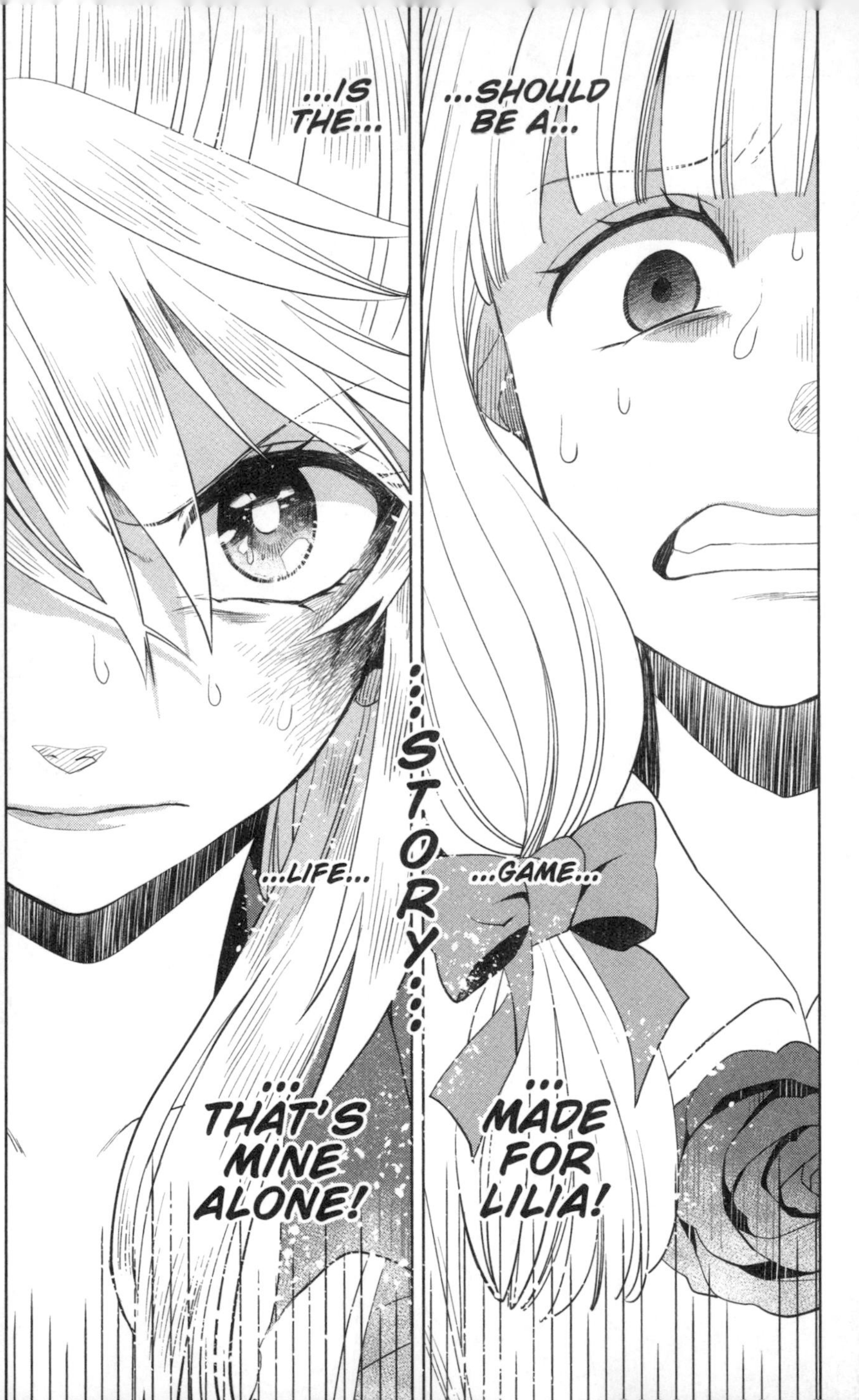
...SHOULD BE A...
...GAME...
...MADE FOR LILIA!
...STORY...
...IS THE...
...LIFE...
...THAT'S MINE ALONE!

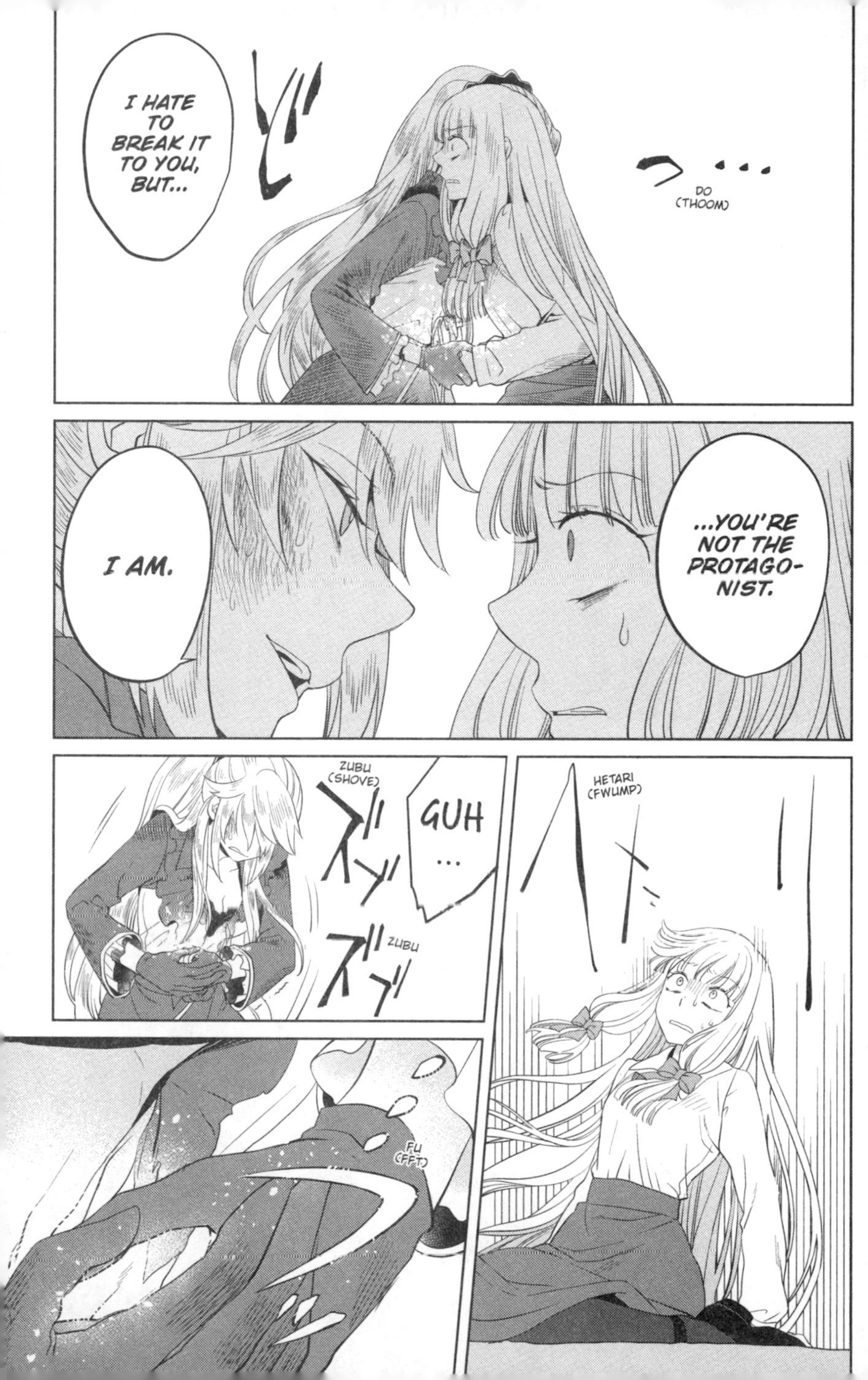
DO
(THOOM)
I HATE TO BREAK IT TO YOU, BUT...
...YOU'RE NOT THE PROTAGO-NIST.
I AM.
HETARI
(FWUMP)
GUH ...
ZUBU
(SHOVE)
ZUBU
FU
(FFT)

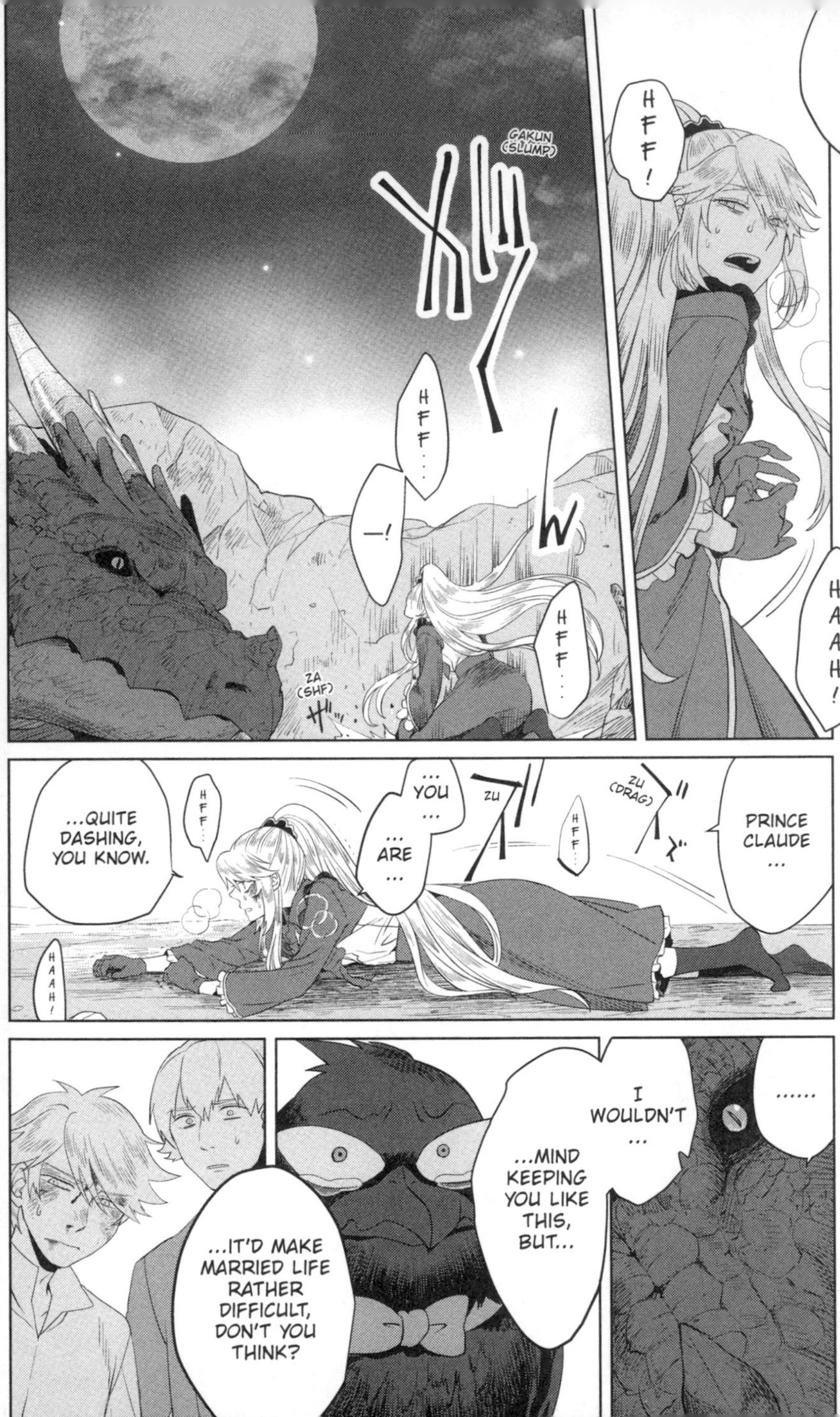
HFF!
HFF!
HAAAH!
GAKUN (SLUMP)
HFF...
—!
HFF...
ZA (SHF)
PRINCE CLAUDE...
ZU (DRAG)
HFF...
ZU
...YOU... ...ARE...
HFF...
...QUITE DASHING, YOU KNOW.
HAAAH!
......
I WOULDN'T... ...MIND KEEPING YOU LIKE THIS, BUT...
...IT'D MAKE MARRIED LIFE RATHER DIFFICULT, DON'T YOU THINK?

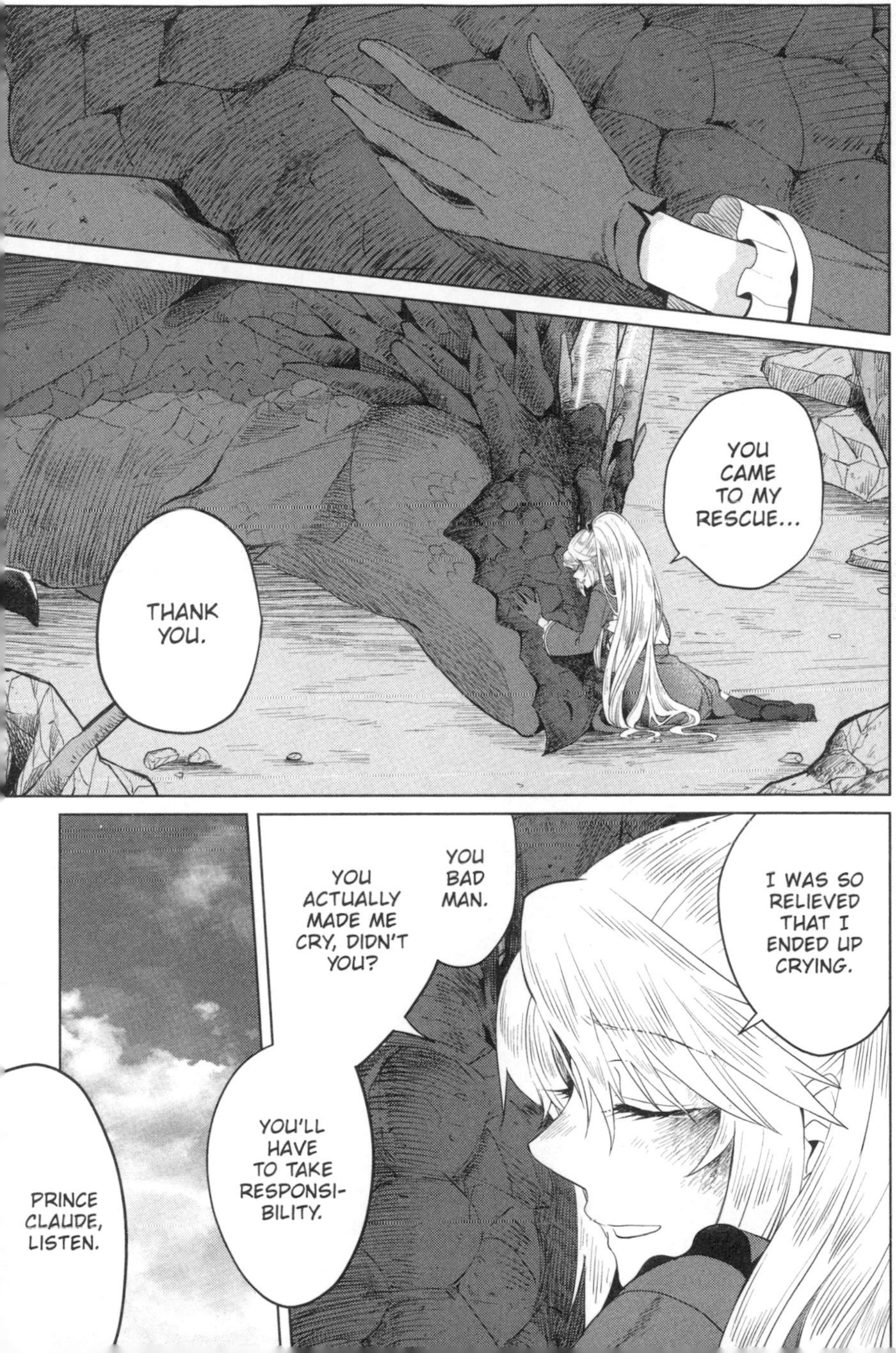
YOU CAME TO MY RESCUE...
THANK YOU.
I WAS SO RELIEVED THAT I ENDED UP CRYING.
YOU BAD MAN.
YOU ACTUALLY MADE ME CRY, DIDN'T YOU?
YOU'LL HAVE TO TAKE RESPONSIBILITY.
PRINCE CLAUDE, LISTEN.

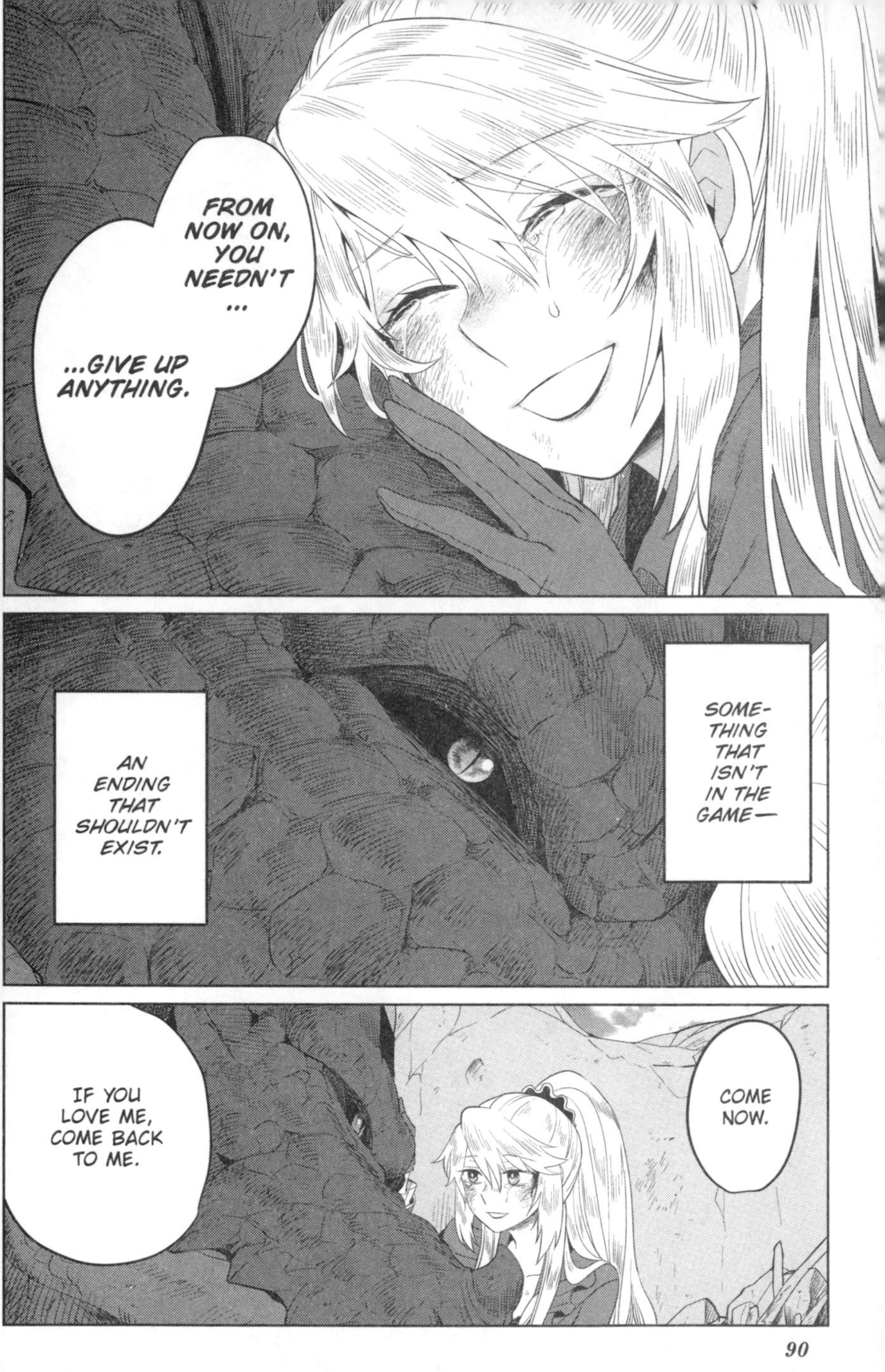
FROM NOW ON, YOU NEEDN'T ...
...GIVE UP ANYTHING.
SOME-THING THAT ISN'T IN THE GAME—
AN ENDING THAT SHOULDN'T EXIST.
COME NOW.
IF YOU LOVE ME, COME BACK TO ME.

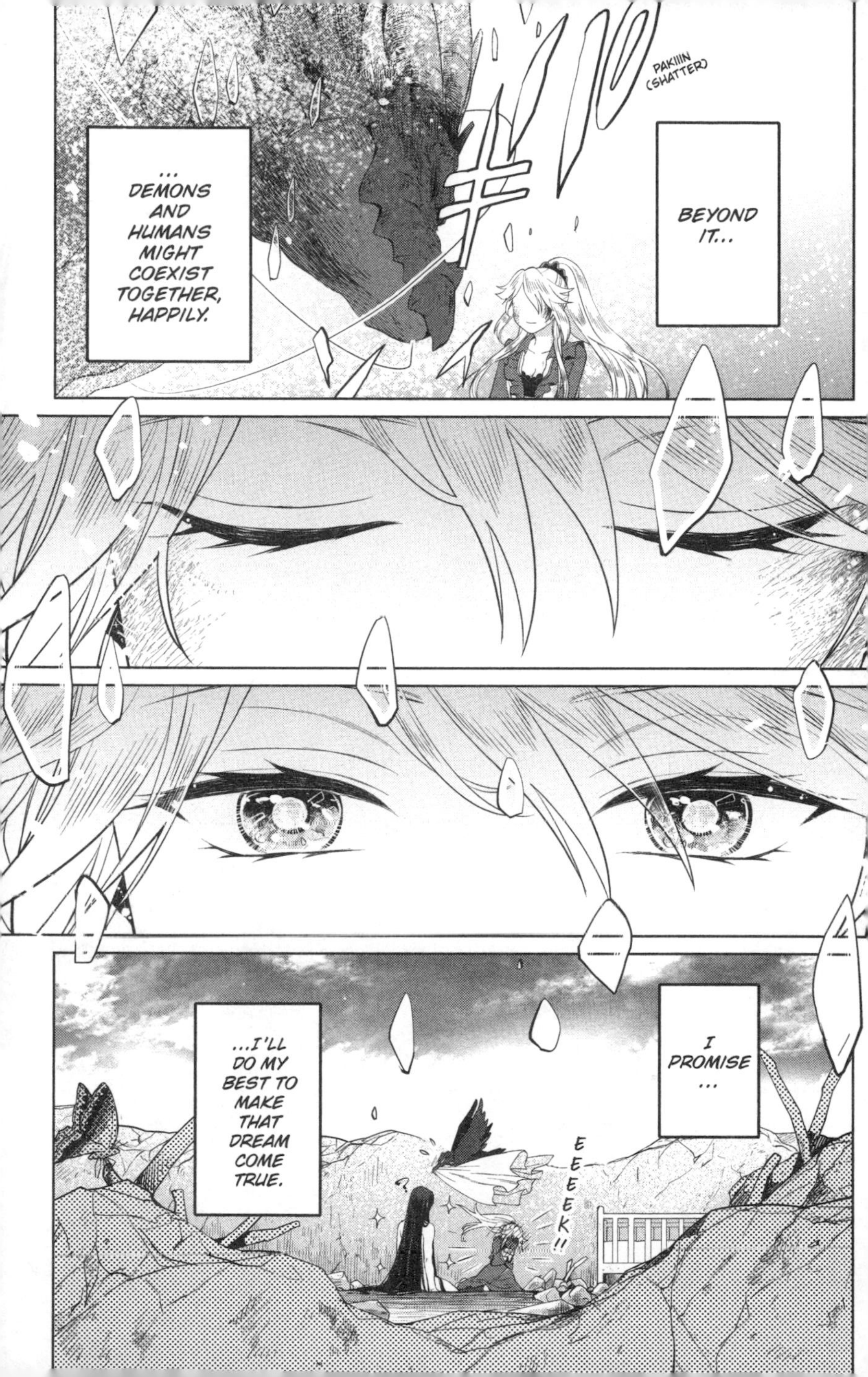
PAKIIIN (SHATTER)
BEYOND IT...
... DEMONS AND HUMANS MIGHT COEXIST TOGETHER, HAPPILY.
I PROMISE ...
...I'LL DO MY BEST TO MAKE THAT DREAM COME TRUE.
EEEEEK!!

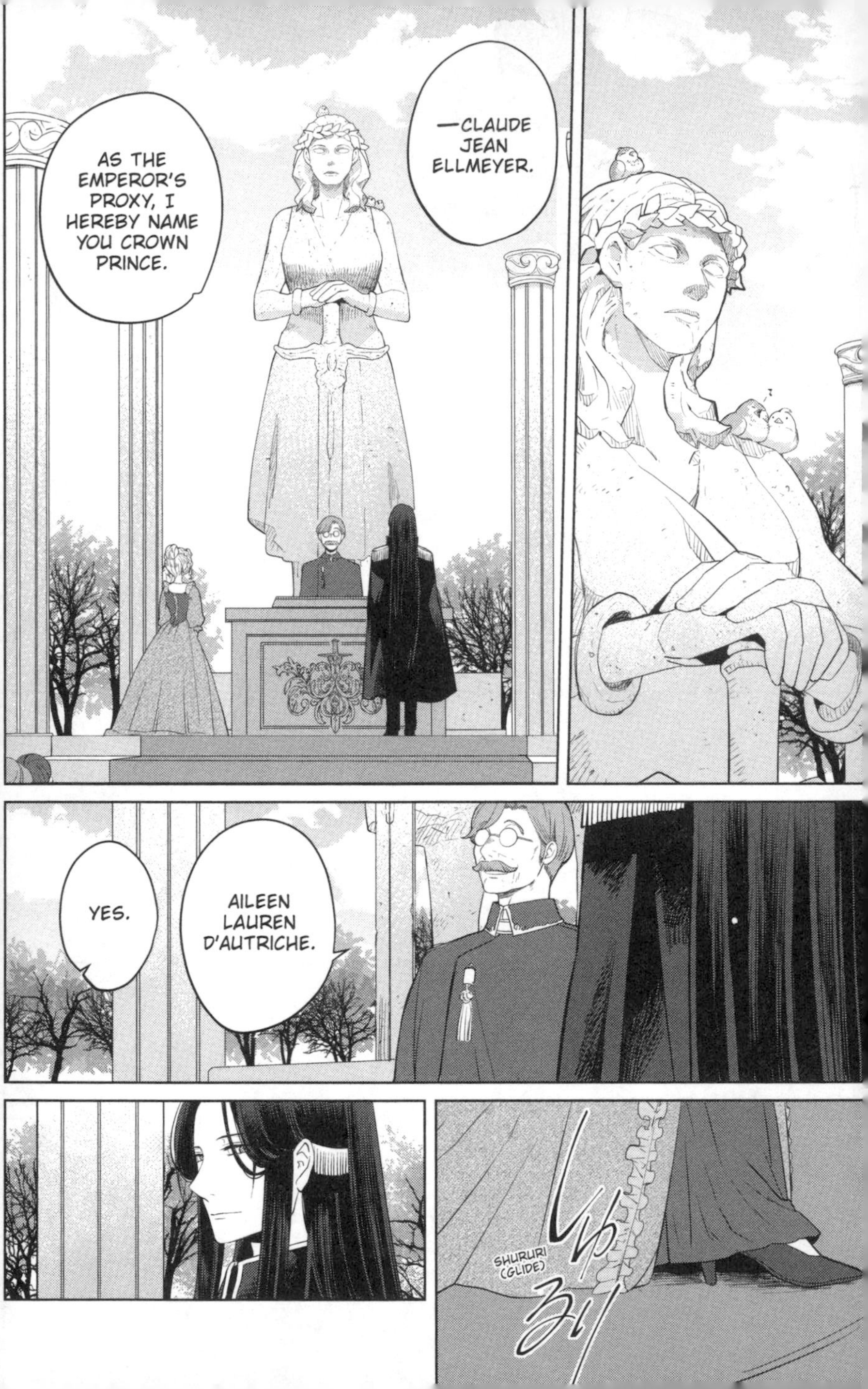
—CLAUDE JEAN ELLMEYER.
AS THE EMPEROR'S PROXY, I HEREBY NAME YOU CROWN PRINCE.
AILEEN LAUREN D'AUTRICHE.
YES.
しゅるり
SHURURI (GLIDE)

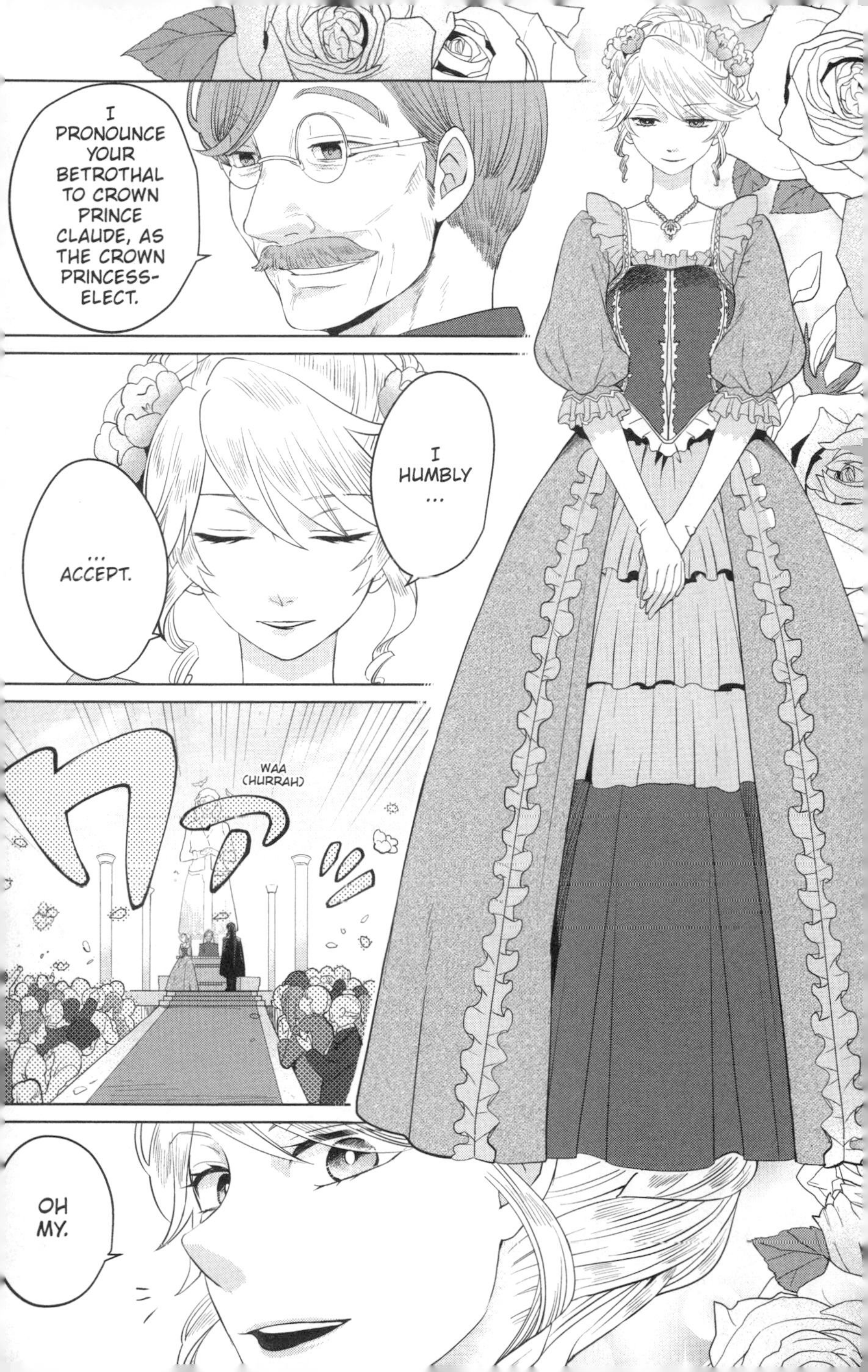
I PRONOUNCE YOUR BETROTHAL TO CROWN PRINCE CLAUDE, AS THE CROWN PRINCESS-ELECT.
I HUMBLY ...
... ACCEPT.
WAA (HURRAH)
OH MY.

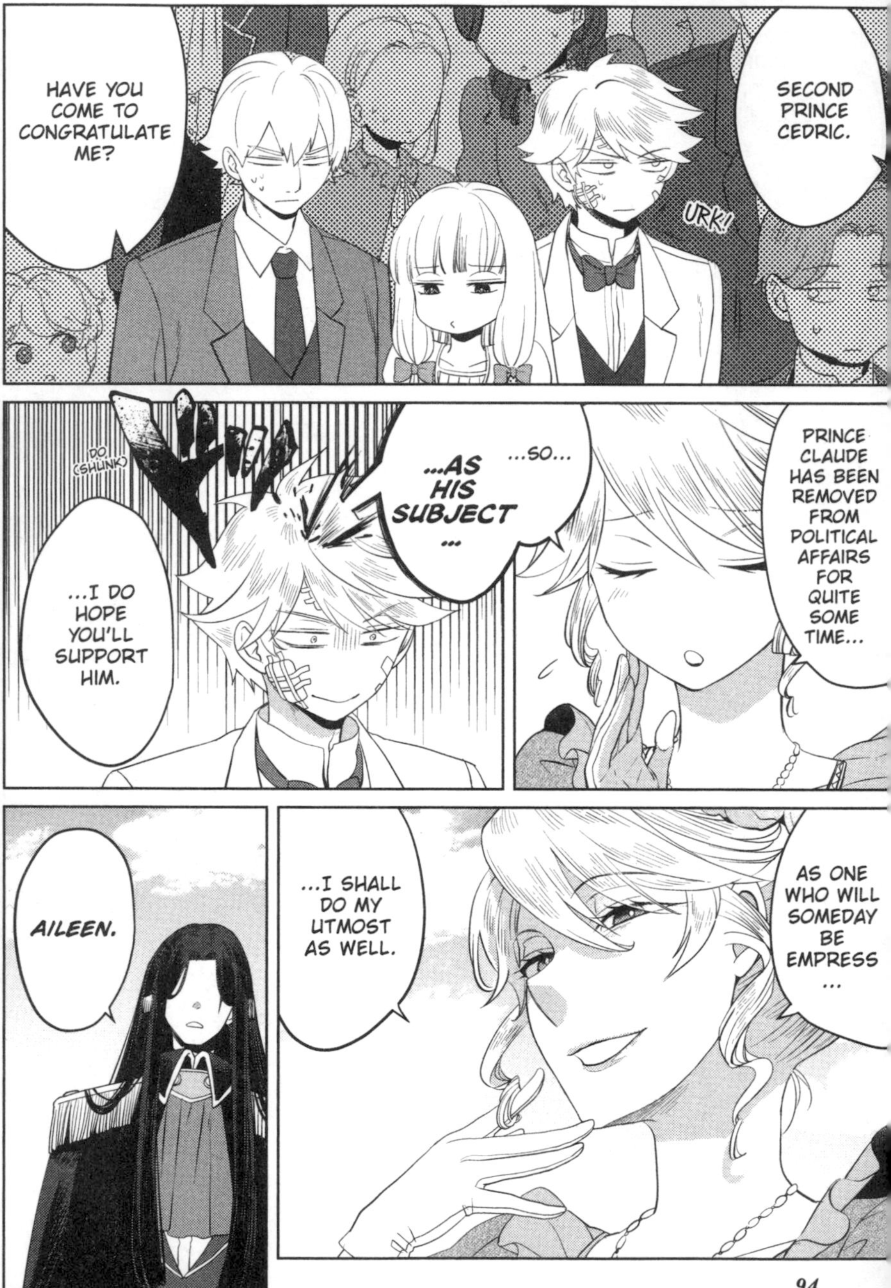
SECOND PRINCE CEDRIC.
URK!
HAVE YOU COME TO CONGRATULATE ME?
PRINCE CLAUDE HAS BEEN REMOVED FROM POLITICAL AFFAIRS FOR QUITE SOME TIME...
...SO...
...AS HIS SUBJECT ...
DO (SHUNK)
...I DO HOPE YOU'LL SUPPORT HIM.
AS ONE WHO WILL SOMEDAY BE EMPRESS ...
...I SHALL DO MY UTMOST AS WELL.
AILEEN.

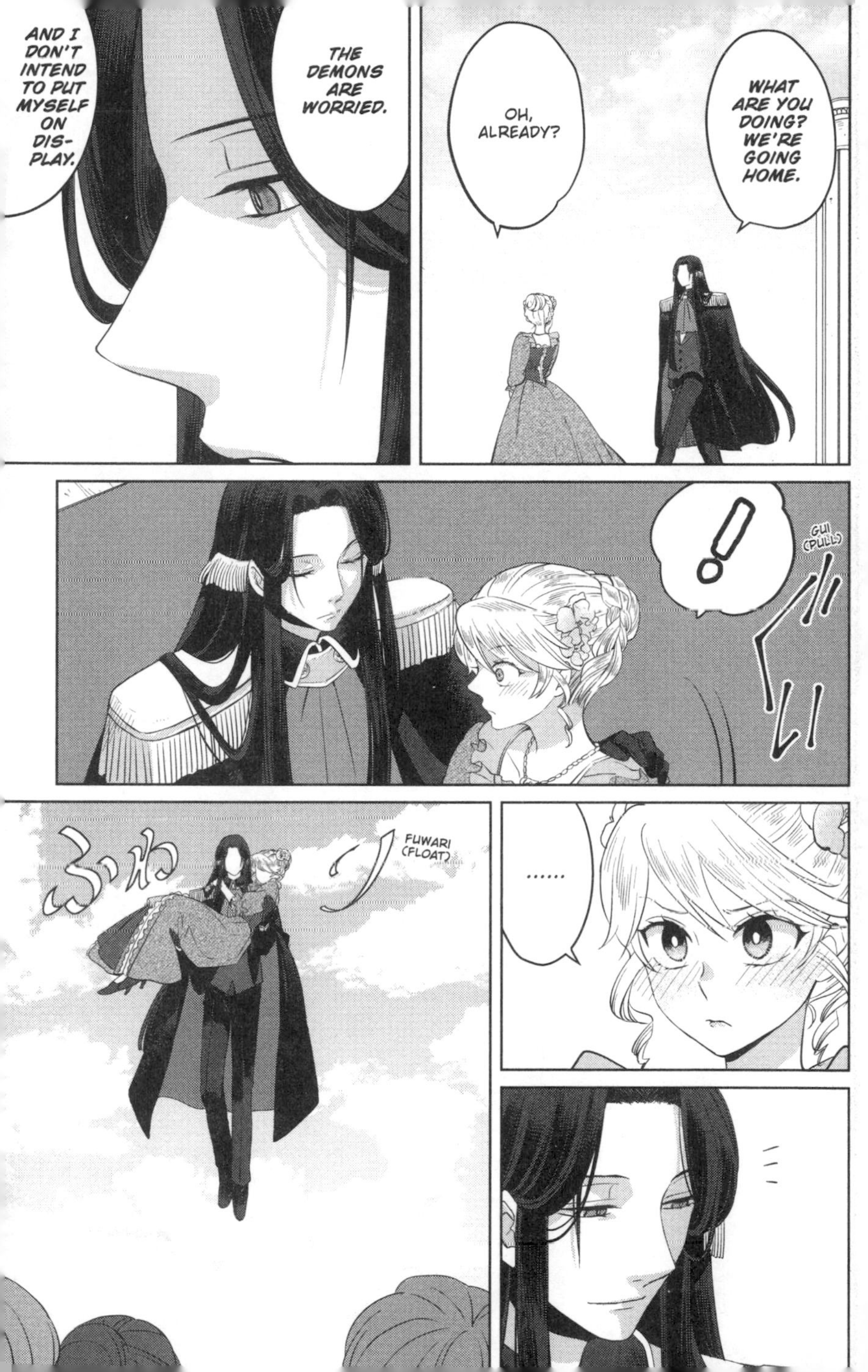
WHAT ARE YOU DOING? WE'RE GOING HOME.
OH, ALREADY?
THE DEMONS ARE WORRIED.
AND I DON'T INTEND TO PUT MYSELF ON DIS-PLAY.
!
GUI (PULL)
......
FUWARI (FLOAT)

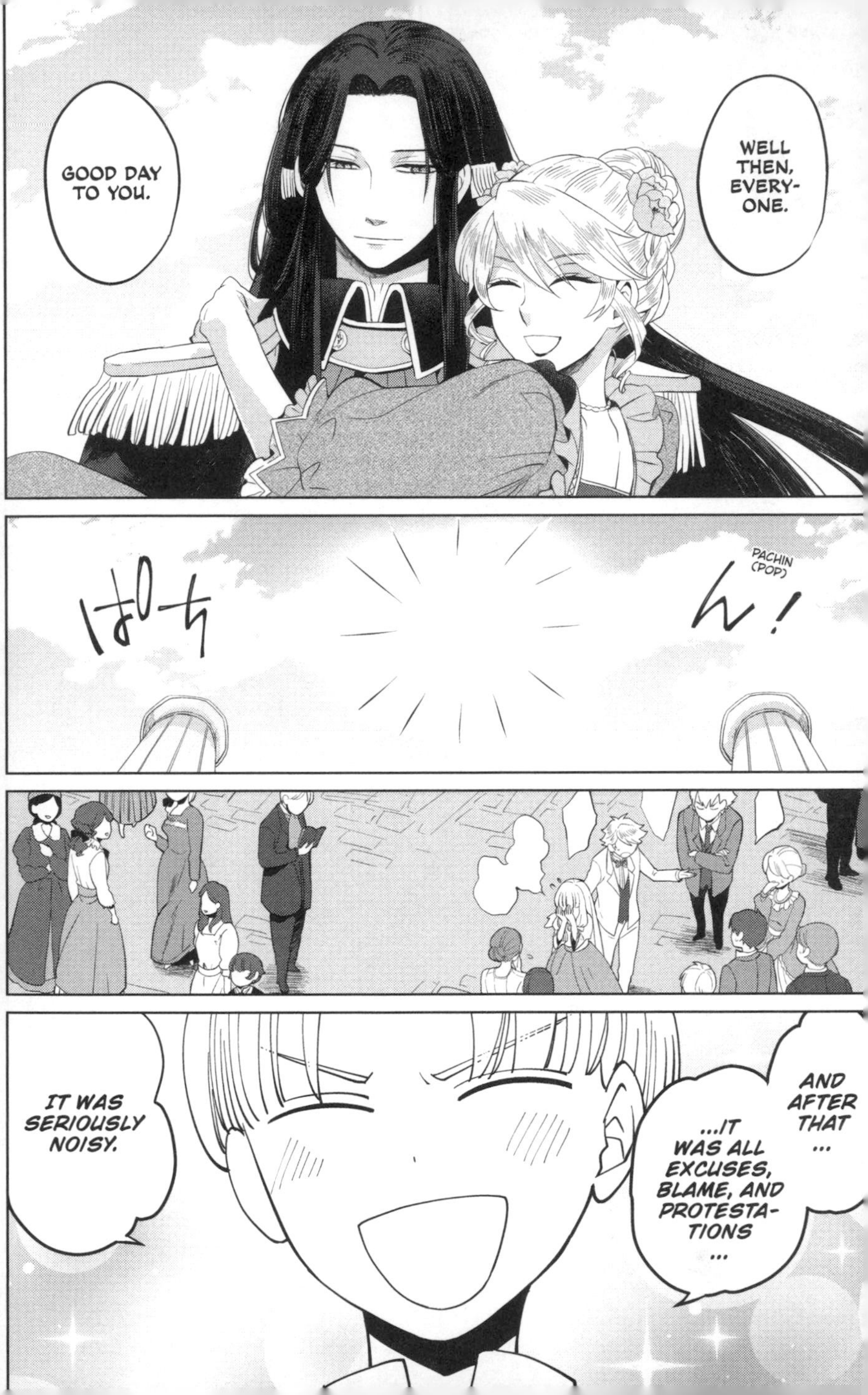
WELL THEN, EVERY-ONE.
GOOD DAY TO YOU.
PACHIN (POP)
ぱちん!
AND AFTER THAT...
...IT WAS ALL EXCUSES, BLAME, AND PROTESTATIONS...
IT WAS SERIOUSLY NOISY.

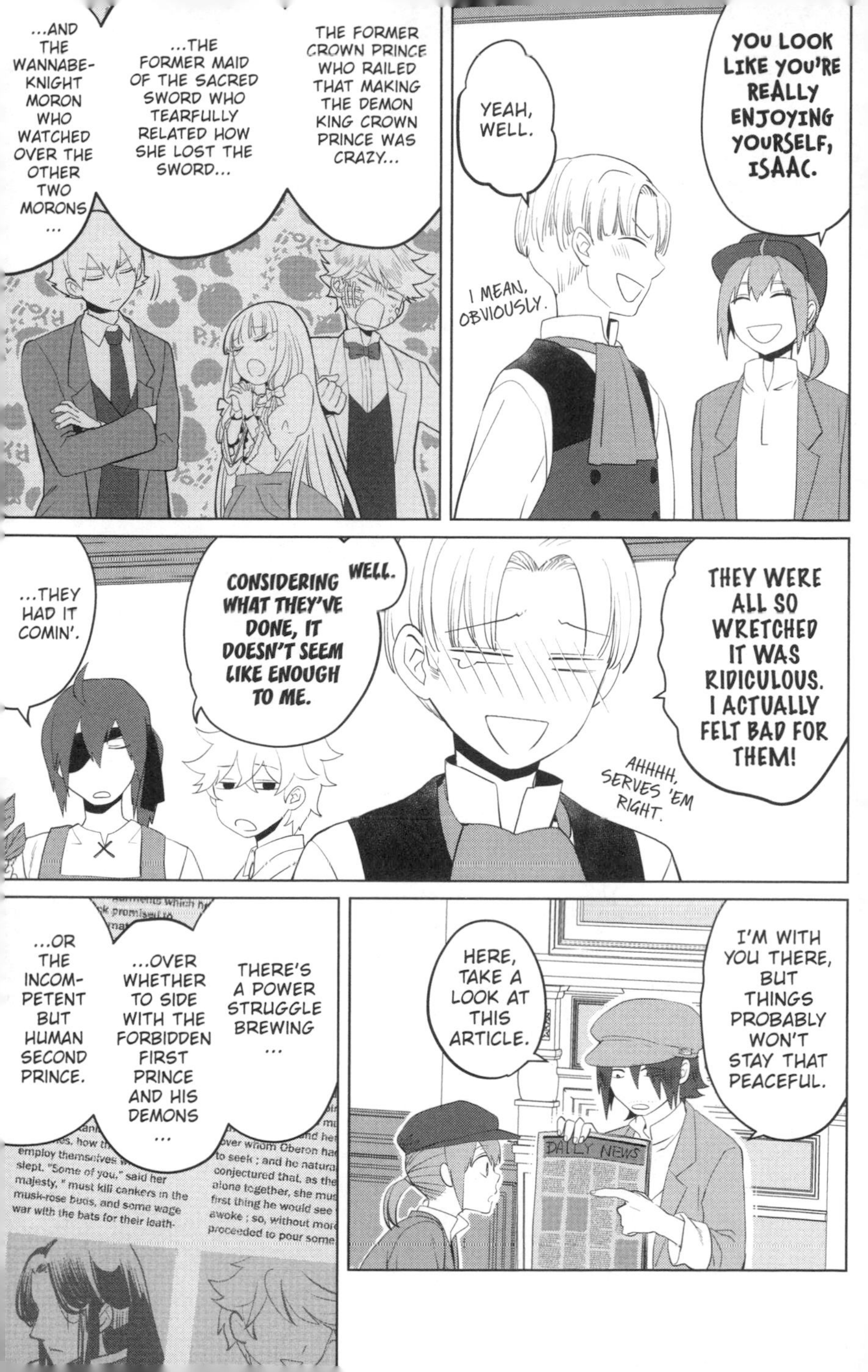
YOU LOOK LIKE YOU'RE REALLY ENJOYING YOURSELF, ISAAC.
YEAH, WELL.
I MEAN, OBVIOUSLY.
THE FORMER CROWN PRINCE WHO RAILED THAT MAKING THE DEMON KING CROWN PRINCE WAS CRAZY...
...THE FORMER MAID OF THE SACRED SWORD WHO TEARFULLY RELATED HOW SHE LOST THE SWORD...
...AND THE WANNABE-KNIGHT MORON WHO WATCHED OVER THE OTHER TWO MORONS...
THEY WERE ALL SO WRETCHED IT WAS RIDICULOUS. I ACTUALLY FELT BAD FOR THEM!
AHHHH, SERVES 'EM RIGHT.
WELL.
CONSIDERING WHAT THEY'VE DONE, IT DOESN'T SEEM LIKE ENOUGH TO ME.
...THEY HAD IT COMIN'.
I'M WITH YOU THERE, BUT THINGS PROBABLY WON'T STAY THAT PEACEFUL.
HERE, TAKE A LOOK AT THIS ARTICLE.
DAILY NEWS
THERE'S A POWER STRUGGLE BREWING...
...OVER WHETHER TO SIDE WITH THE FORBIDDEN FIRST PRINCE AND HIS DEMONS...
...OR THE INCOMPETENT BUT HUMAN SECOND PRINCE.

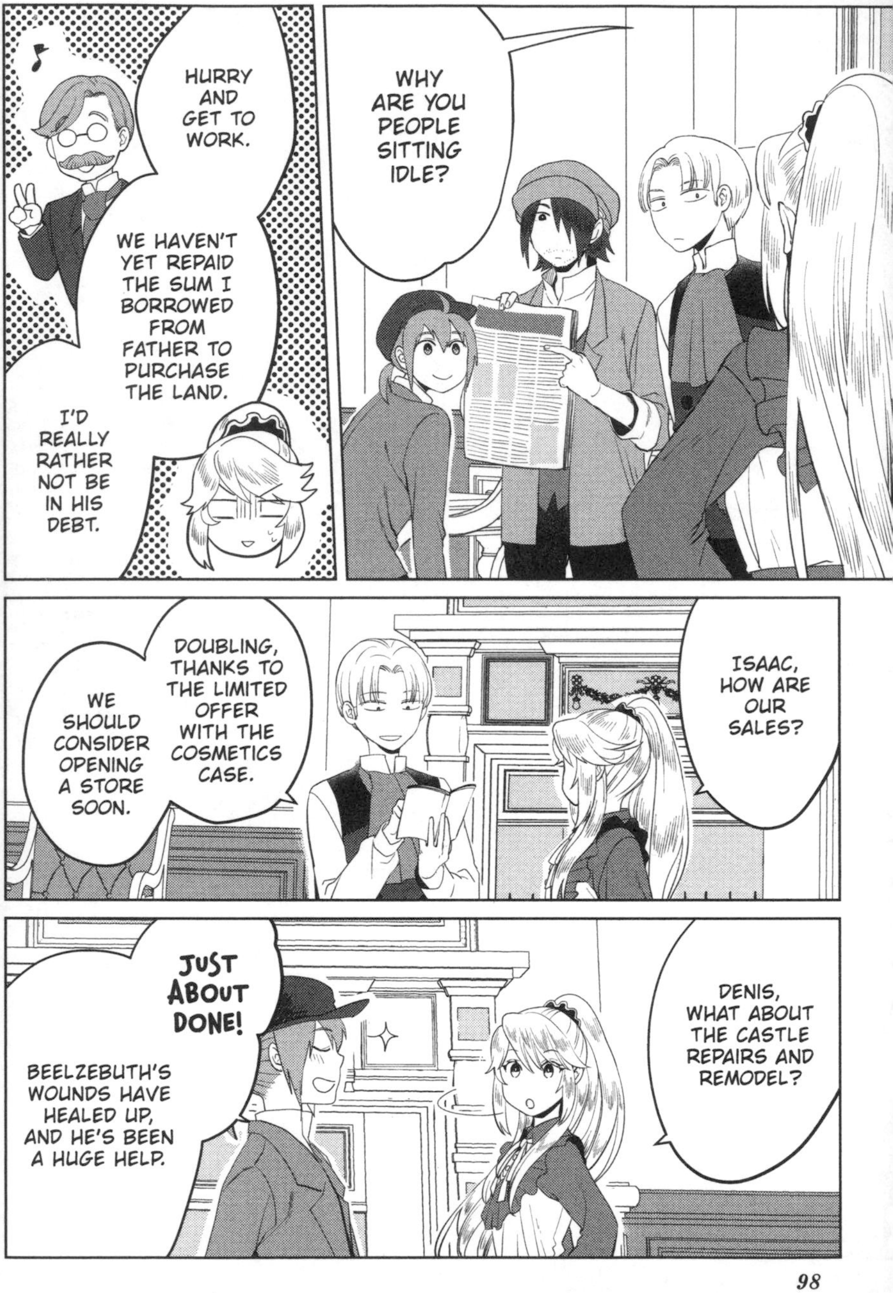
WHY ARE YOU PEOPLE SITTING IDLE?
HURRY AND GET TO WORK.
WE HAVEN'T YET REPAID THE SUM I BORROWED FROM FATHER TO PURCHASE THE LAND.
I'D REALLY RATHER NOT BE IN HIS DEBT.
ISAAC, HOW ARE OUR SALES?
DOUBLING, THANKS TO THE LIMITED OFFER WITH THE COSMETICS CASE.
WE SHOULD CONSIDER OPENING A STORE SOON.
DENIS, WHAT ABOUT THE CASTLE REPAIRS AND REMODEL?
JUST ABOUT DONE!
BEELZEBUTH'S WOUNDS HAVE HEALED UP, AND HE'S BEEN A HUGE HELP.

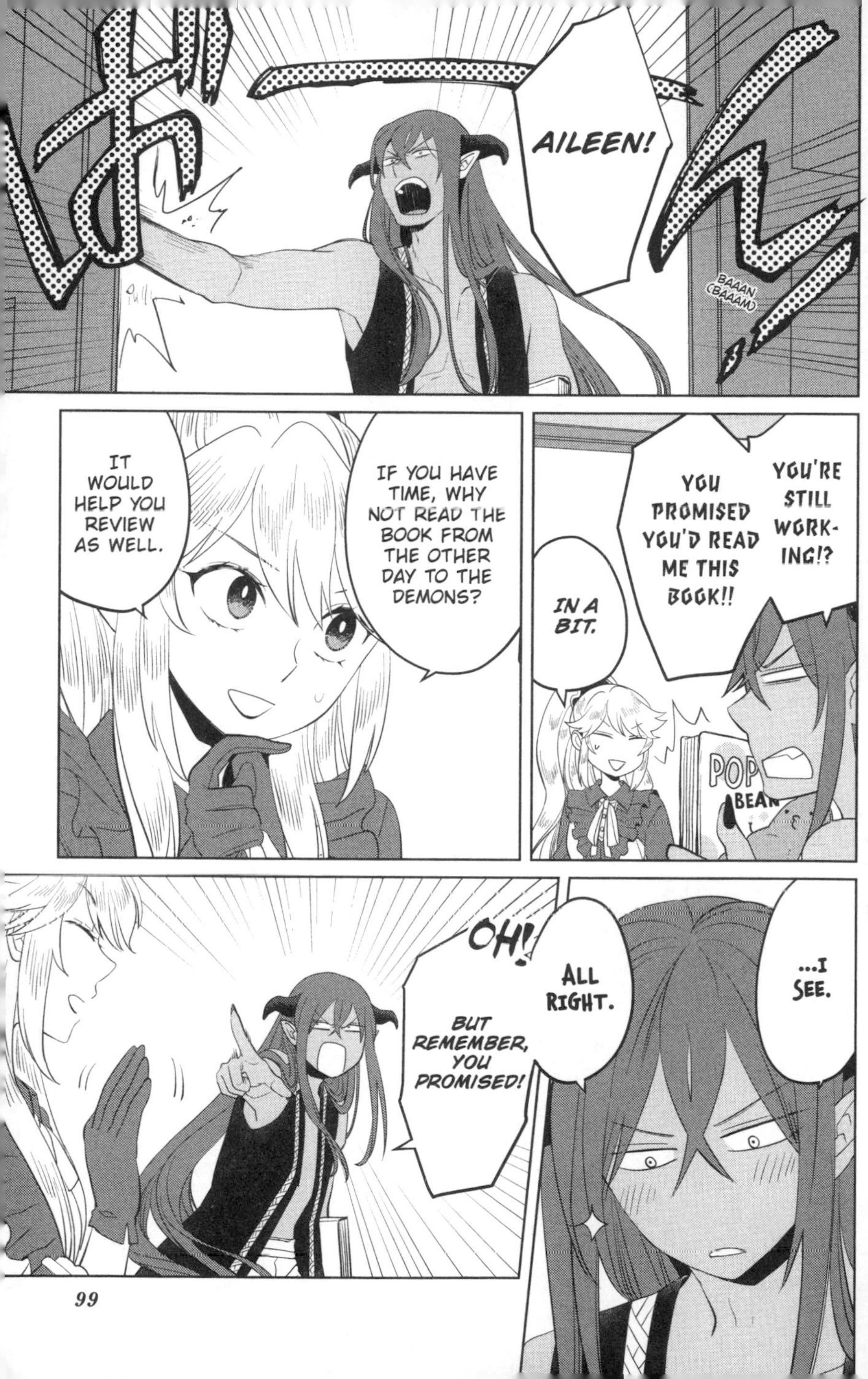
AILEEN!
BAAAN (BAAAM)
YOU'RE STILL WORKING!?
YOU PROMISED YOU'D READ ME THIS BOOK!!
IN A BIT.
IF YOU HAVE TIME, WHY NOT READ THE BOOK FROM THE OTHER DAY TO THE DEMONS?
IT WOULD HELP YOU REVIEW AS WELL.
...I SEE.
ALL RIGHT.
OH!
BUT REMEMBER, YOU PROMISED!

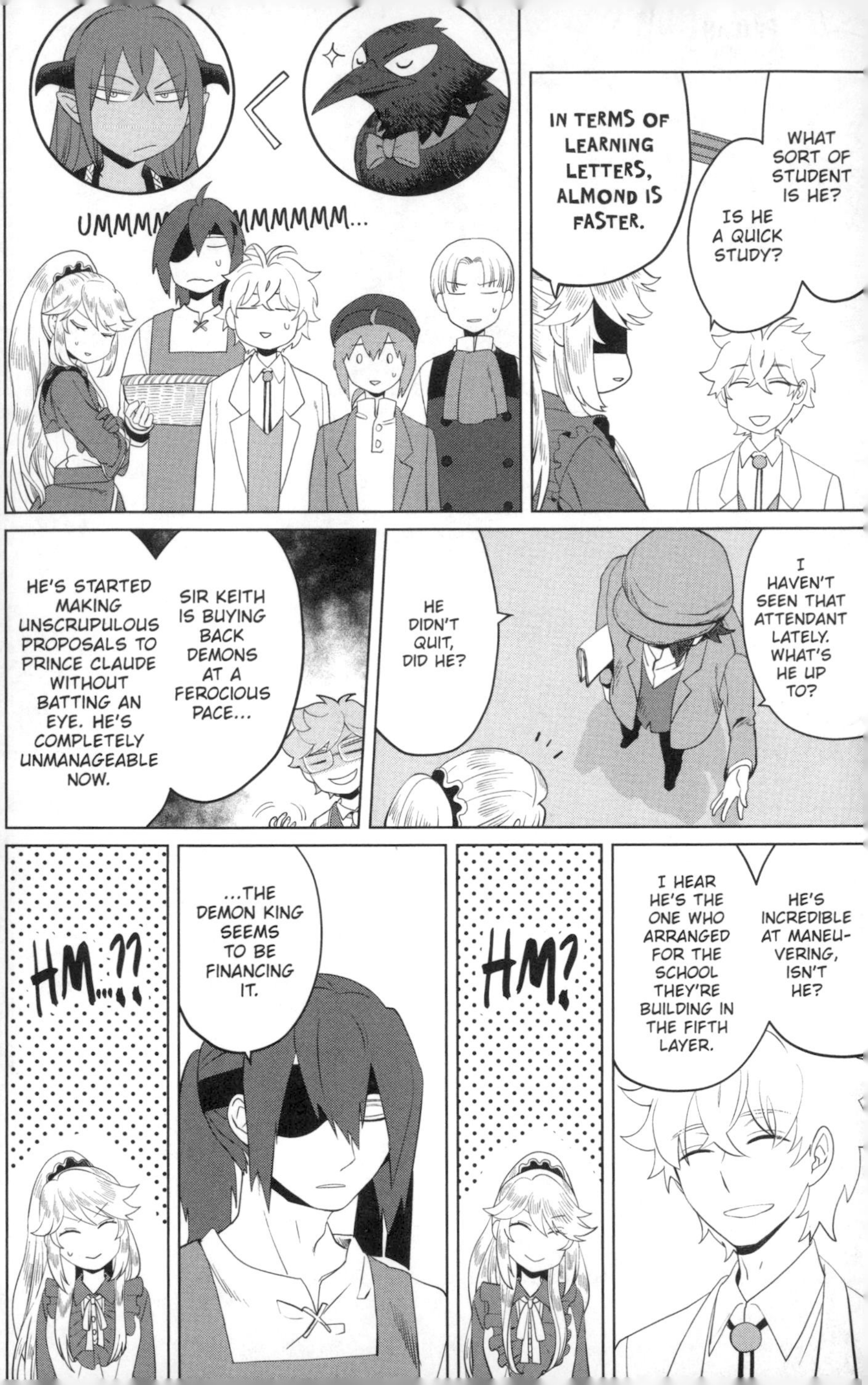
WHAT SORT OF STUDENT IS HE?
IS HE A QUICK STUDY?
IN TERMS OF LEARNING LETTERS, ALMOND IS FASTER.
UMMMM MMMMMM...
I HAVEN'T SEEN THAT ATTENDANT LATELY. WHAT'S HE UP TO?
HE DIDN'T QUIT, DID HE?
SIR KEITH IS BUYING BACK DEMONS AT A FEROCIOUS PACE...
HE'S STARTED MAKING UNSCRUPULOUS PROPOSALS TO PRINCE CLAUDE WITHOUT BATTING AN EYE. HE'S COMPLETELY UNMANAGEABLE NOW.
HE'S INCREDIBLE AT MANEU-VERING, ISN'T HE?
I HEAR HE'S THE ONE WHO ARRANGED FOR THE SCHOOL THEY'RE BUILDING IN THE FIFTH LAYER.
HM?
...THE DEMON KING SEEMS TO BE FINANCING IT.
HM...??

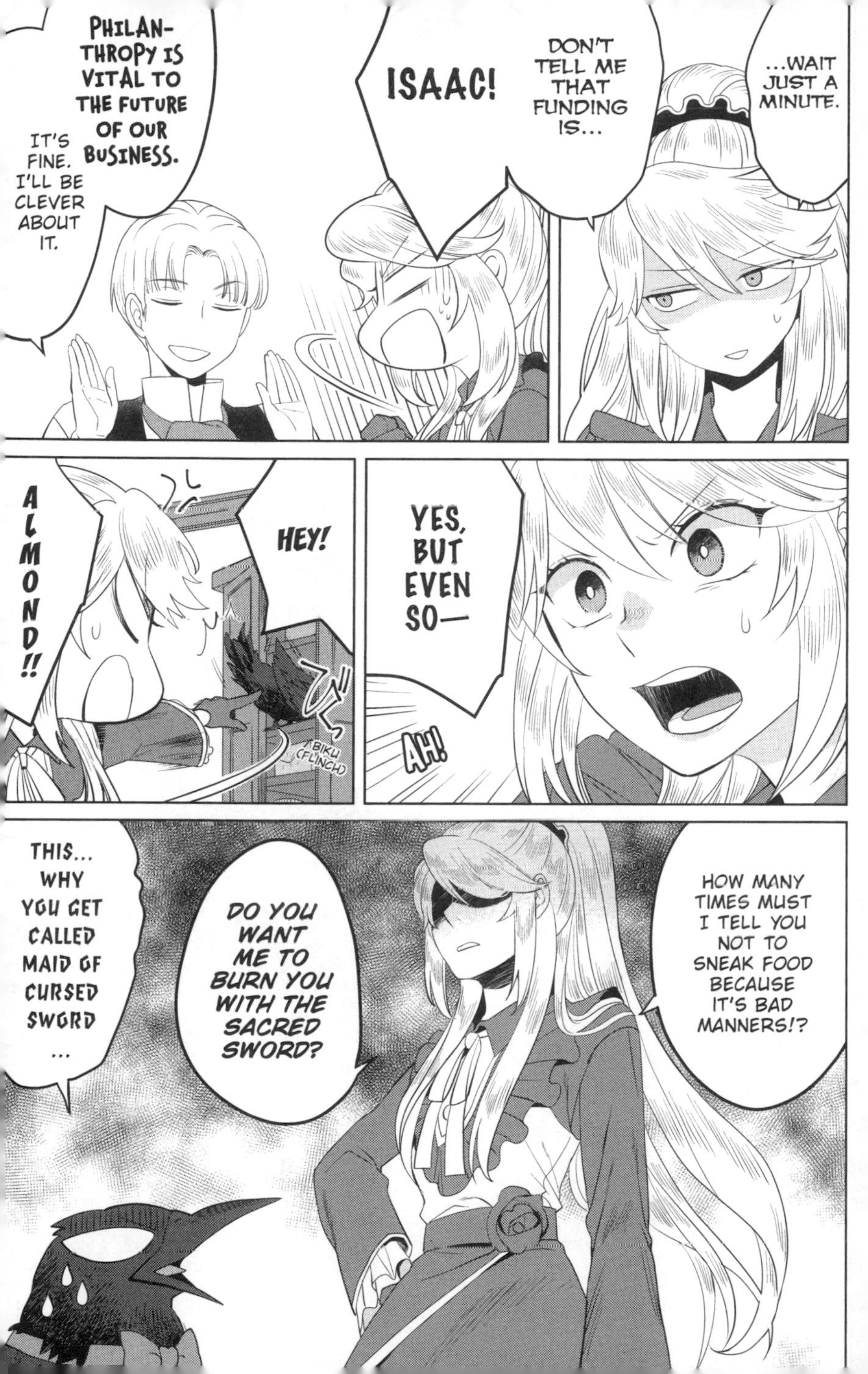
...WAIT JUST A MINUTE.
DON'T TELL ME THAT FUNDING IS...
ISAAC!
PHILAN-THROPY IS VITAL TO THE FUTURE OF OUR BUSINESS.
IT'S FINE. I'LL BE CLEVER ABOUT IT.
YES, BUT EVEN SO—
AH!
HEY!
ALMOND!!
BIKU (FLINCH)
HOW MANY TIMES MUST I TELL YOU NOT TO SNEAK FOOD BECAUSE IT'S BAD MANNERS!?
DO YOU WANT ME TO BURN YOU WITH THE SACRED SWORD?
THIS... WHY YOU GET CALLED MAID OF CURSED SWORD ...

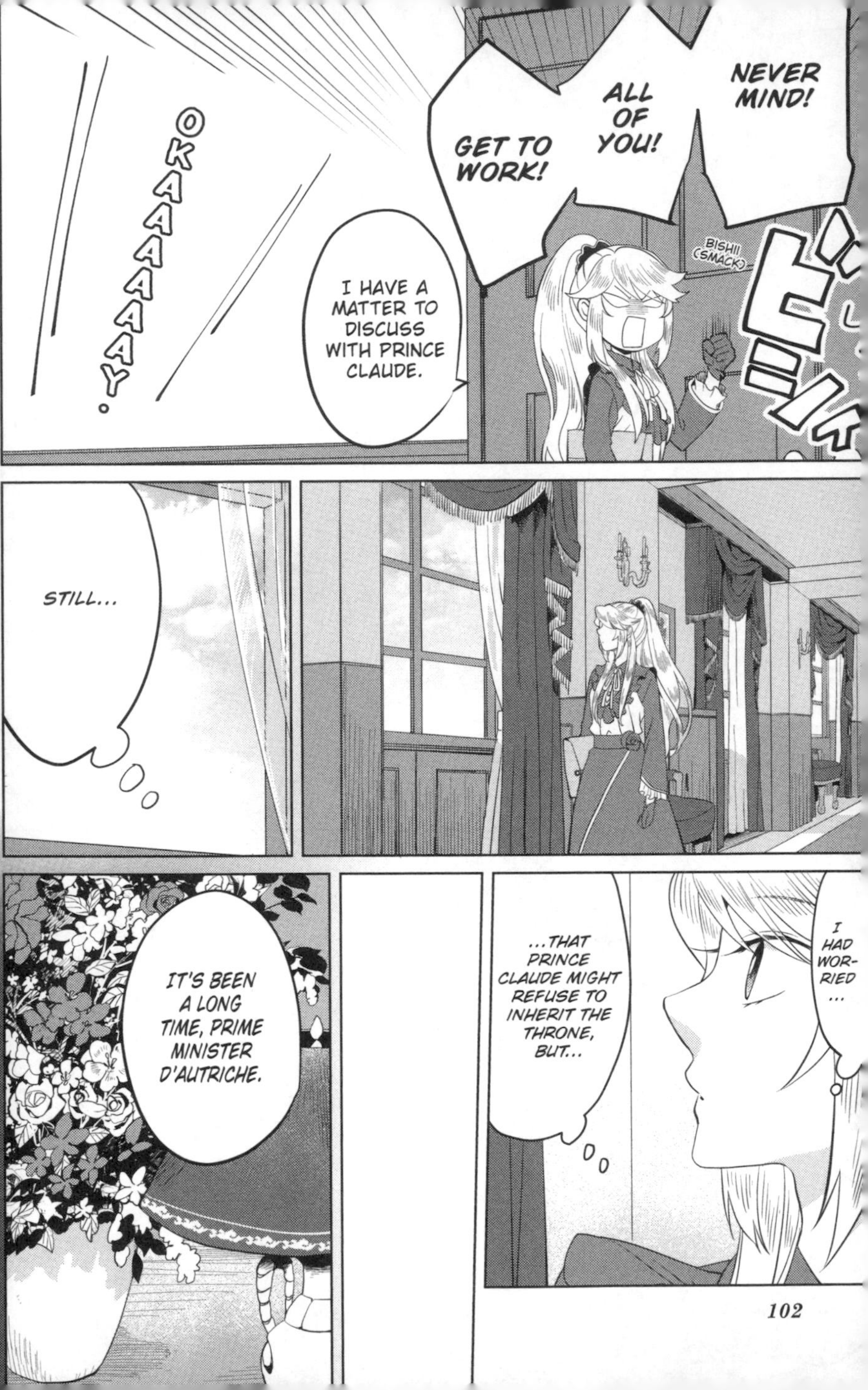
NEVER MIND!
ALL OF YOU!
GET TO WORK!
BISHII (SMACK)
I HAVE A MATTER TO DISCUSS WITH PRINCE CLAUDE.
OKAAAAAAAY.
STILL...
I HAD WOR-RIED...
...THAT PRINCE CLAUDE MIGHT REFUSE TO INHERIT THE THRONE, BUT...
IT'S BEEN A LONG TIME, PRIME MINISTER D'AUTRICHE.

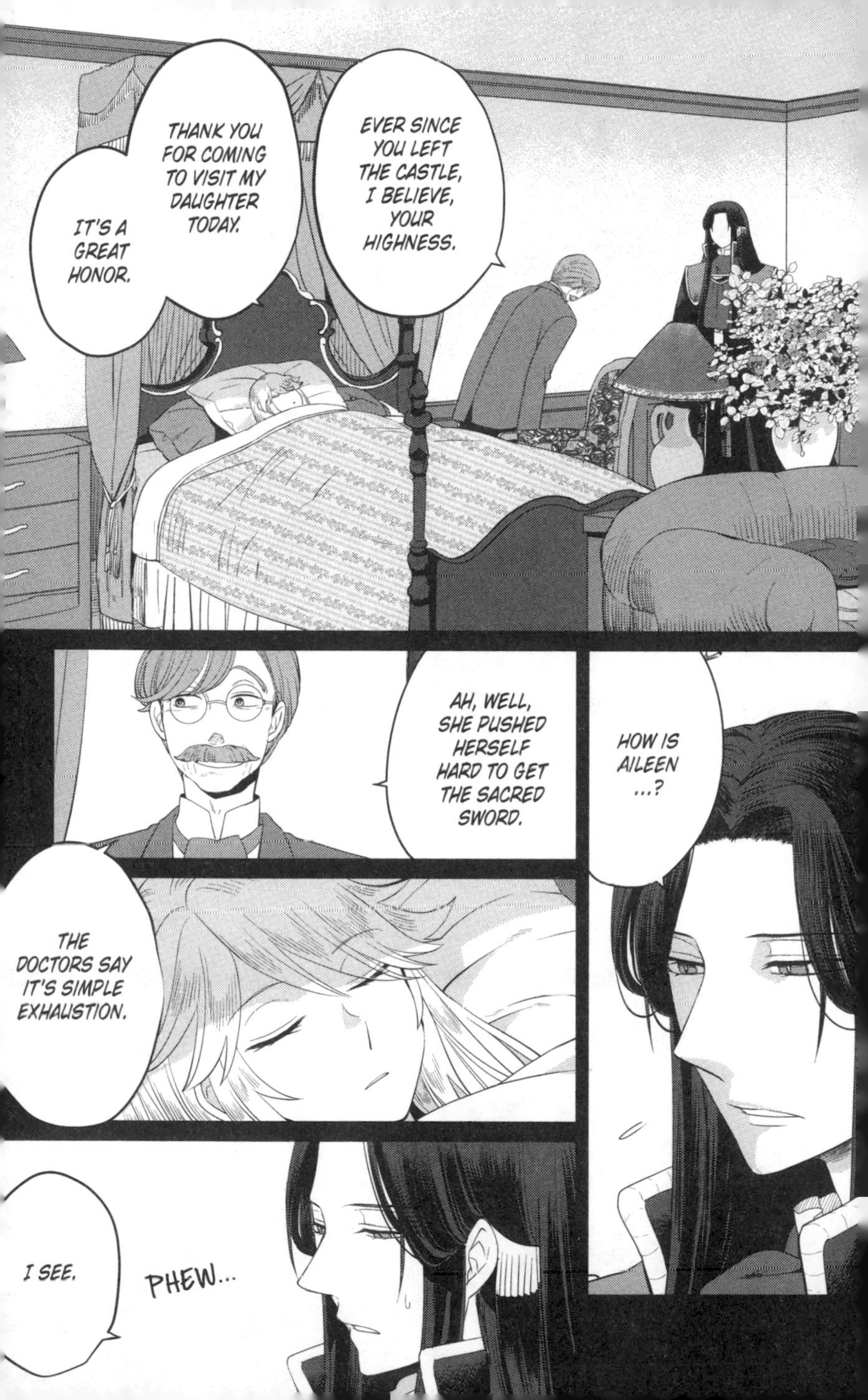
EVER SINCE YOU LEFT THE CASTLE, I BELIEVE, YOUR HIGHNESS.
THANK YOU FOR COMING TO VISIT MY DAUGHTER TODAY.
IT'S A GREAT HONOR.
HOW IS AILEEN ...?
AH, WELL, SHE PUSHED HERSELF HARD TO GET THE SACRED SWORD.
THE DOCTORS SAY IT'S SIMPLE EXHAUSTION.
PHEW...
I SEE.

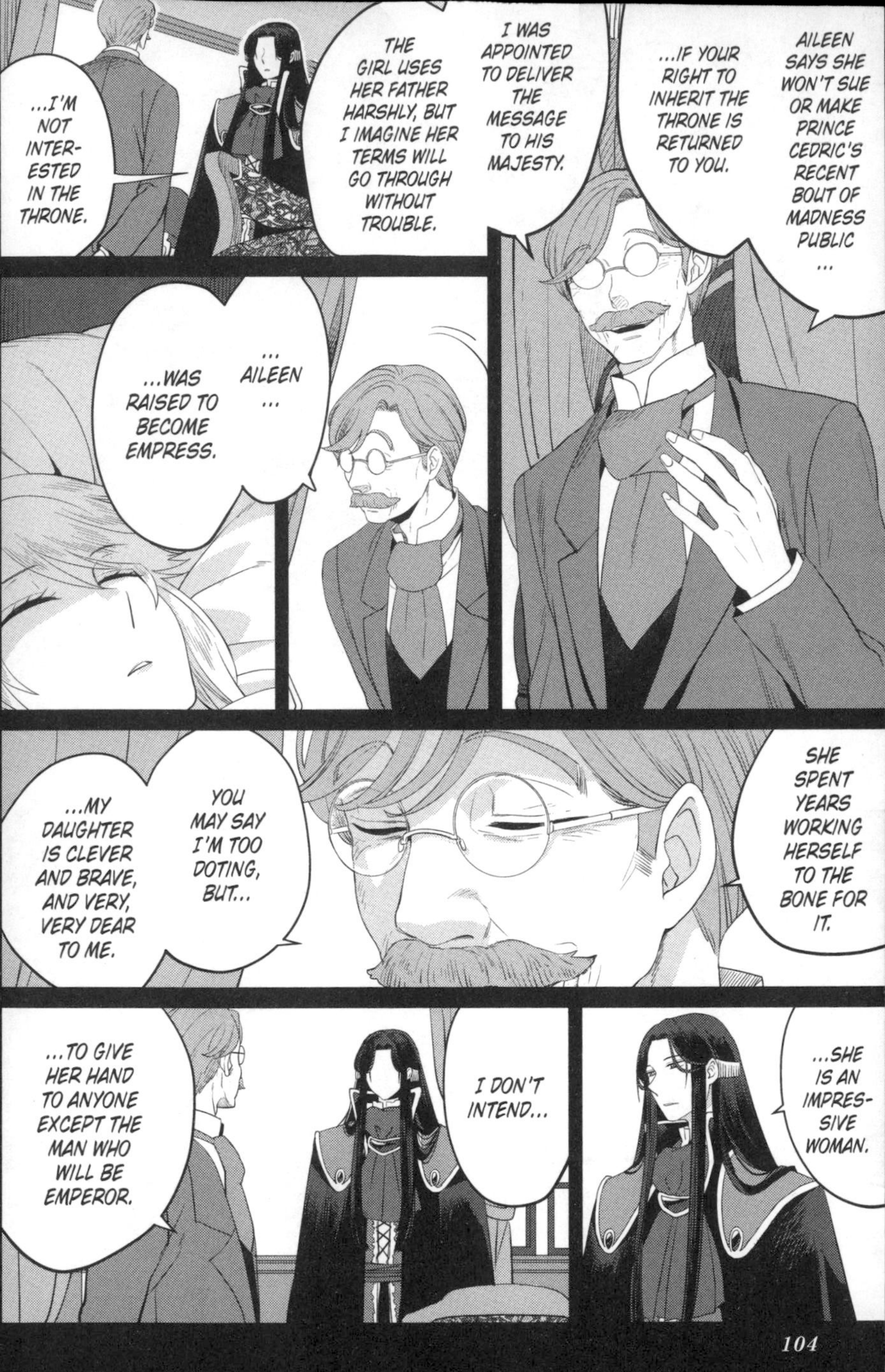
AILEEN SAYS SHE WON'T SUE OR MAKE PRINCE CEDRIC'S RECENT BOUT OF MADNESS PUBLIC...
...IF YOUR RIGHT TO INHERIT THE THRONE IS RETURNED TO YOU.
I WAS APPOINTED TO DELIVER THE MESSAGE TO HIS MAJESTY.
THE GIRL USES HER FATHER HARSHLY, BUT I IMAGINE HER TERMS WILL GO THROUGH WITHOUT TROUBLE.
...I'M NOT INTER-ESTED IN THE THRONE.
...AILEEN...
...WAS RAISED TO BECOME EMPRESS.
SHE SPENT YEARS WORKING HERSELF TO THE BONE FOR IT.
YOU MAY SAY I'M TOO DOTING, BUT...
...MY DAUGHTER IS CLEVER AND BRAVE, AND VERY, VERY DEAR TO ME.
...SHE IS AN IMPRES-SIVE WOMAN.
I DON'T INTEND...
...TO GIVE HER HAND TO ANYONE EXCEPT THE MAN WHO WILL BE EMPEROR.

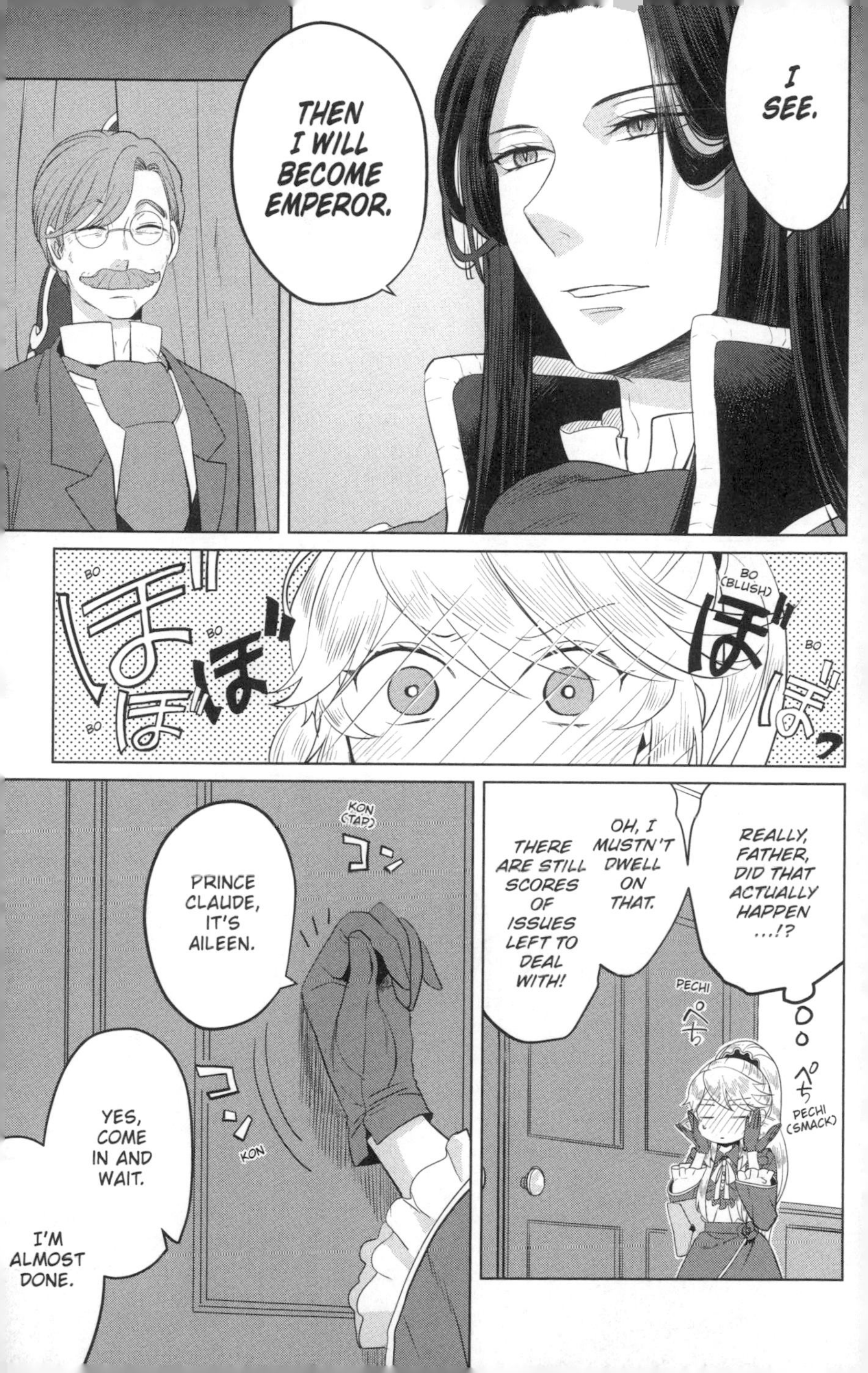
I SEE.
THEN I WILL BECOME EMPEROR.
BO (BLUSH)
BO
BO
BO
BO
REALLY, FATHER, DID THAT ACTUALLY HAPPEN ...!?
OH, I MUSTN'T DWELL ON THAT.
THERE ARE STILL SCORES OF ISSUES LEFT TO DEAL WITH!
PECHI
PECHI (SMACK)
KON (TAP)
PRINCE CLAUDE, IT'S AILEEN.
KON
YES, COME IN AND WAIT.
I'M ALMOST DONE.

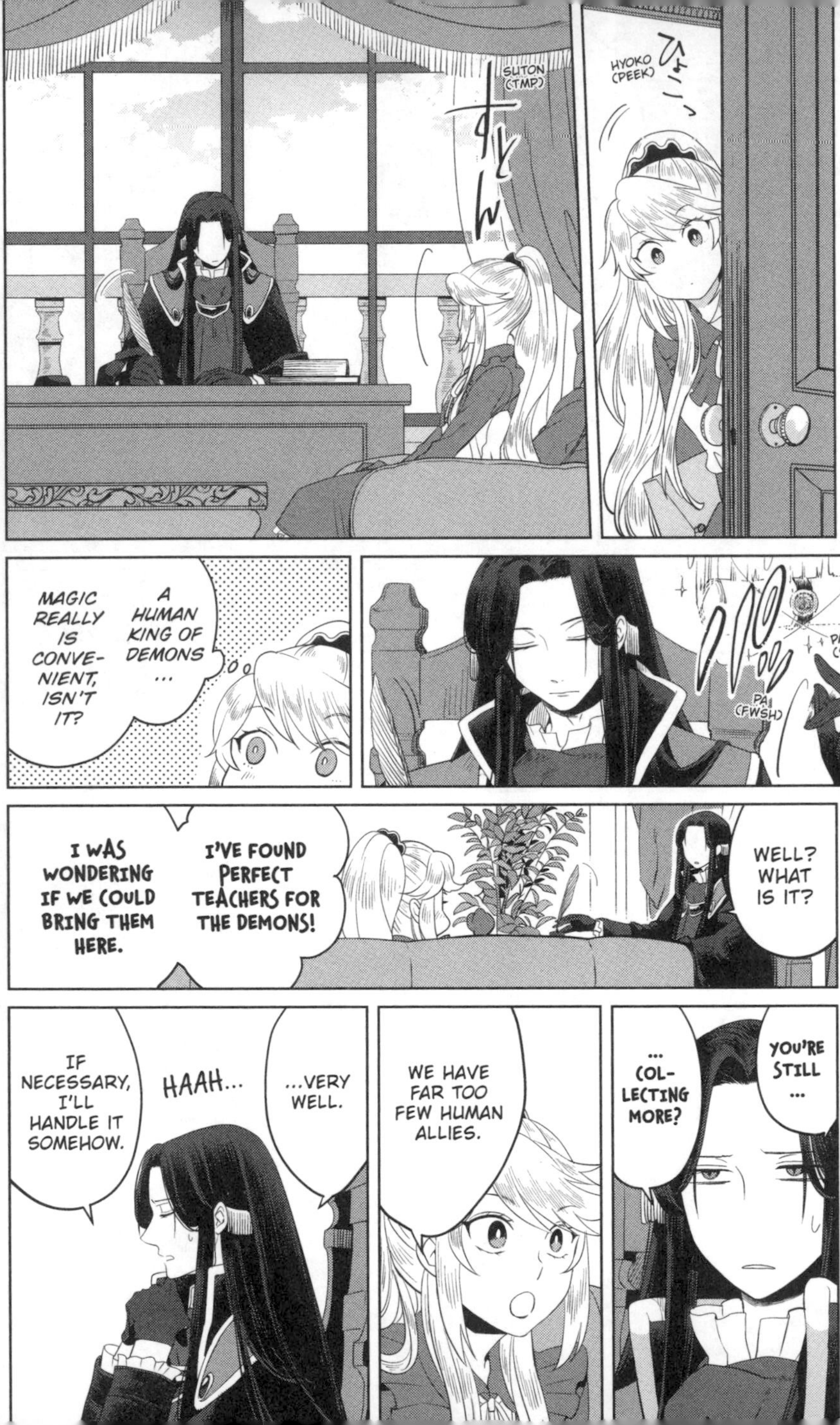
ひょこっ
HYOKO (PEEK)
すとん
SUTON (TMP)
PACHIN (SNAP)
PA (FWSH)
A HUMAN KING OF DEMONS...
MAGIC REALLY IS CONVENIENT, ISN'T IT?
WELL? WHAT IS IT?
I'VE FOUND PERFECT TEACHERS FOR THE DEMONS!
I WAS WONDERING IF WE COULD BRING THEM HERE.
YOU'RE STILL...
...COLLECTING MORE?
WE HAVE FAR TOO FEW HUMAN ALLIES.
...VERY WELL.
HAAH...
IF NECESSARY, I'LL HANDLE IT SOMEHOW.

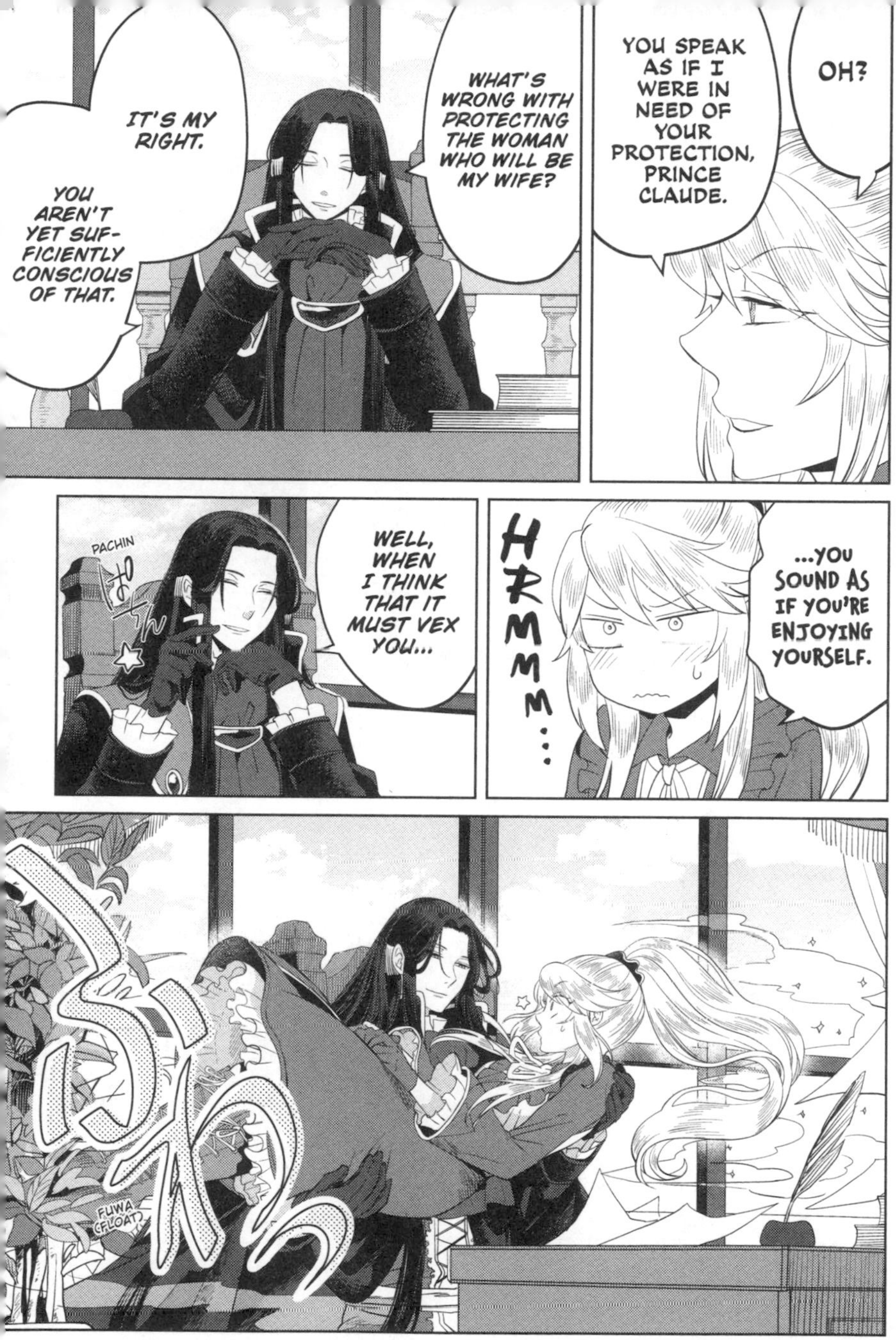
OH?
YOU SPEAK AS IF I WERE IN NEED OF YOUR PROTECTION, PRINCE CLAUDE.
WHAT'S WRONG WITH PROTECTING THE WOMAN WHO WILL BE MY WIFE?
IT'S MY RIGHT.
YOU AREN'T YET SUF-FICIENTLY CONSCIOUS OF THAT.
HRMMM...
...YOU SOUND AS IF YOU'RE ENJOYING YOURSELF.
WELL, WHEN I THINK THAT IT MUST VEX YOU...
PACHIN
FUWA (FLOAT)

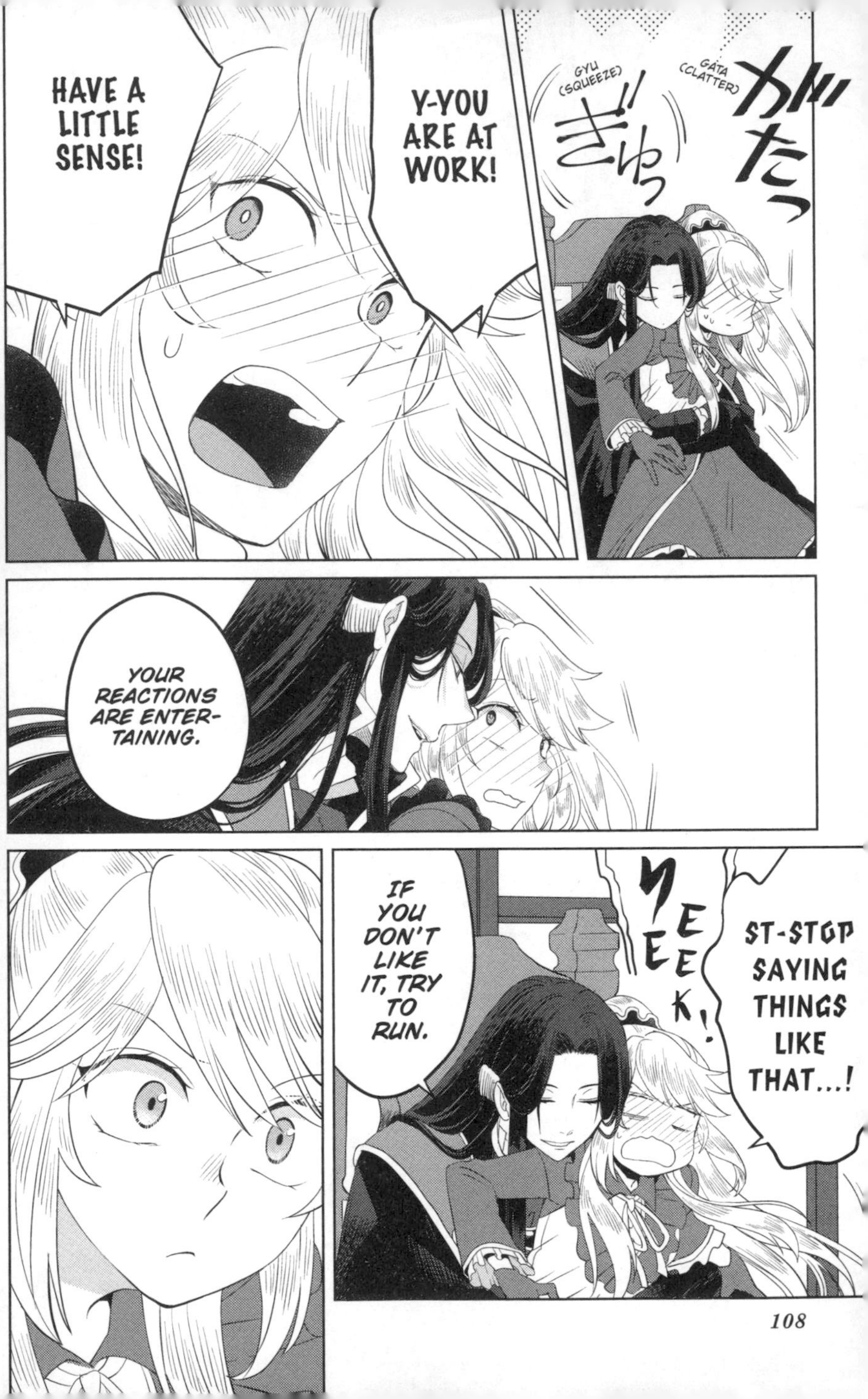
ガタッ
GATA (CLATTER)
ぎゅっ
GYU (SQUEEZE)
Y-YOU ARE AT WORK!
HAVE A LITTLE SENSE!
YOUR REACTIONS ARE ENTER-TAINING.
ST-STOP SAYING THINGS LIKE THAT...!
EEEK!
IF YOU DON'T LIKE IT, TRY TO RUN.

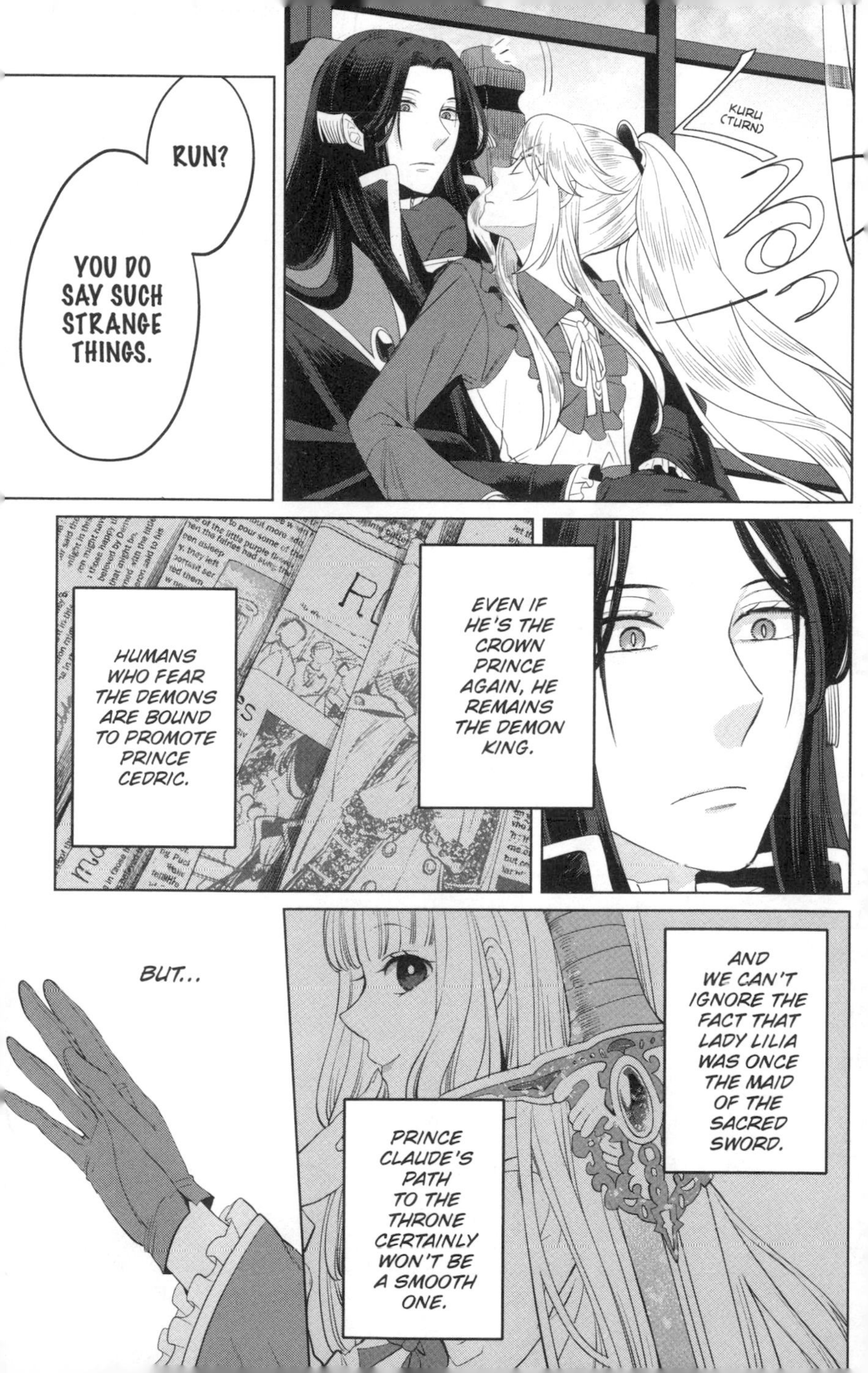
KURU (TURN)
RUN?
YOU DO SAY SUCH STRANGE THINGS.
EVEN IF HE'S THE CROWN PRINCE AGAIN, HE REMAINS THE DEMON KING.
HUMANS WHO FEAR THE DEMONS ARE BOUND TO PROMOTE PRINCE CEDRIC.
AND WE CAN'T IGNORE THE FACT THAT LADY LILIA WAS ONCE THE MAID OF THE SACRED SWORD.
BUT...
PRINCE CLAUDE'S PATH TO THE THRONE CERTAINLY WON'T BE A SMOOTH ONE.

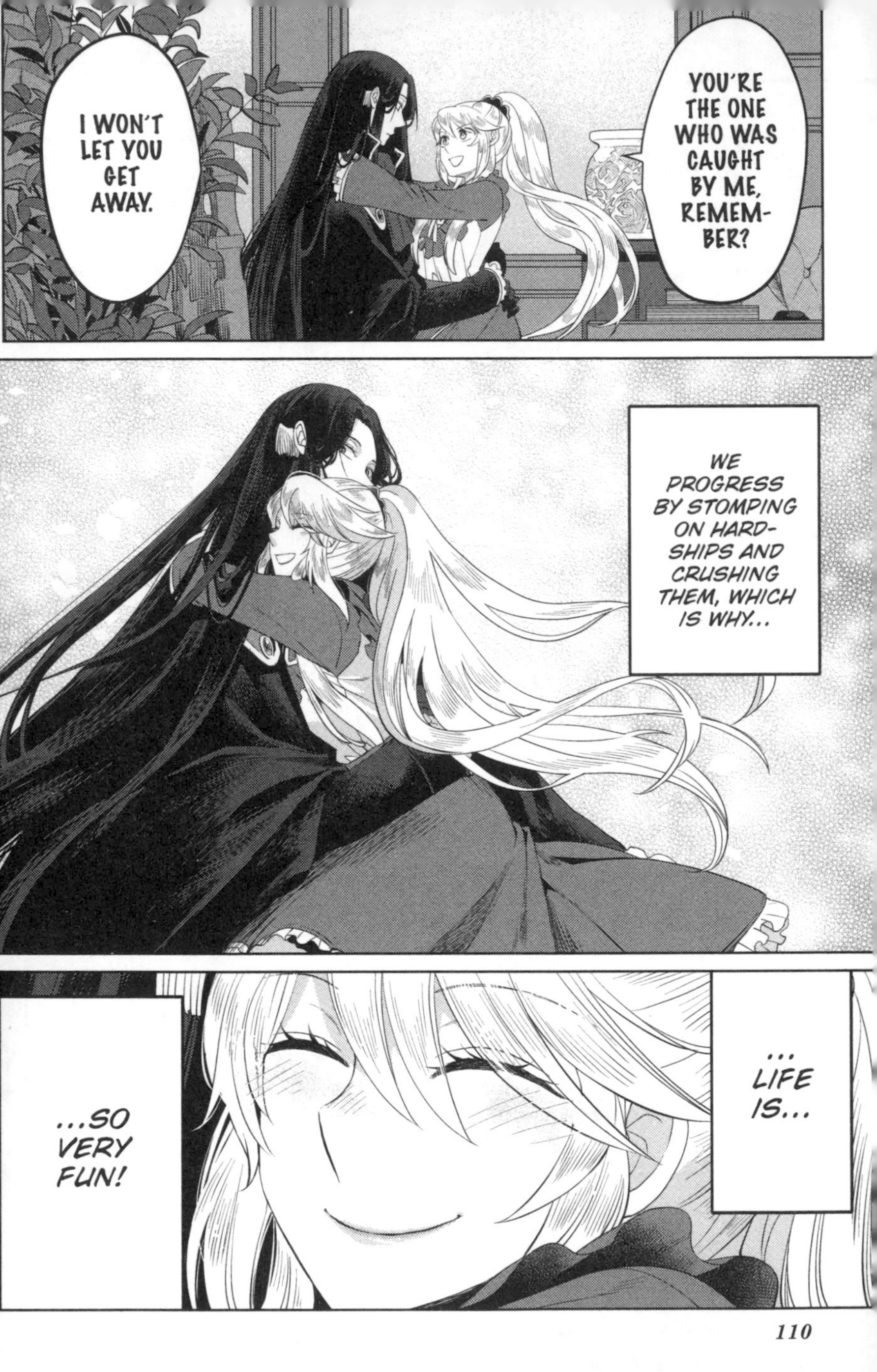
YOU'RE THE ONE WHO WAS CAUGHT BY ME, REMEMBER?
I WON'T LET YOU GET AWAY.
WE PROGRESS BY STOMPING ON HARDSHIPS AND CRUSHING THEM, WHICH IS WHY...
...LIFE IS...
...SO VERY FUN!

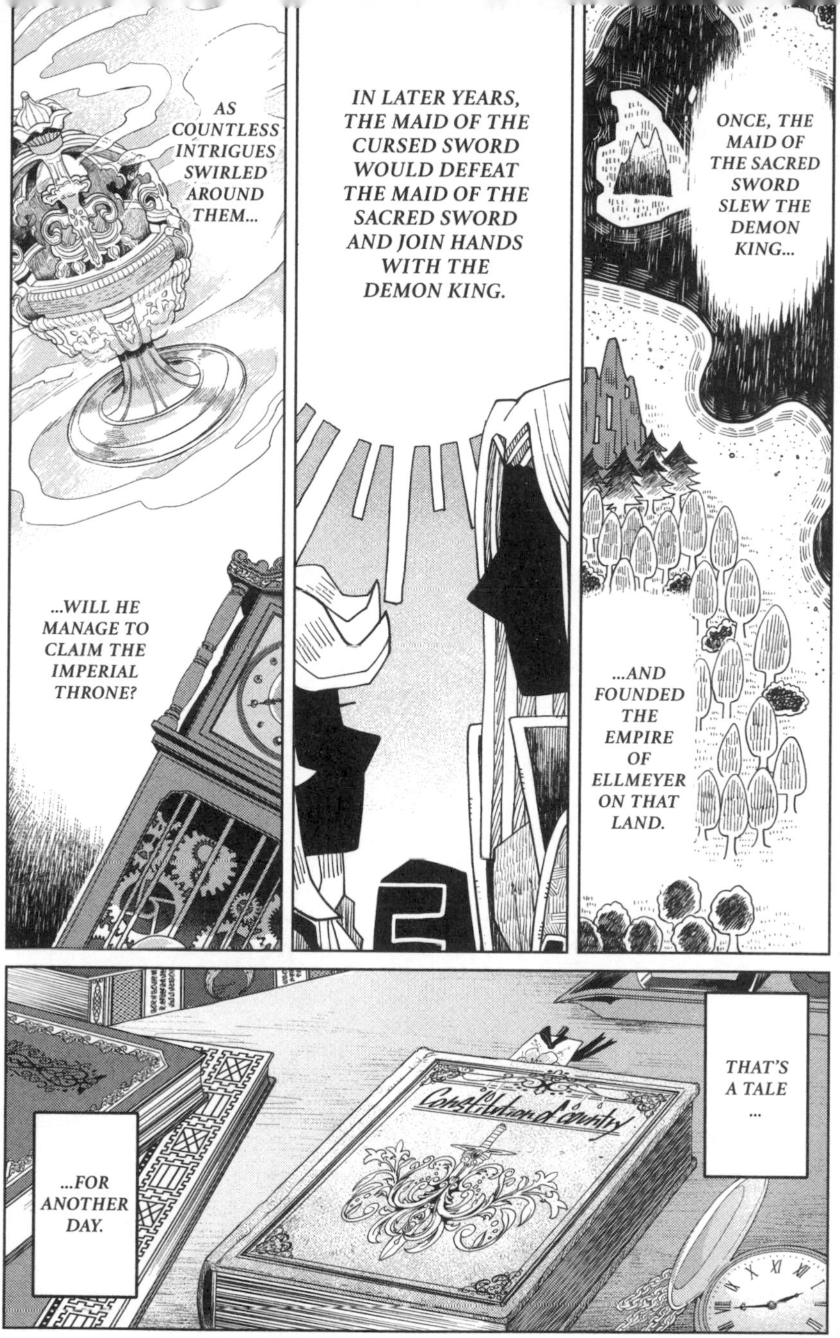
ONCE, THE MAID OF THE SACRED SWORD SLEW THE DEMON KING...
...AND FOUNDED THE EMPIRE OF ELLMEYER ON THAT LAND.
IN LATER YEARS, THE MAID OF THE CURSED SWORD WOULD DEFEAT THE MAID OF THE SACRED SWORD AND JOIN HANDS WITH THE DEMON KING.
AS COUNTLESS INTRIGUES SWIRLED AROUND THEM...
...WILL HE MANAGE TO CLAIM THE IMPERIAL THRONE?
THAT'S A TALE ...
...FOR ANOTHER DAY.

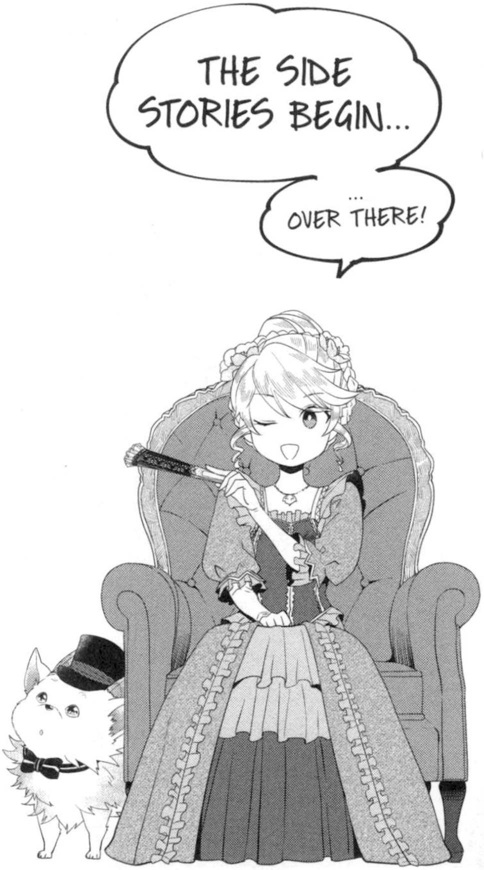
THE SIDE STORIES BEGIN...
... OVER THERE!

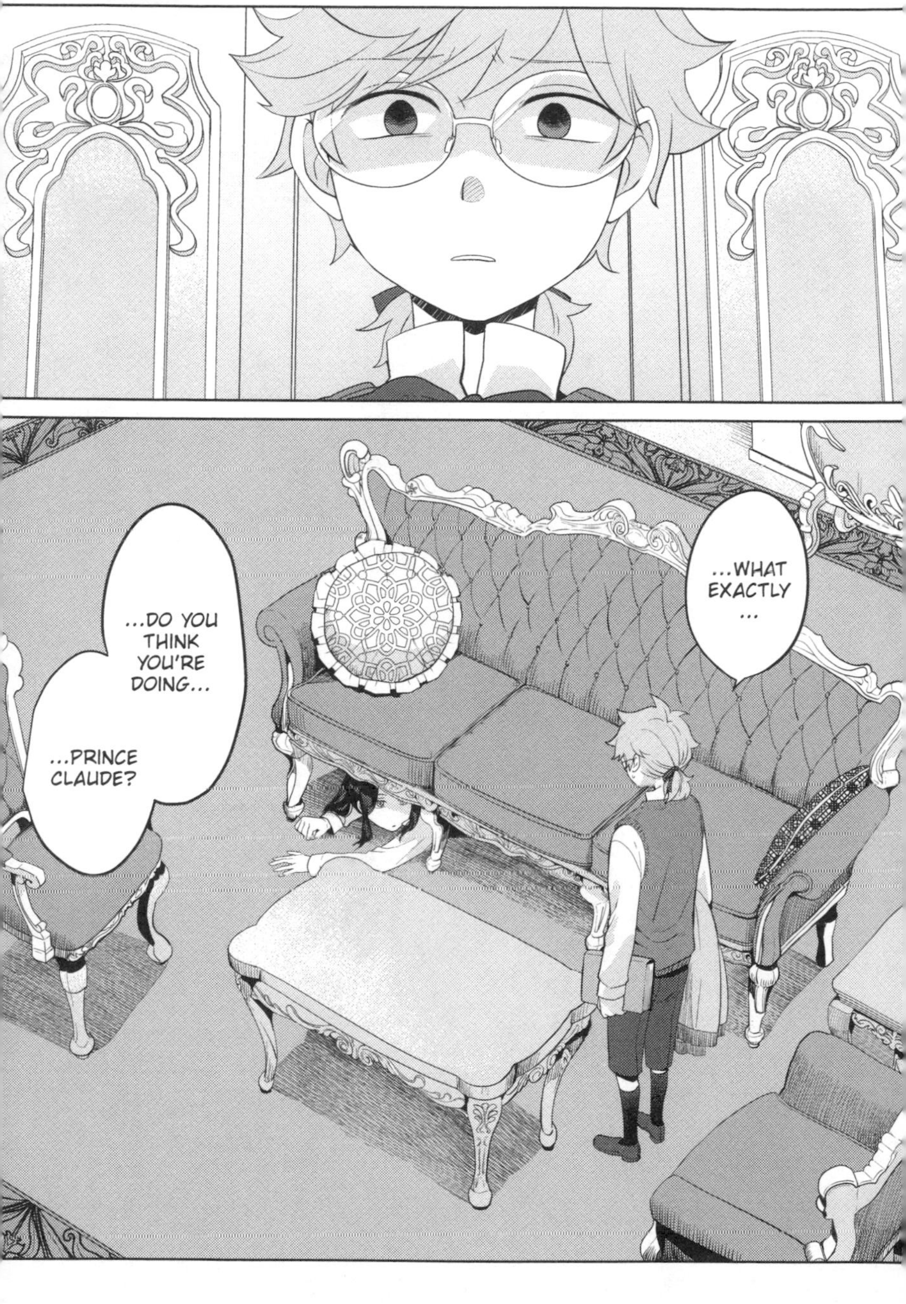
…WHAT EXACTLY …
…DO YOU THINK YOU'RE DOING…
…PRINCE CLAUDE?

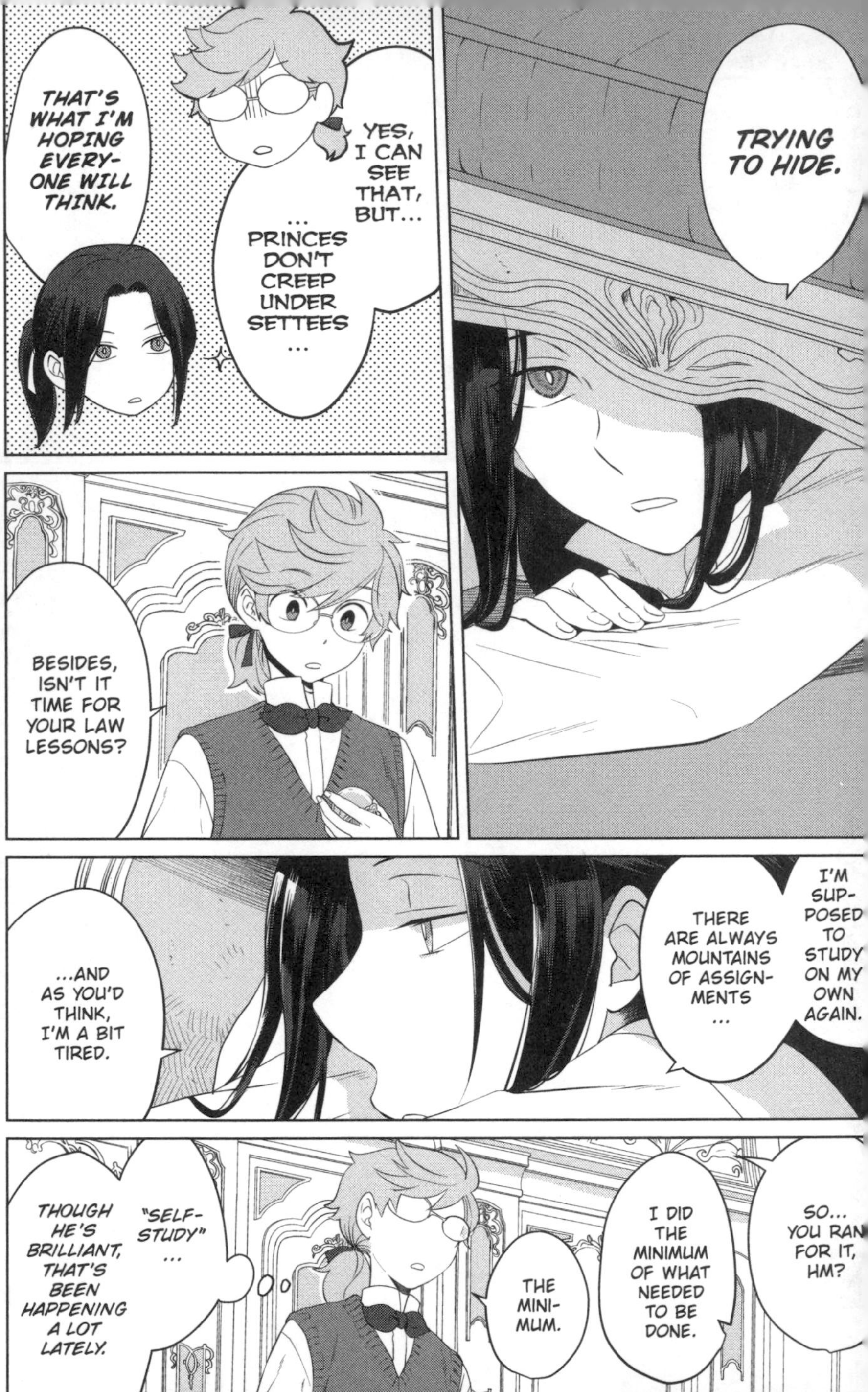
TRYING TO HIDE.
YES, I CAN SEE THAT, BUT...
... PRINCES DON'T CREEP UNDER SETTEES ...
THAT'S WHAT I'M HOPING EVERYONE WILL THINK.
BESIDES, ISN'T IT TIME FOR YOUR LAW LESSONS?
I'M SUPPOSED TO STUDY ON MY OWN AGAIN.
THERE ARE ALWAYS MOUNTAINS OF ASSIGNMENTS ...
...AND AS YOU'D THINK, I'M A BIT TIRED.
SO... YOU RAN FOR IT, HM?
I DID THE MINIMUM OF WHAT NEEDED TO BE DONE.
THE MINIMUM.
"SELF-STUDY" ...
THOUGH HE'S BRILLIANT, THAT'S BEEN HAPPENING A LOT LATELY.

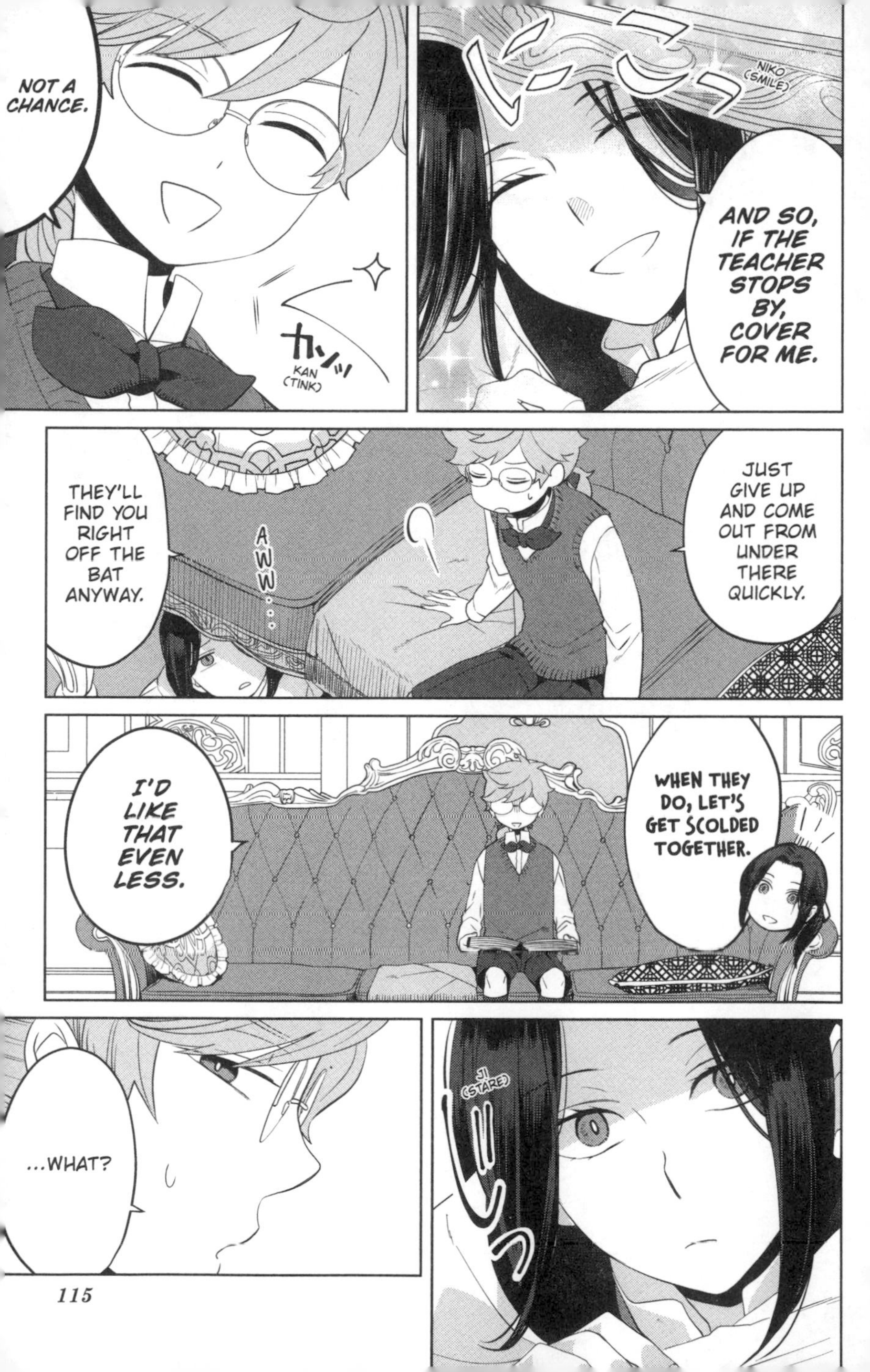
NIKO (SMILE)
AND SO, IF THE TEACHER STOPS BY, COVER FOR ME.
NOT A CHANCE.
KAN (TINK)
JUST GIVE UP AND COME OUT FROM UNDER THERE QUICKLY.
THEY'LL FIND YOU RIGHT OFF THE BAT ANYWAY.
AWW...
WHEN THEY DO, LET'S GET SCOLDED TOGETHER.
I'D LIKE THAT EVEN LESS.
JI (STARE)
...WHAT?

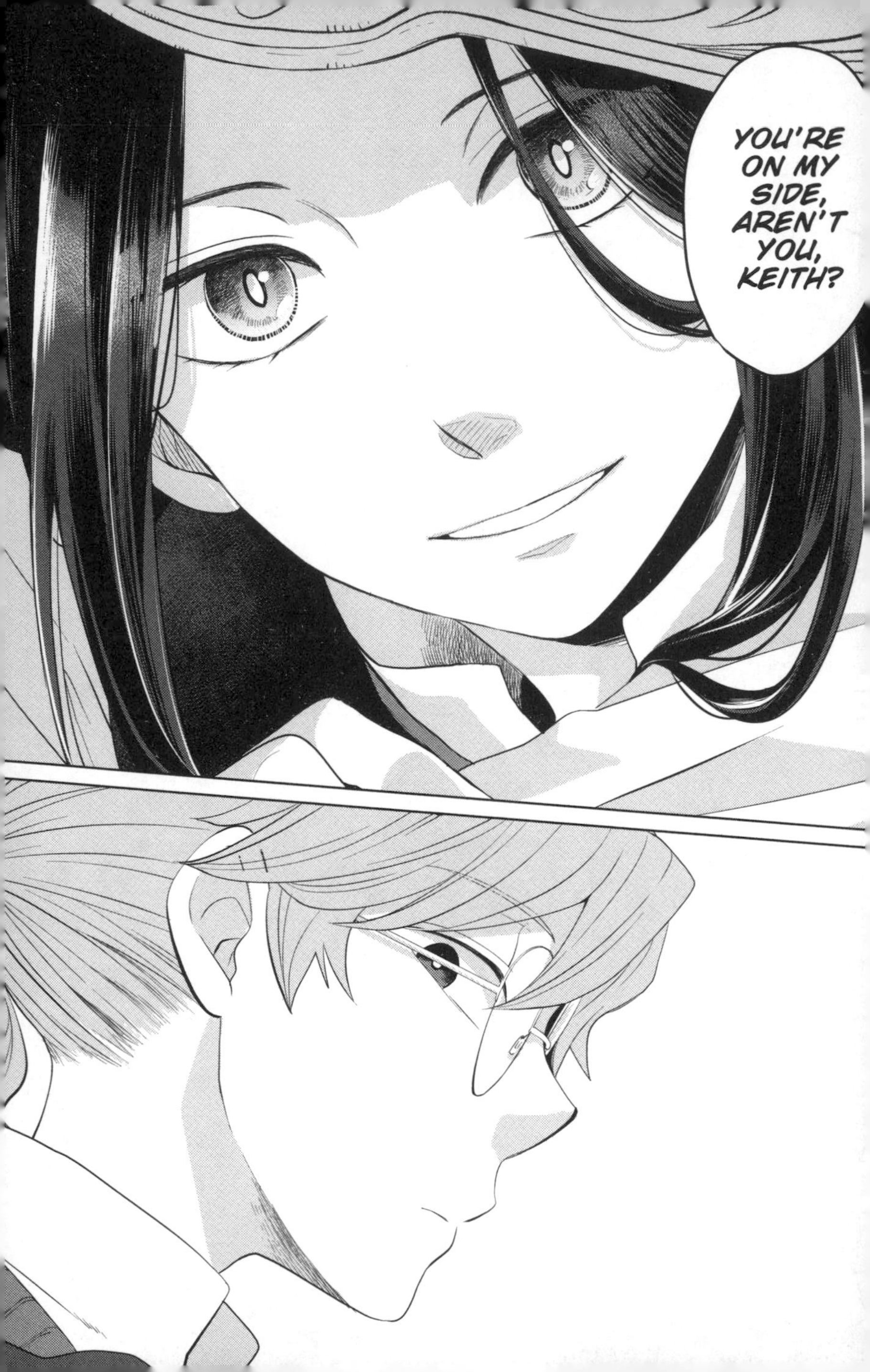
YOU'RE ON MY SIDE, AREN'T YOU, KEITH?

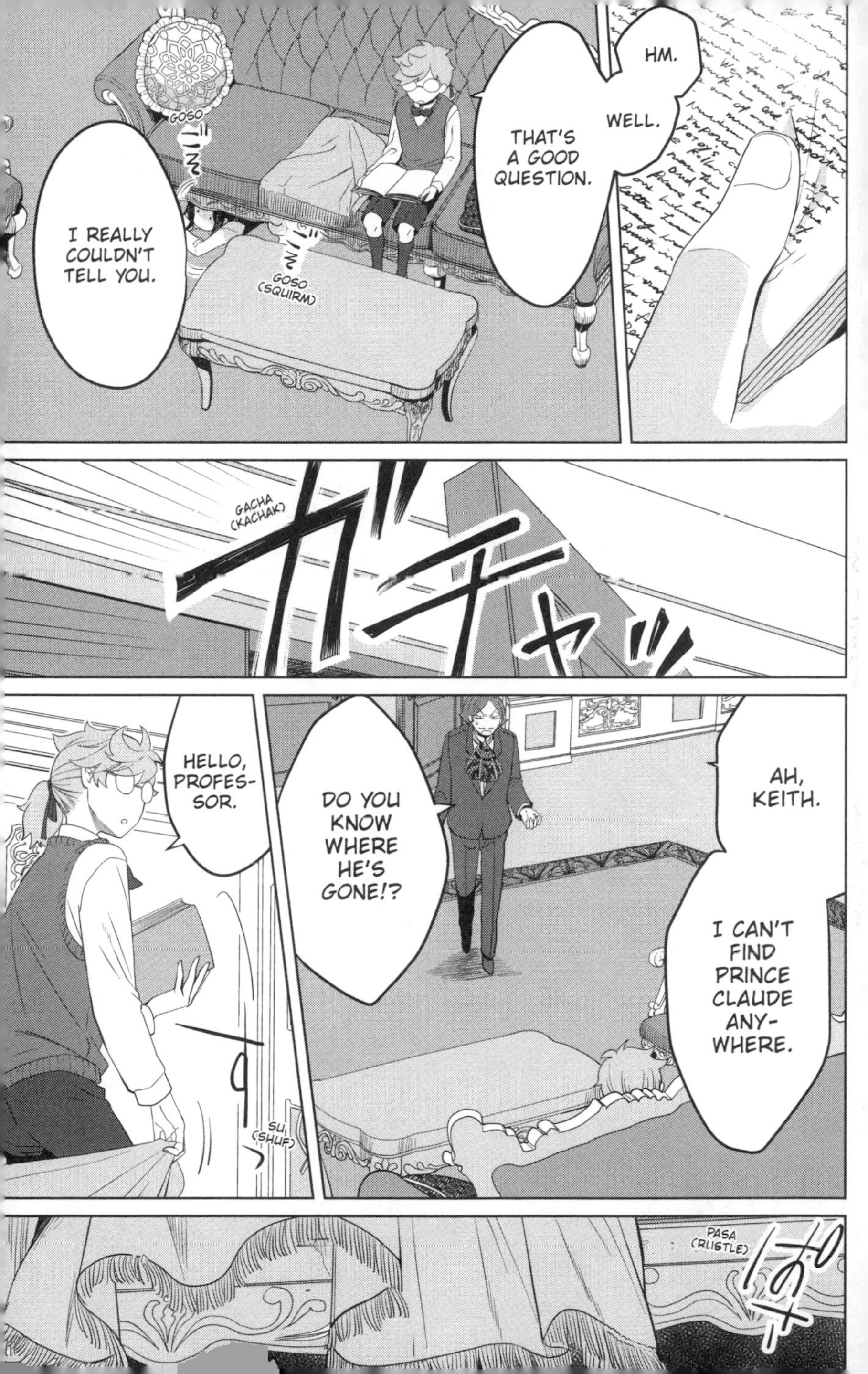
HM.
WELL.
THAT'S A GOOD QUESTION.
GOSO
I REALLY COULDN'T TELL YOU.
GOSO (SQUIRM)
GACHA (KACHAK)
AH, KEITH.
I CAN'T FIND PRINCE CLAUDE ANY-WHERE.
DO YOU KNOW WHERE HE'S GONE!?
HELLO, PROFES-SOR.
SU (SHUF)
PASA (RUSTLE)

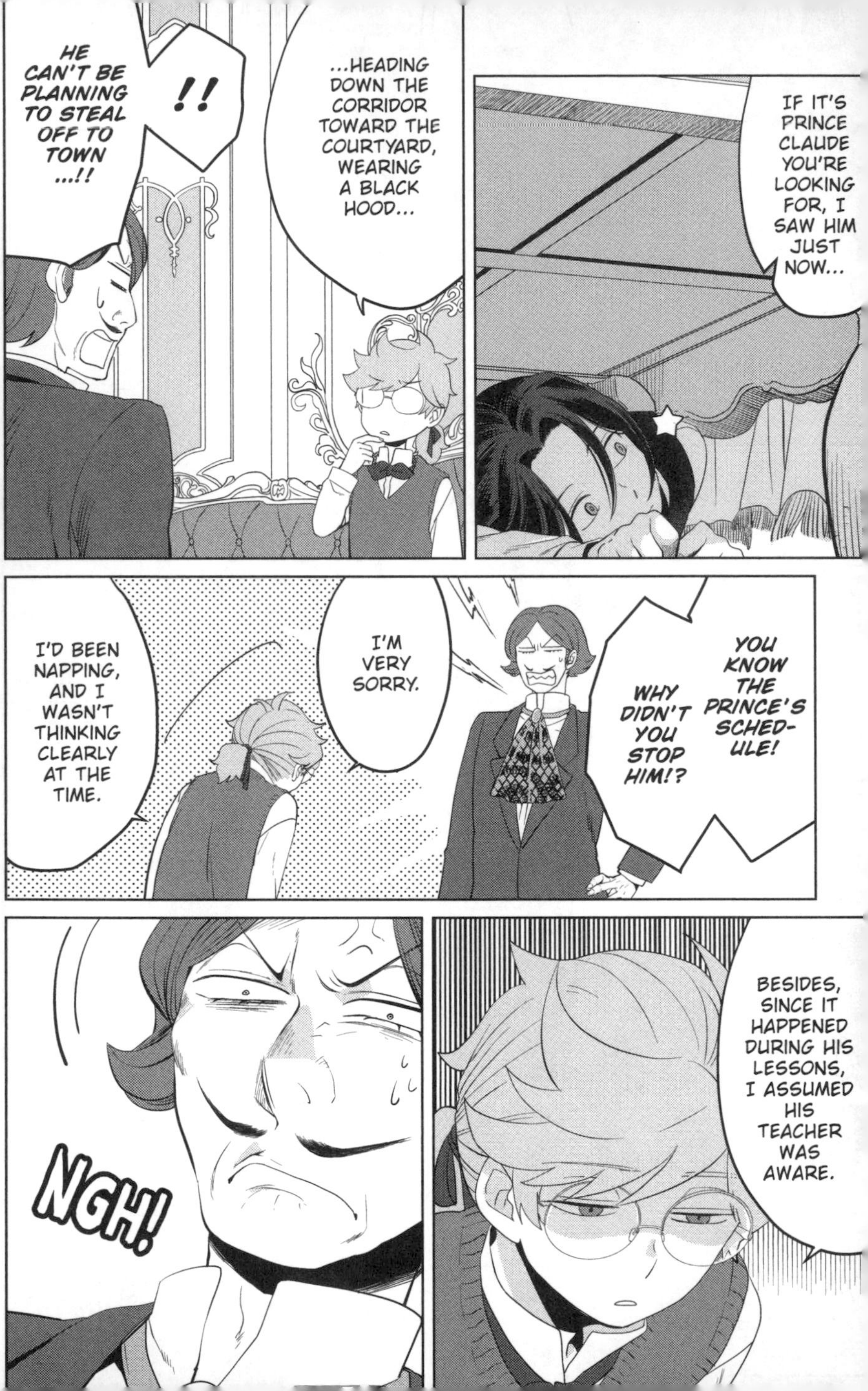
IF IT'S PRINCE CLAUDE YOU'RE LOOKING FOR, I SAW HIM JUST NOW...
...HEADING DOWN THE CORRIDOR TOWARD THE COURTYARD, WEARING A BLACK HOOD...
!!
HE CAN'T BE PLANNING TO STEAL OFF TO TOWN ...!!
YOU KNOW THE PRINCE'S SCHED-ULE!
WHY DIDN'T YOU STOP HIM!?
I'M VERY SORRY.
I'D BEEN NAPPING, AND I WASN'T THINKING CLEARLY AT THE TIME.
BESIDES, SINCE IT HAPPENED DURING HIS LESSONS, I ASSUMED HIS TEACHER WAS AWARE.
NGH!

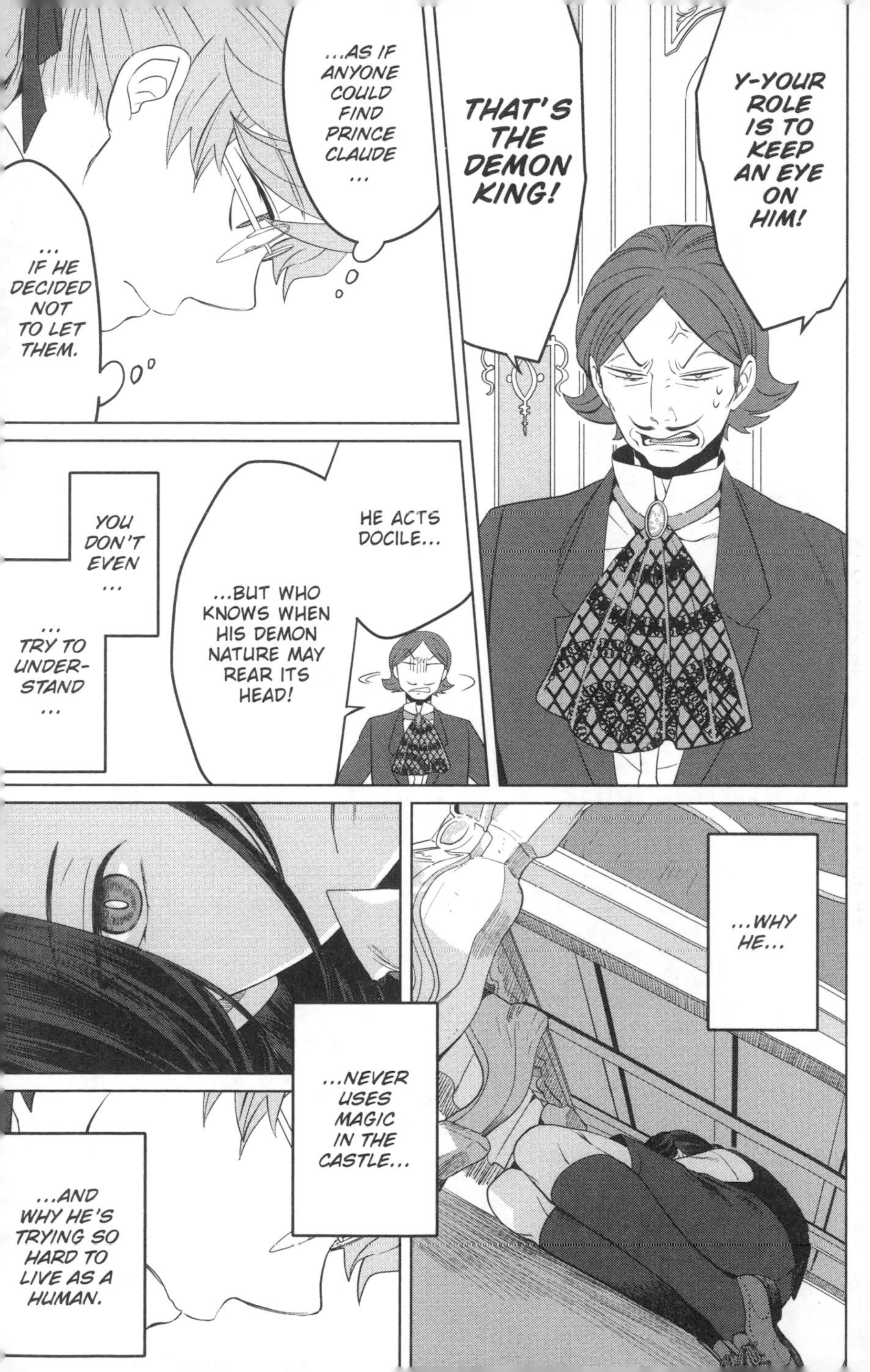
Y-YOUR ROLE IS TO KEEP AN EYE ON HIM!
THAT'S THE DEMON KING!
...AS IF ANYONE COULD FIND PRINCE CLAUDE...
...IF HE DECIDED NOT TO LET THEM.
HE ACTS DOCILE...
...BUT WHO KNOWS WHEN HIS DEMON NATURE MAY REAR ITS HEAD!
YOU DON'T EVEN...
...TRY TO UNDERSTAND...
...WHY HE...
...NEVER USES MAGIC IN THE CASTLE...
...AND WHY HE'S TRYING SO HARD TO LIVE AS A HUMAN.

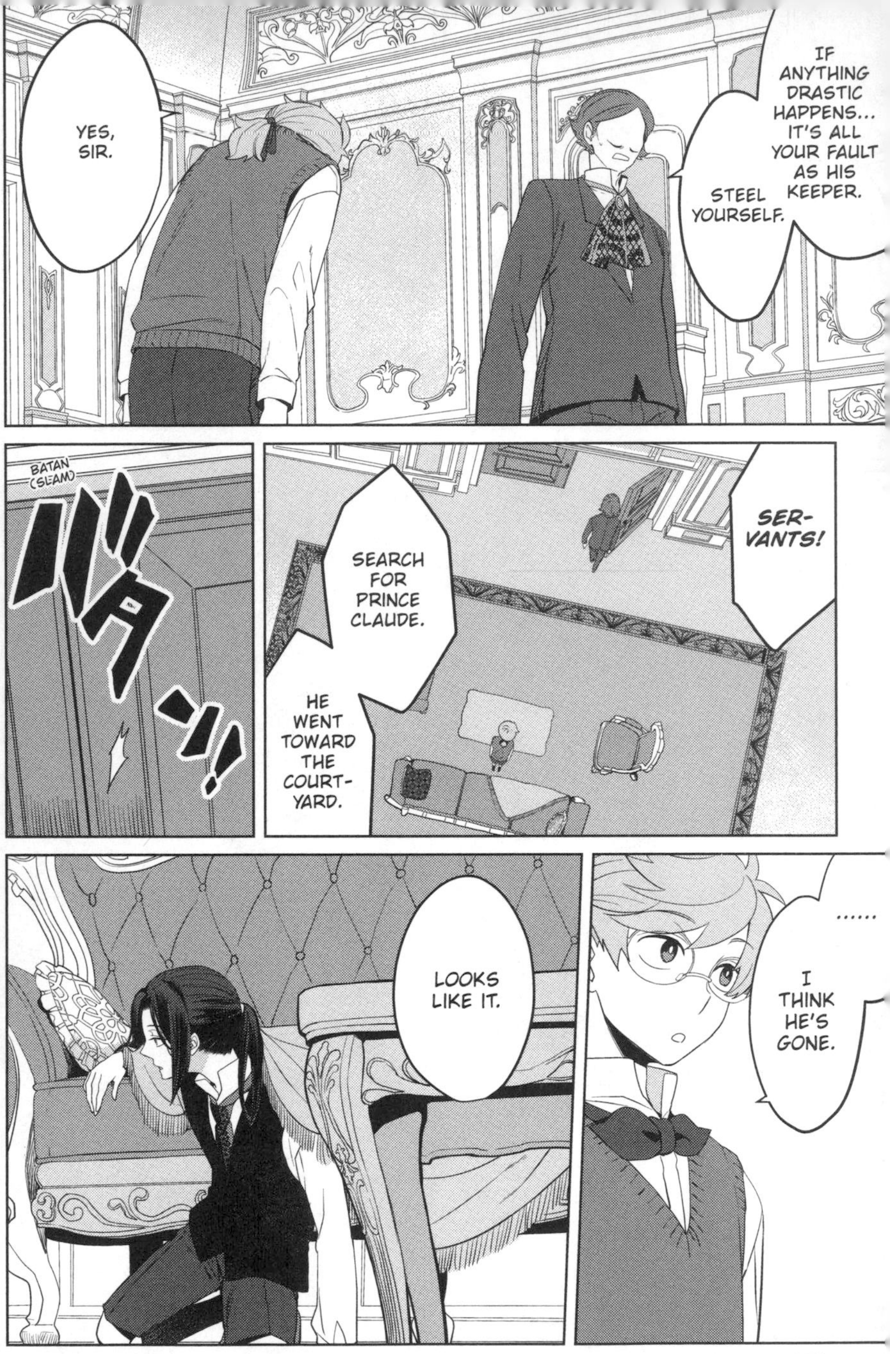
IF ANYTHING DRASTIC HAPPENS... IT'S ALL YOUR FAULT AS HIS KEEPER.
STEEL YOURSELF.
YES, SIR.
SER-VANTS!
SEARCH FOR PRINCE CLAUDE.
HE WENT TOWARD THE COURT-YARD.
BATAN (SLAM)
......
I THINK HE'S GONE.
LOOKS LIKE IT.

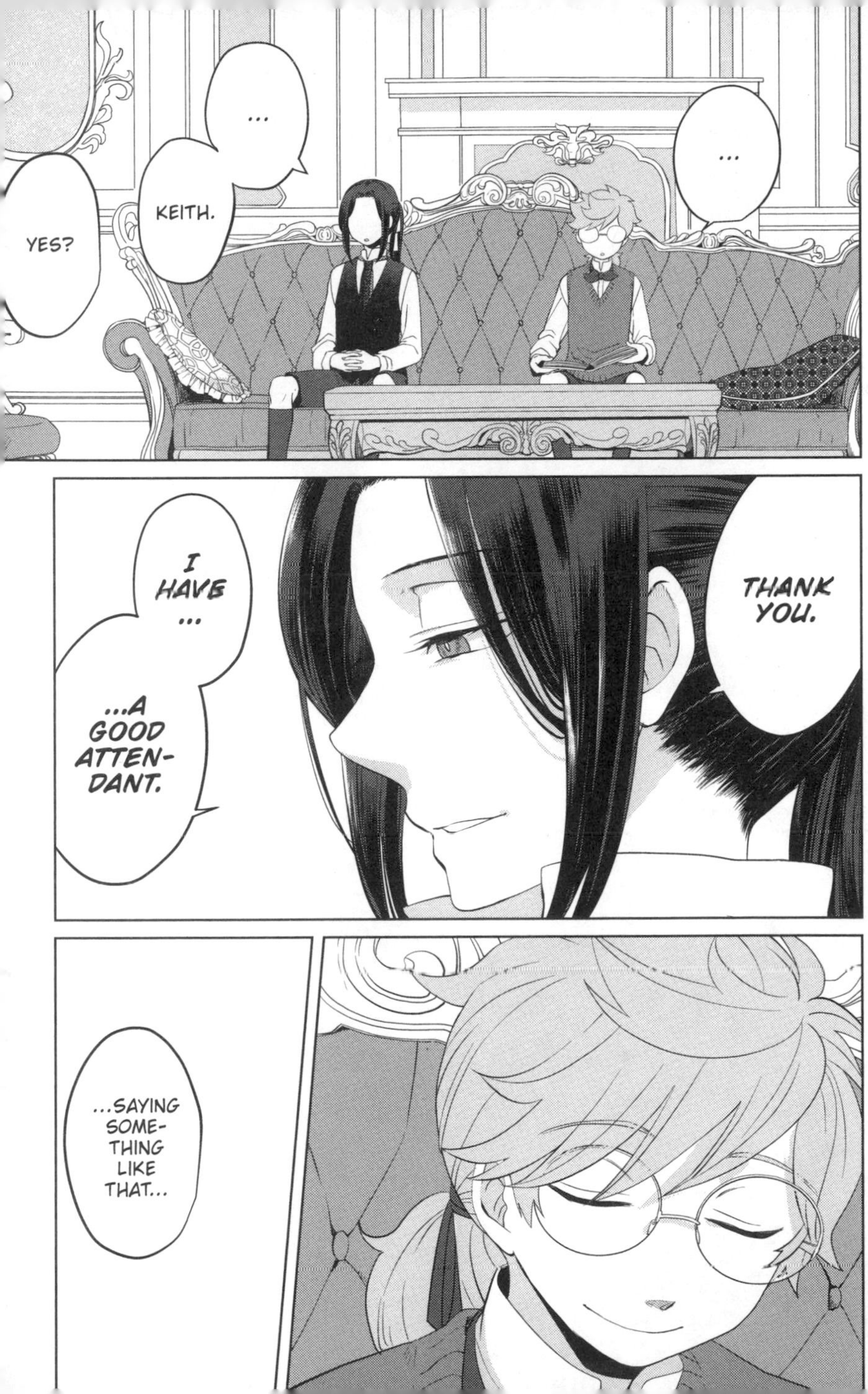
...
...
KEITH.
YES?
THANK YOU.
I HAVE ...
...A GOOD ATTENDANT.
...SAYING SOMETHING LIKE THAT...

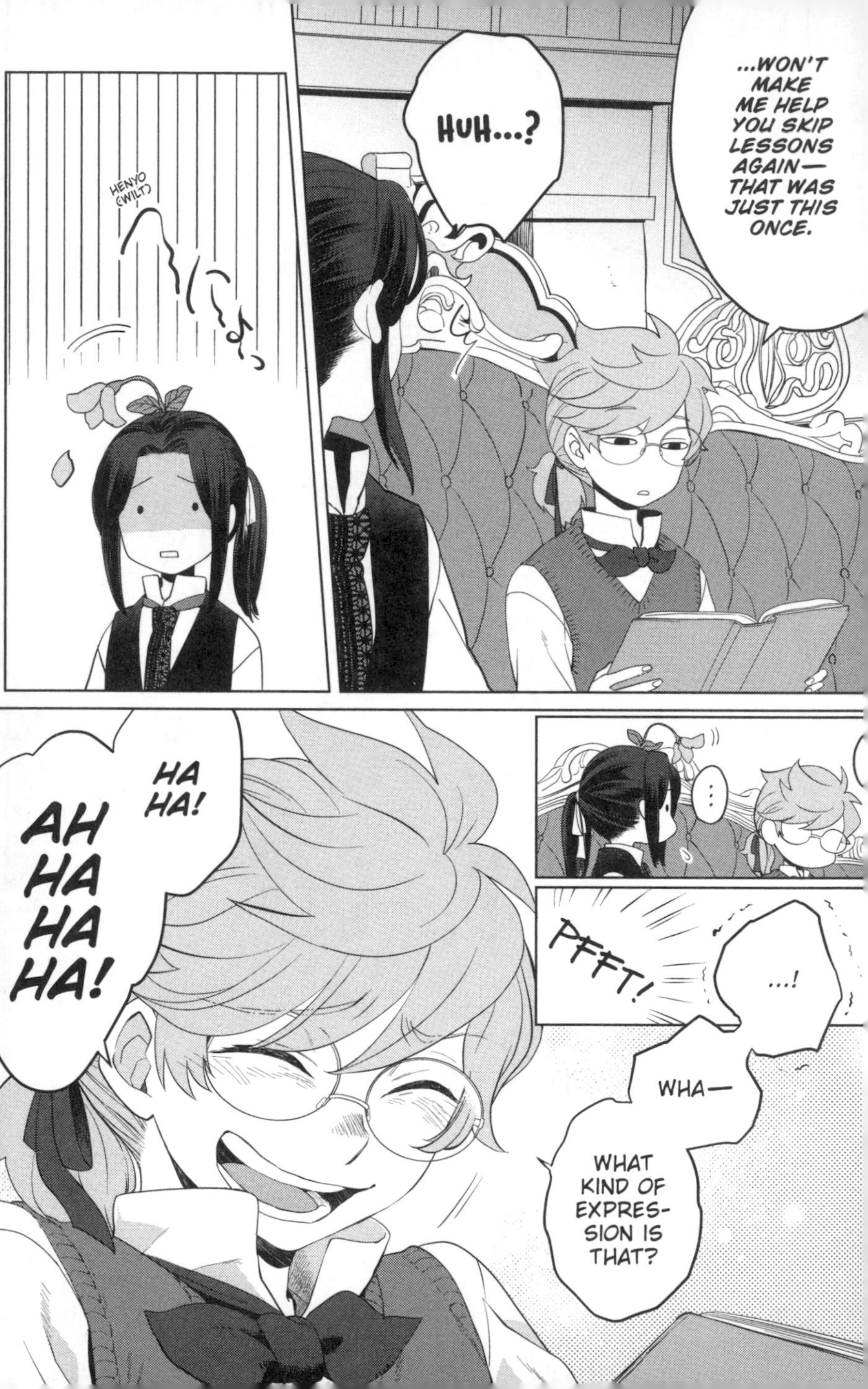
...WON'T MAKE ME HELP YOU SKIP LESSONS AGAIN—THAT WAS JUST THIS ONCE.
HUH...?
HENYO (WILT)
...
PFFFT!
...!
HA HA!
AH HA HA HA HA!
WHA—
WHAT KIND OF EXPRESSION IS THAT?

AGH, I CAAAN'T! THAT WAS HILARIOUS ...!

AH HA HA HA HA HA HA!

HEEEE!

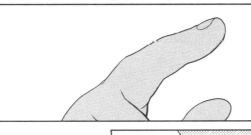

AHHHHH!

BI' BRUVVER!

PWAY WITH MEEE! SHOW ME MAGIC!

LISTEN, CEDRIC.

DON'T TELL ANYONE I'M HERE. IT'LL BE OUR SECRET.

THE MAGIC TOO.

...SEE-KWET!

WOOO-OOW!!

SHH...

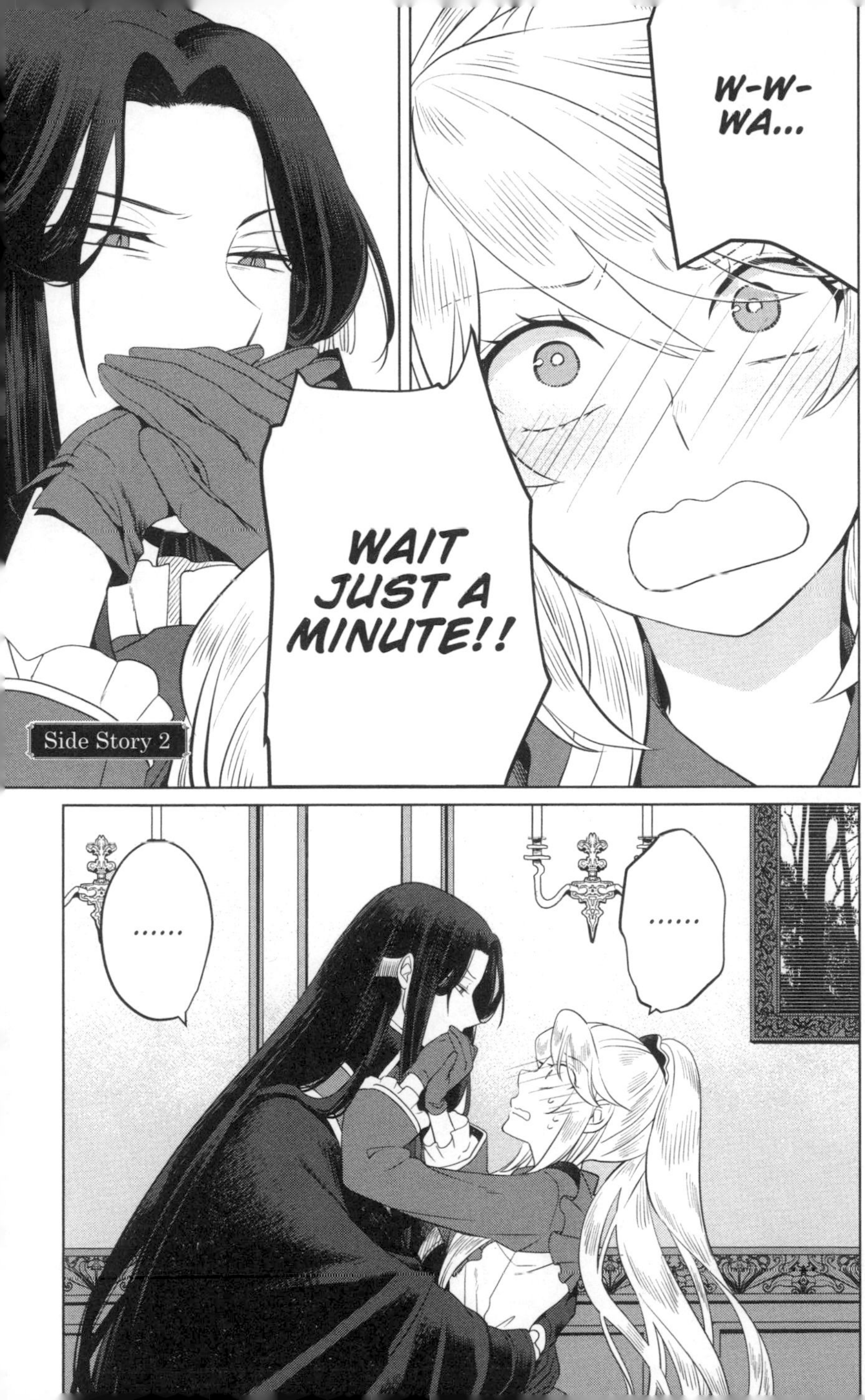
W-W-WA...
WAIT JUST A MINUTE!!
Side Story 2
......
......

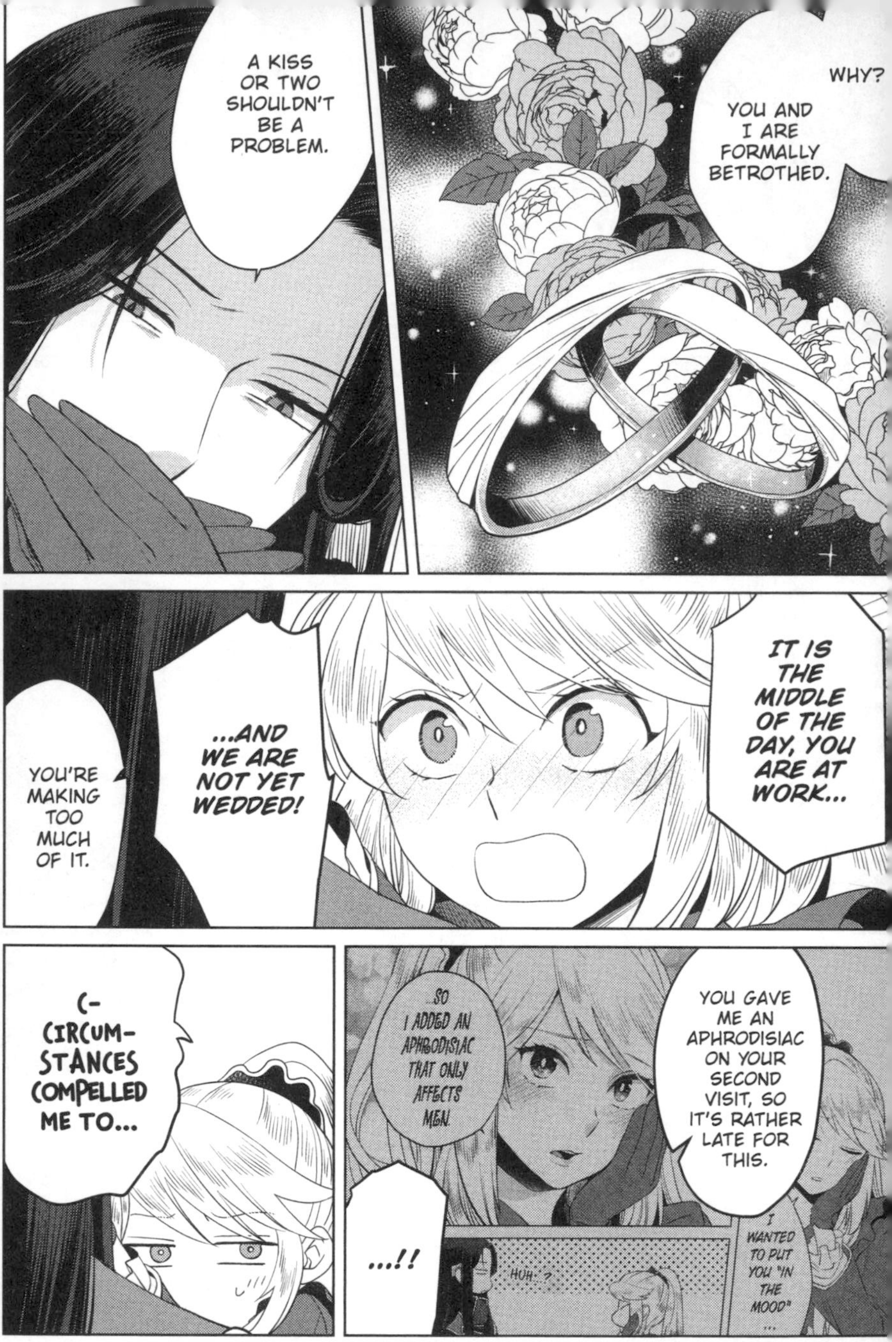

WHY?
YOU AND I ARE FORMALLY BETROTHED.
A KISS OR TWO SHOULDN'T BE A PROBLEM.
IT IS THE MIDDLE OF THE DAY, YOU ARE AT WORK...
...AND WE ARE NOT YET WEDDED!
YOU'RE MAKING TOO MUCH OF IT.
YOU GAVE ME AN APHRODISIAC ON YOUR SECOND VISIT, SO IT'S RATHER LATE FOR THIS.
...SO I ADDED AN APHRODISIAC THAT ONLY AFFECTS MEN.
I WANTED TO PUT YOU "IN THE MOOD"...
HUH...?
...!!
C-CIRCUMSTANCES COMPELLED ME TO...

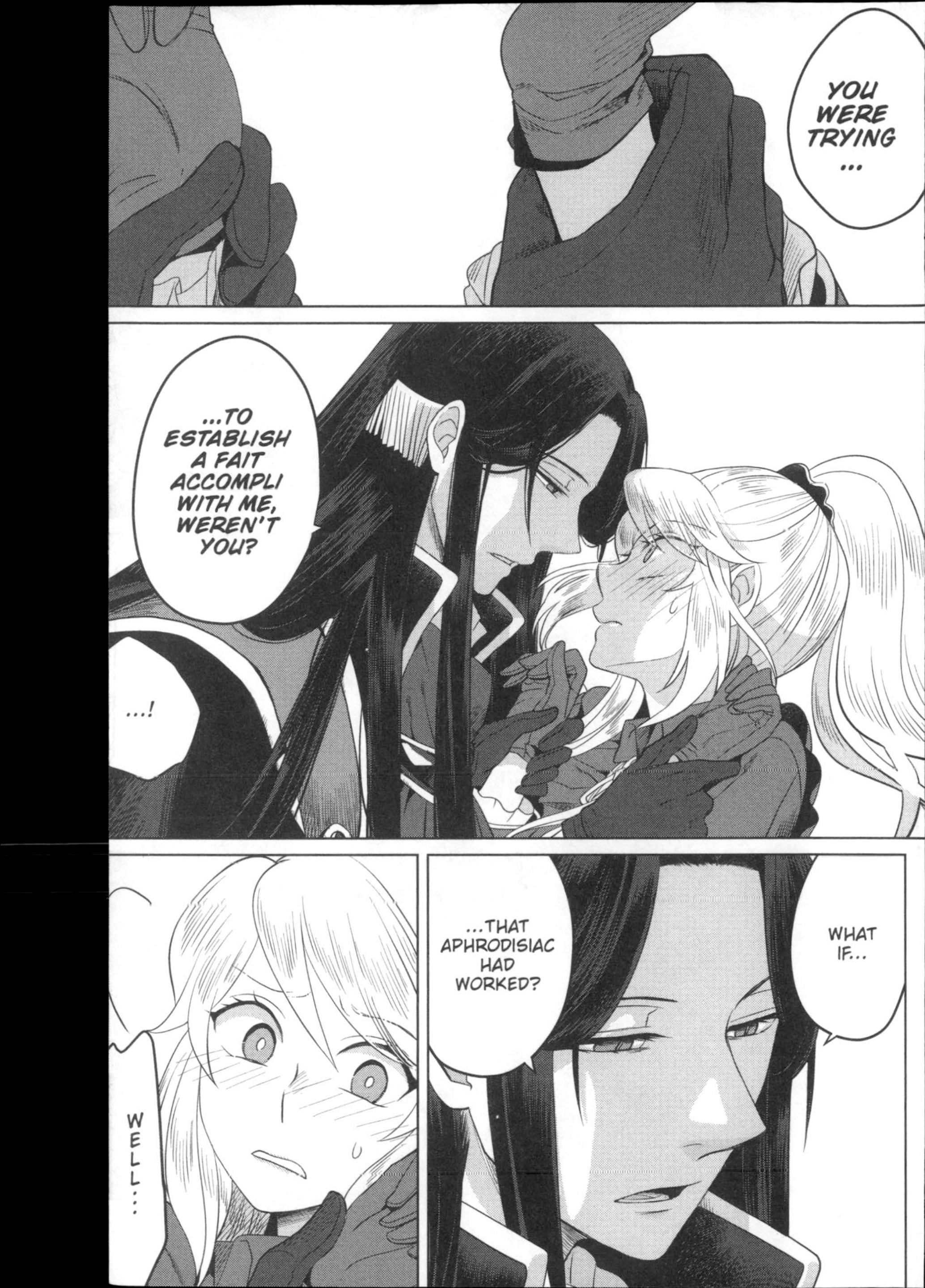
YOU WERE TRYING ...
...TO ESTABLISH A FAIT ACCOMPLI WITH ME, WEREN'T YOU?
...!
WHAT IF...
...THAT APHRODISIAC HAD WORKED?
WELL...

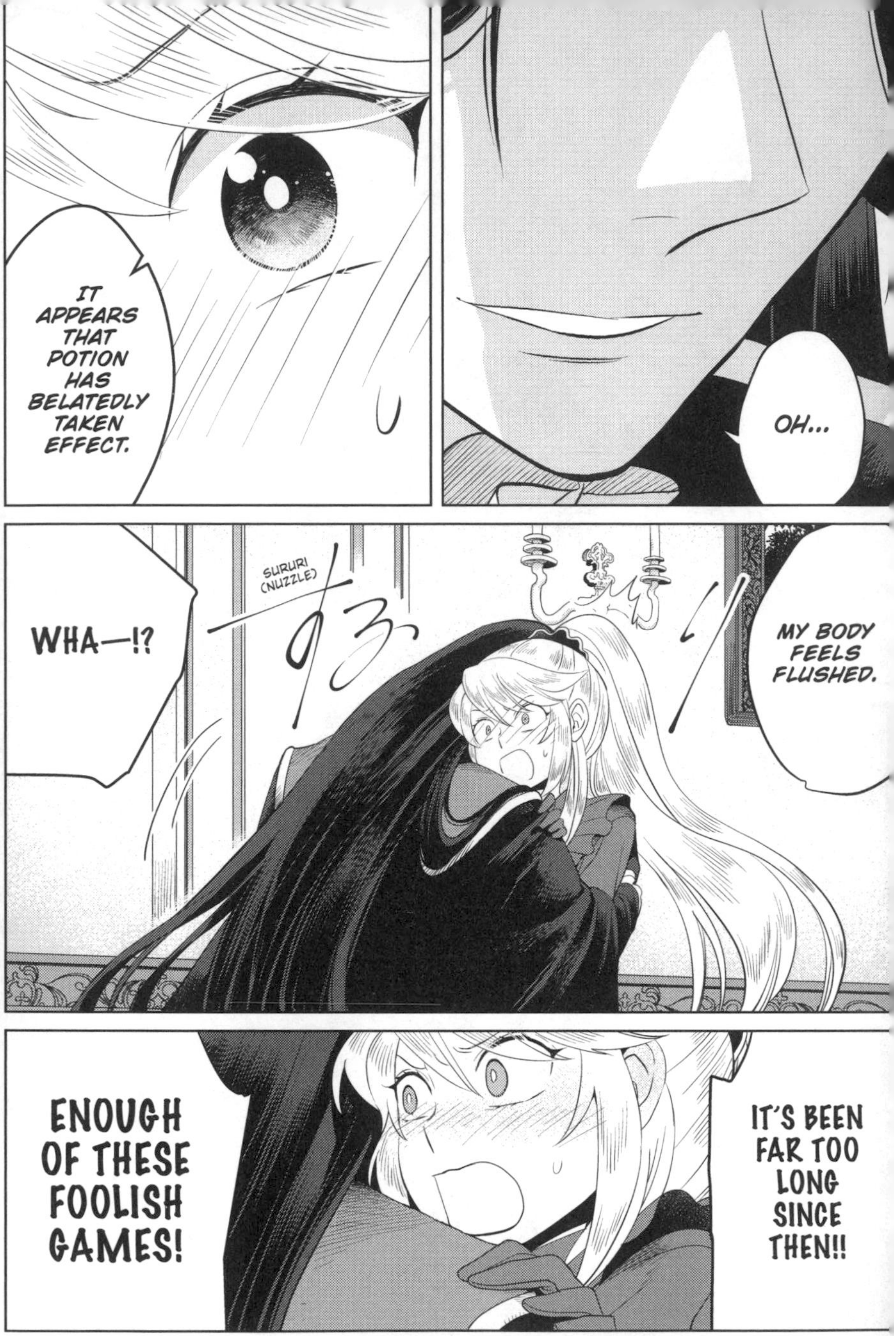
OH...
IT APPEARS THAT POTION HAS BELATEDLY TAKEN EFFECT.
MY BODY FEELS FLUSHED.
SURURI (NUZZLE)
WHA—!?
IT'S BEEN FAR TOO LONG SINCE THEN!!
ENOUGH OF THESE FOOLISH GAMES!

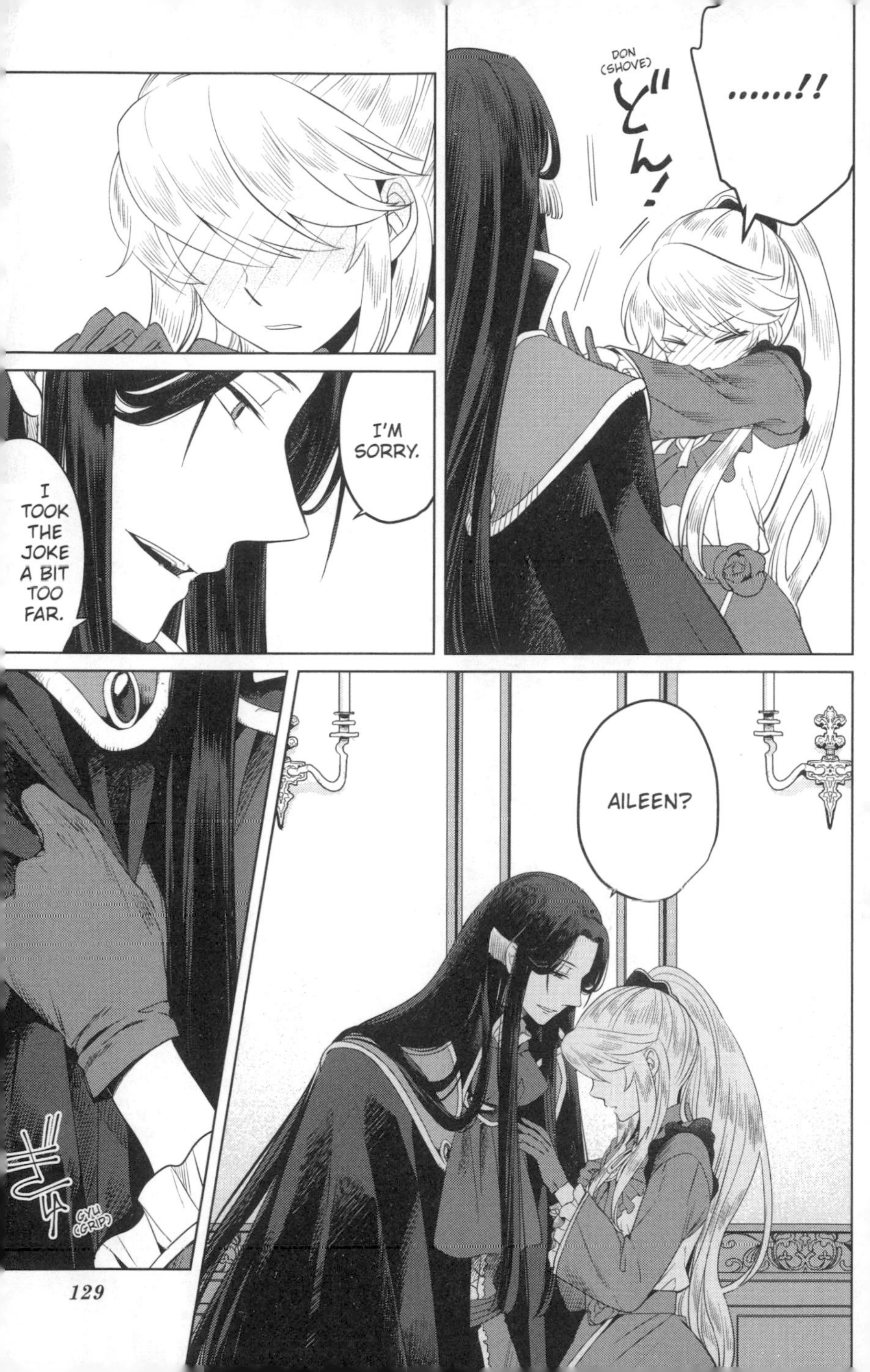

......!!
どん！
DON (SHOVE)
I'M SORRY.
I TOOK THE JOKE A BIT TOO FAR.
AILEEN?
ぎゅ
GYU (GRIP)

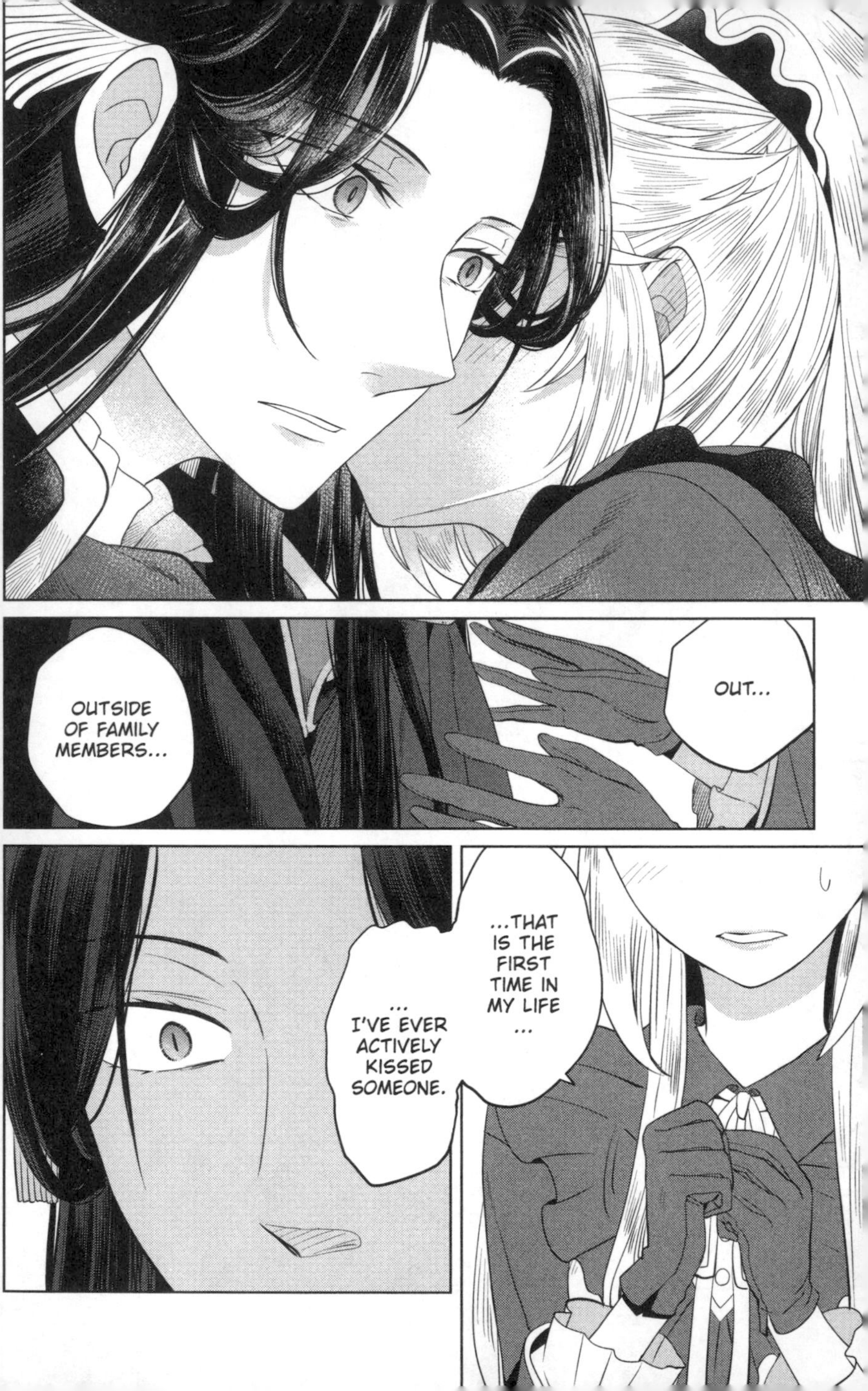
OUT...
OUTSIDE OF FAMILY MEMBERS...
...THAT IS THE FIRST TIME IN MY LIFE ...
... I'VE EVER ACTIVELY KISSED SOMEONE.

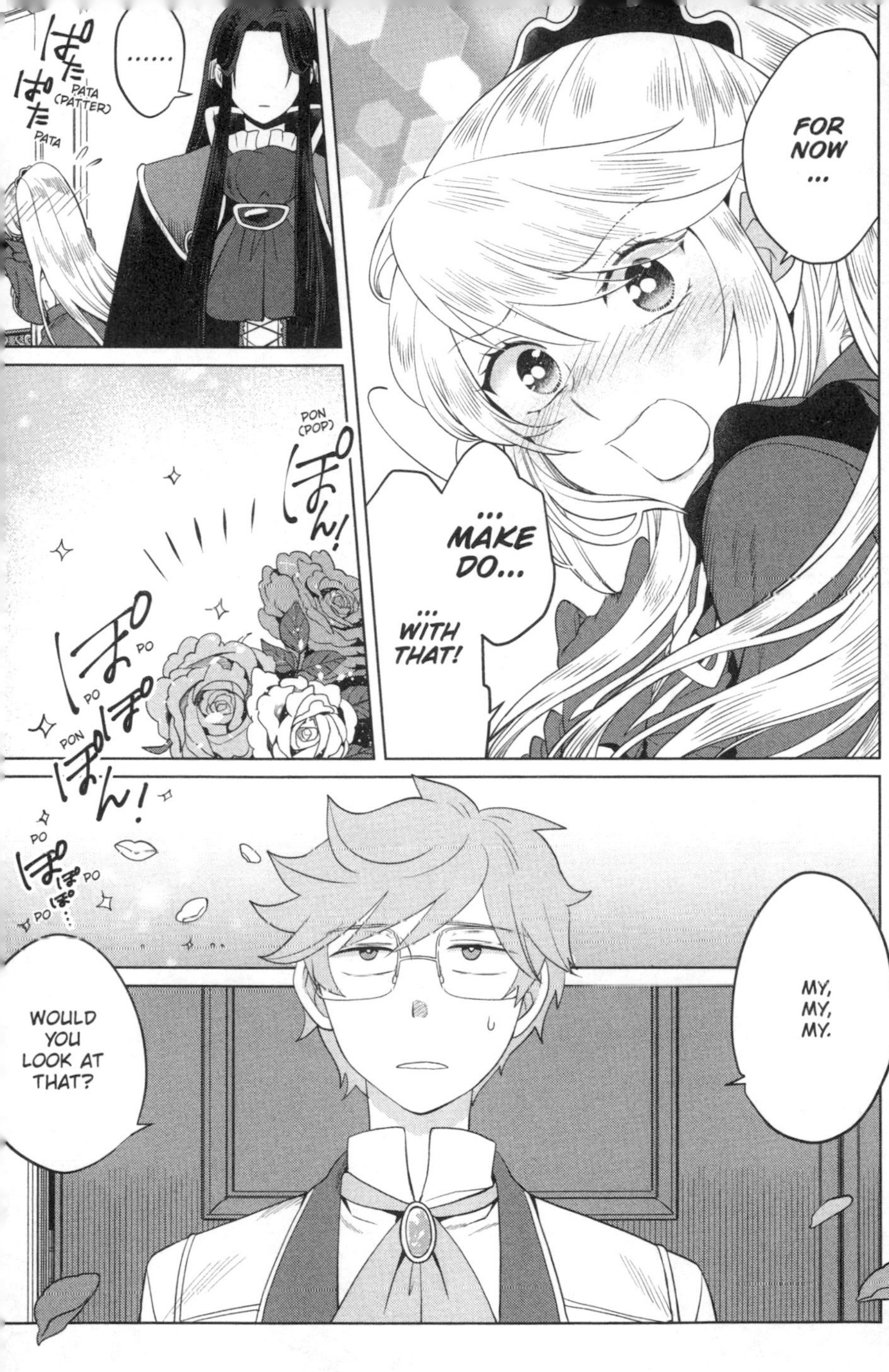
FOR NOW...
... MÄKE DO...
... WITH THAT!
......
ぱた ぱた
PATA (PATTER)
PATA
PON (POP)
ぽん!
ぽ PO ぽ PO ぽ PON ぽん!
PO ぽぽ PO ぽ PO...
MY, MY, MY.
WOULD YOU LOOK AT THAT?

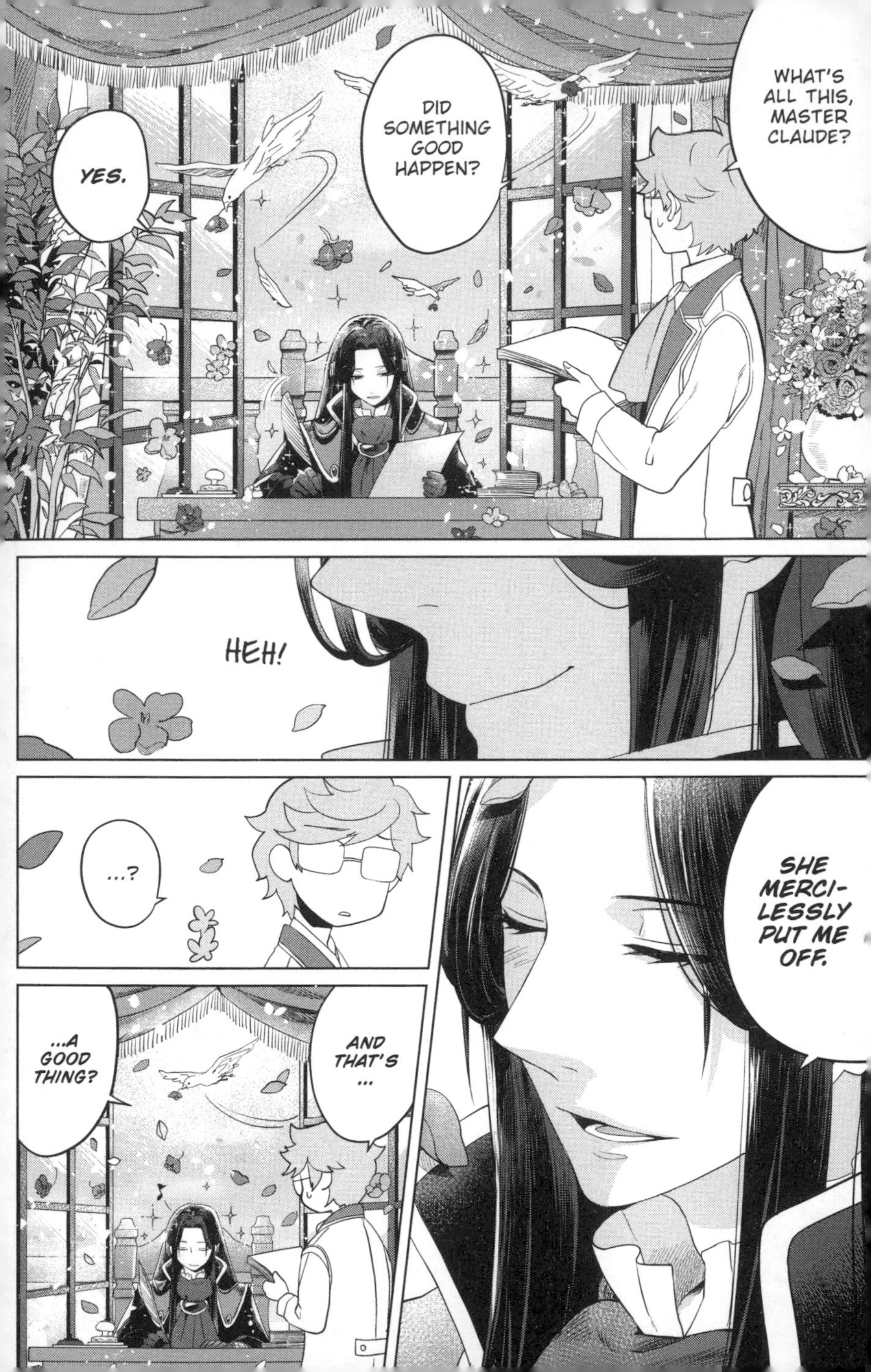
WHAT'S ALL THIS, MASTER CLAUDE?
DID SOMETHING GOOD HAPPEN?
YES.
HEH!
SHE MERCI-LESSLY PUT ME OFF.
...?
AND THAT'S ...
...A GOOD THING?

I'm the VILLAINESS, So I'm Taming the Final Boss

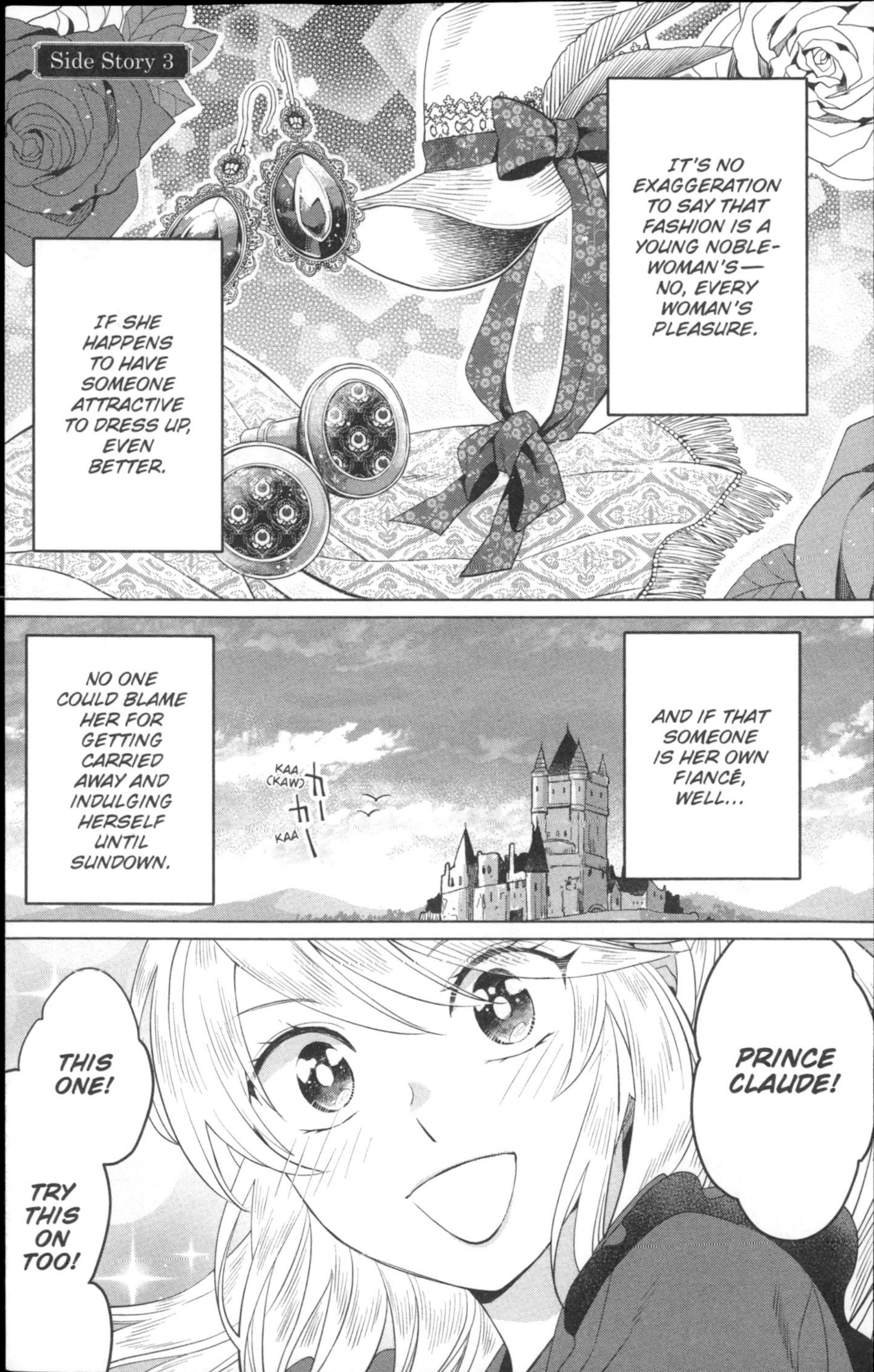
Side Story 3
IT'S NO EXAGGERATION TO SAY THAT FASHION IS A YOUNG NOBLE-WOMAN'S—NO, EVERY WOMAN'S PLEASURE.
IF SHE HAPPENS TO HAVE SOMEONE ATTRACTIVE TO DRESS UP, EVEN BETTER.
AND IF THAT SOMEONE IS HER OWN FIANCÉ, WELL...
KAA (KAW)
KAA
NO ONE COULD BLAME HER FOR GETTING CARRIED AWAY AND INDULGING HERSELF UNTIL SUNDOWN.
PRINCE CLAUDE!
THIS ONE!
TRY THIS ON TOO!

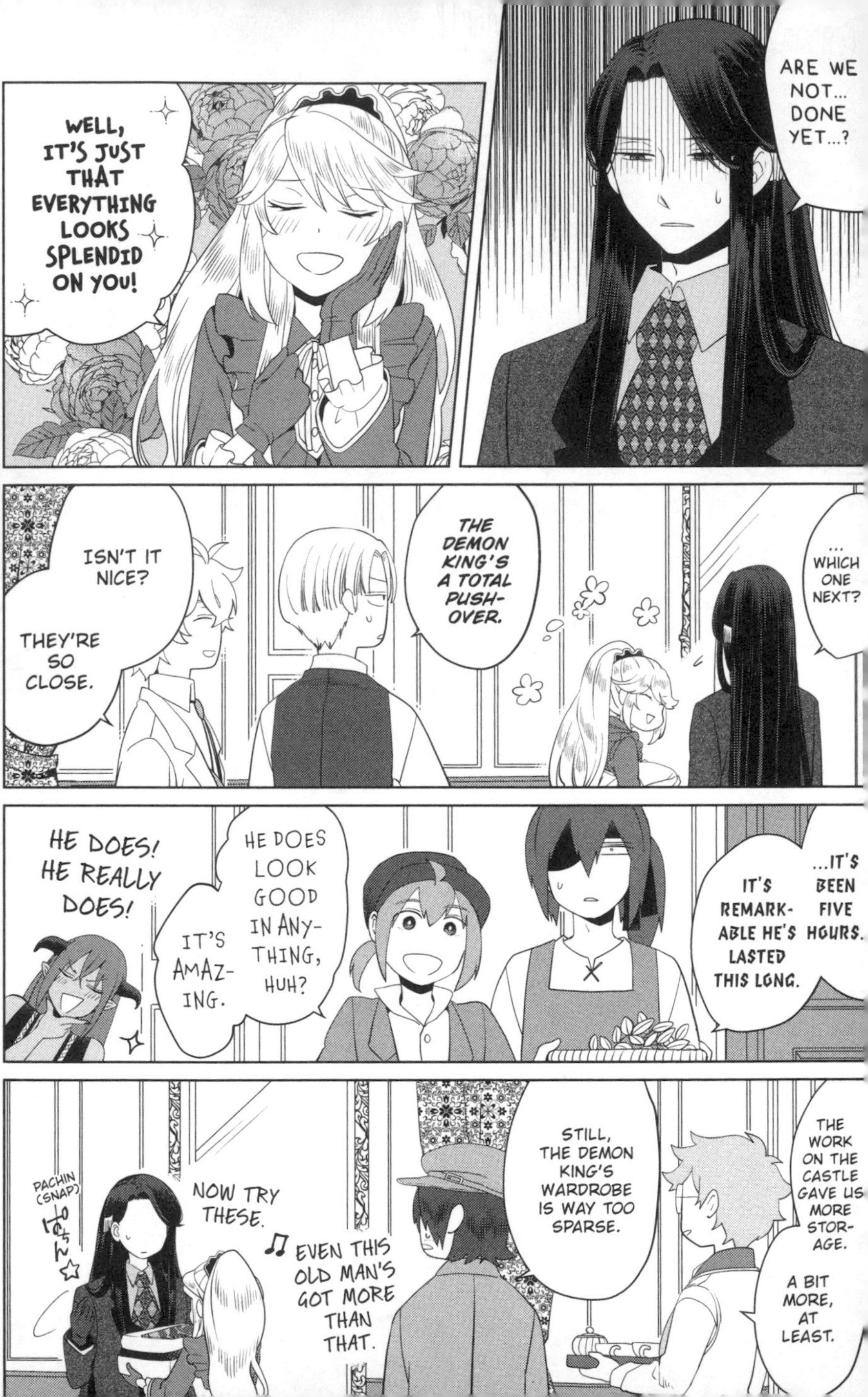
ARE WE NOT... DONE YET...?
WELL, IT'S JUST THAT EVERYTHING LOOKS SPLENDID ON YOU!
...WHICH ONE NEXT?
THE DEMON KING'S A TOTAL PUSH-OVER.
ISN'T IT NICE?
THEY'RE SO CLOSE.
...IT'S BEEN FIVE HOURS.
IT'S REMARKABLE HE'S LASTED THIS LONG.
HE DOES LOOK GOOD IN ANYTHING, HUH?
IT'S AMAZING.
HE DOES! HE REALLY DOES!
THE WORK ON THE CASTLE GAVE US MORE STORAGE.
A BIT MORE, AT LEAST.
STILL, THE DEMON KING'S WARDROBE IS WAY TOO SPARSE.
EVEN THIS OLD MAN'S GOT MORE THAN THAT.
NOW TRY THESE.
PACHIN (SNAP)

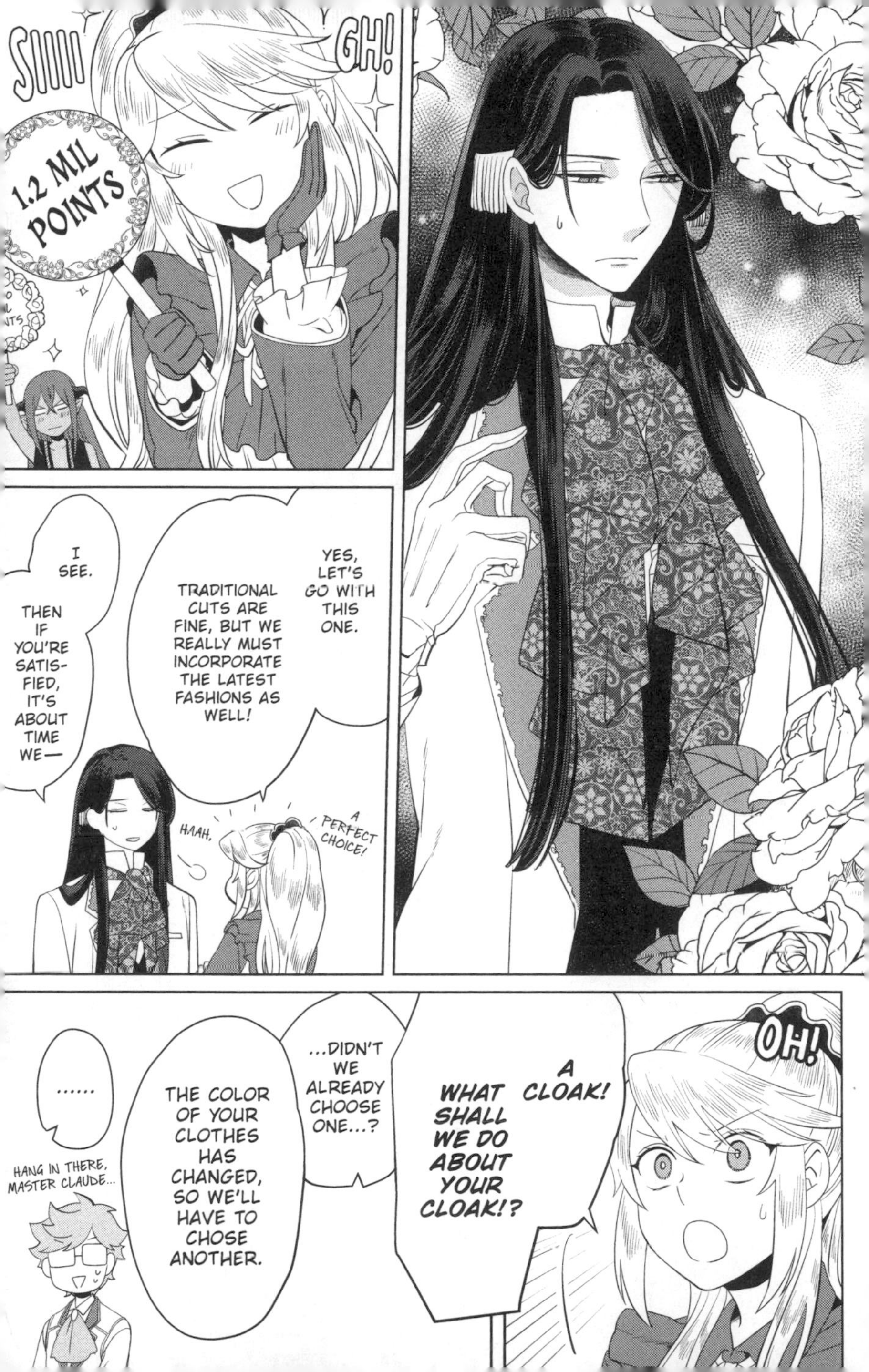
SIIII GH!
1.2 MIL POINTS
YES, LET'S GO WITH THIS ONE.
TRADITIONAL CUTS ARE FINE, BUT WE REALLY MUST INCORPORATE THE LATEST FASHIONS AS WELL!
I SEE.
THEN IF YOU'RE SATIS-FIED, IT'S ABOUT TIME WE—
A PERFECT CHOICE!
HAAH,
OH!
A CLOAK!
WHAT SHALL WE DO ABOUT YOUR CLOAK!?
...DIDN'T WE ALREADY CHOOSE ONE...?
THE COLOR OF YOUR CLOTHES HAS CHANGED, SO WE'LL HAVE TO CHOSE ANOTHER.
......
HANG IN THERE, MASTER CLAUDE...

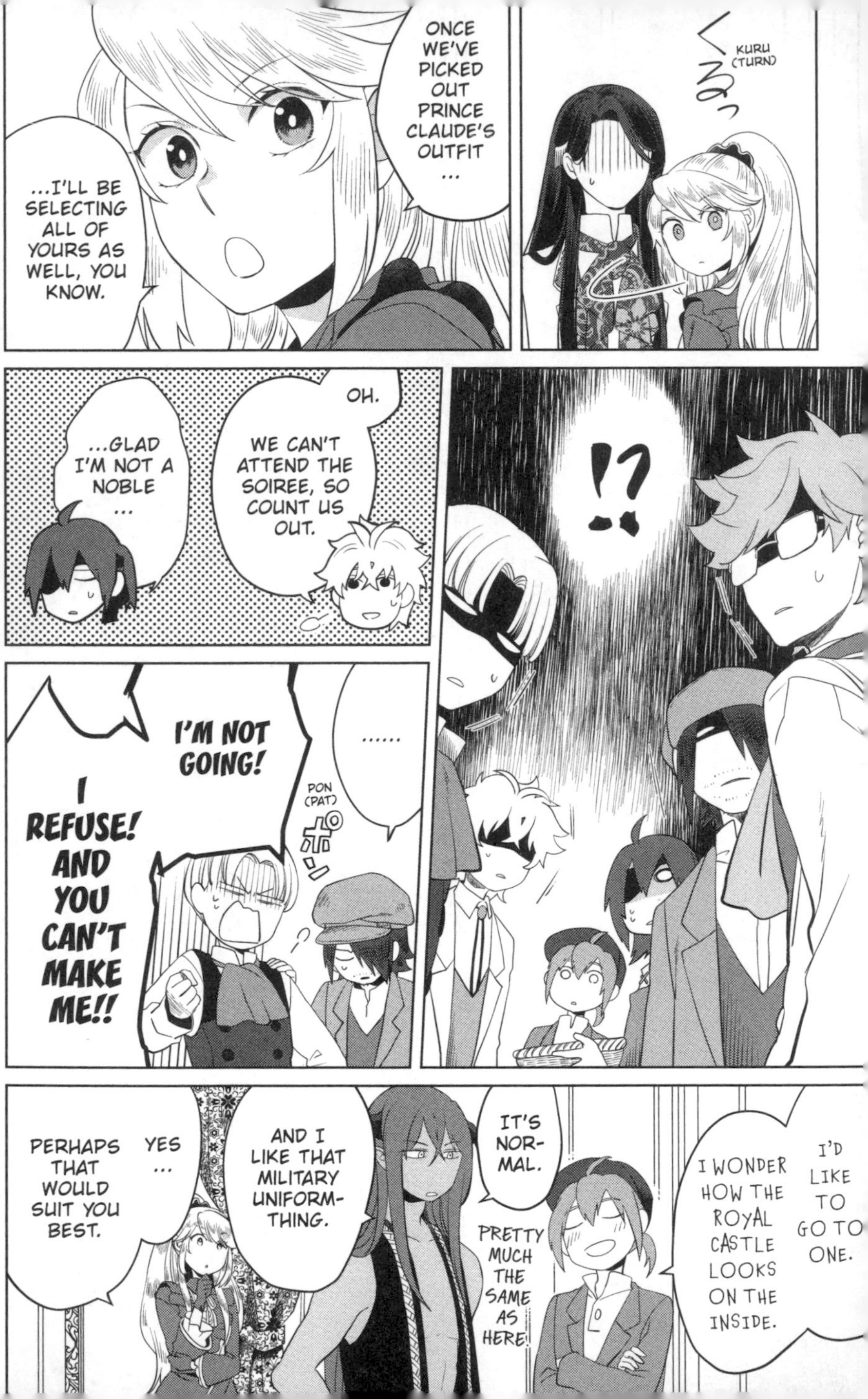
KURU (TURN)
くるっ
ONCE WE'VE PICKED OUT PRINCE CLAUDE'S OUTFIT...
...I'LL BE SELECTING ALL OF YOURS AS WELL, YOU KNOW.
!?
OH.
WE CAN'T ATTEND THE SOIREE, SO COUNT US OUT.
...GLAD I'M NOT A NOBLE...
......
PON (PAT)
ポンッ
I'M NOT GOING!
I REFUSE! AND YOU CAN'T MAKE ME!!
I'D LIKE TO GO TO ONE.
I WONDER HOW THE ROYAL CASTLE LOOKS ON THE INSIDE.
IT'S NOR-MAL.
PRETTY MUCH THE SAME AS HERE.
AND I LIKE THAT MILITARY UNIFORM-THING.
YES...
PERHAPS THAT WOULD SUIT YOU BEST.

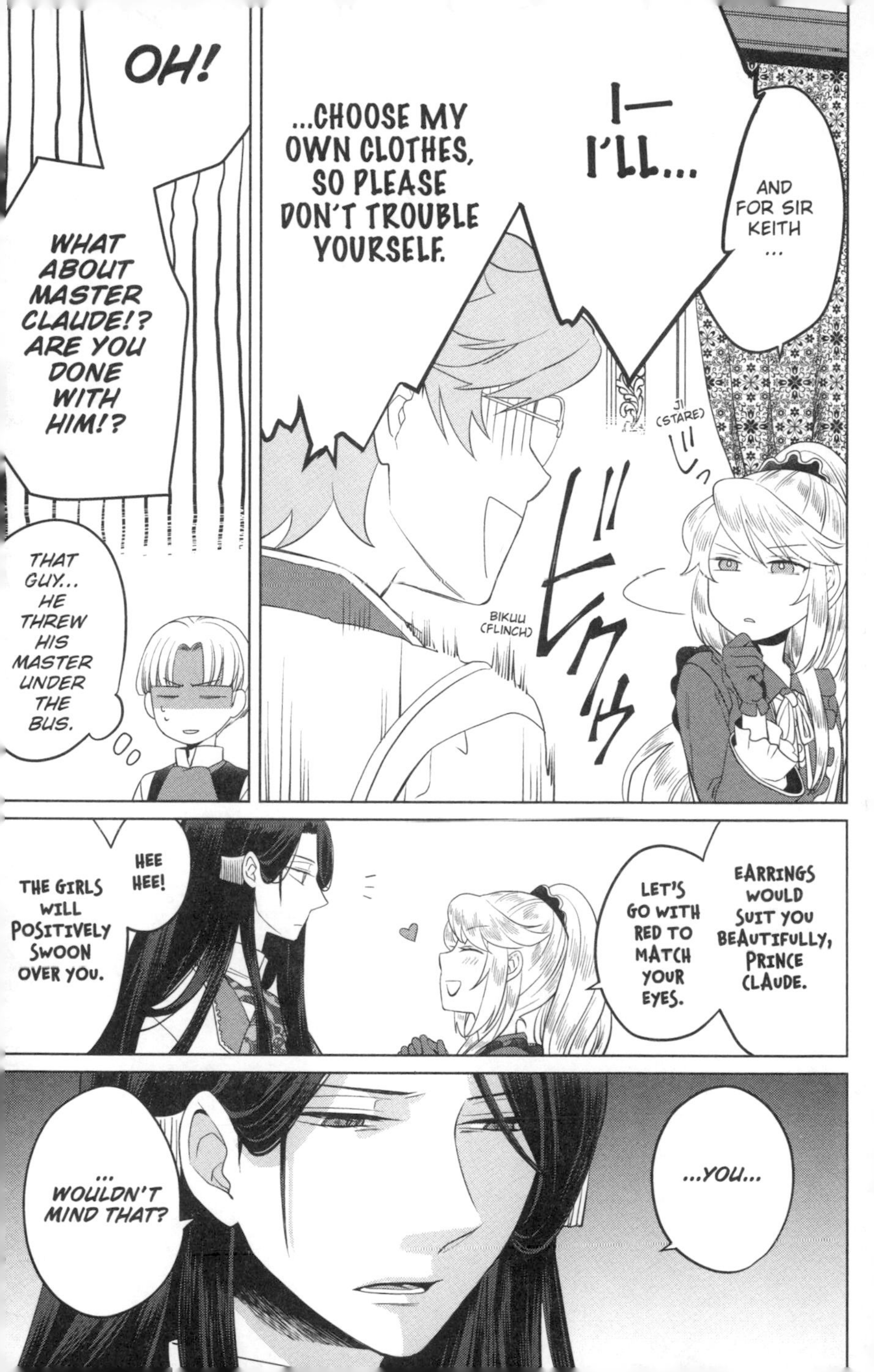
AND FOR SIR KEITH ...
I— I'LL...
...CHOOSE MY OWN CLOTHES, SO PLEASE DON'T TROUBLE YOURSELF.
JI (STARE)
BIKUU (FLINCH)
OH!
WHAT ABOUT MASTER CLAUDE!? ARE YOU DONE WITH HIM!?
THAT GUY... HE THREW HIS MASTER UNDER THE BUS.
EARRINGS WOULD SUIT YOU BEAUTIFULLY, PRINCE CLAUDE.
LET'S GO WITH RED TO MATCH YOUR EYES.
HEE HEE!
THE GIRLS WILL POSITIVELY SWOON OVER YOU.
...YOU...
... WOULDN'T MIND THAT?

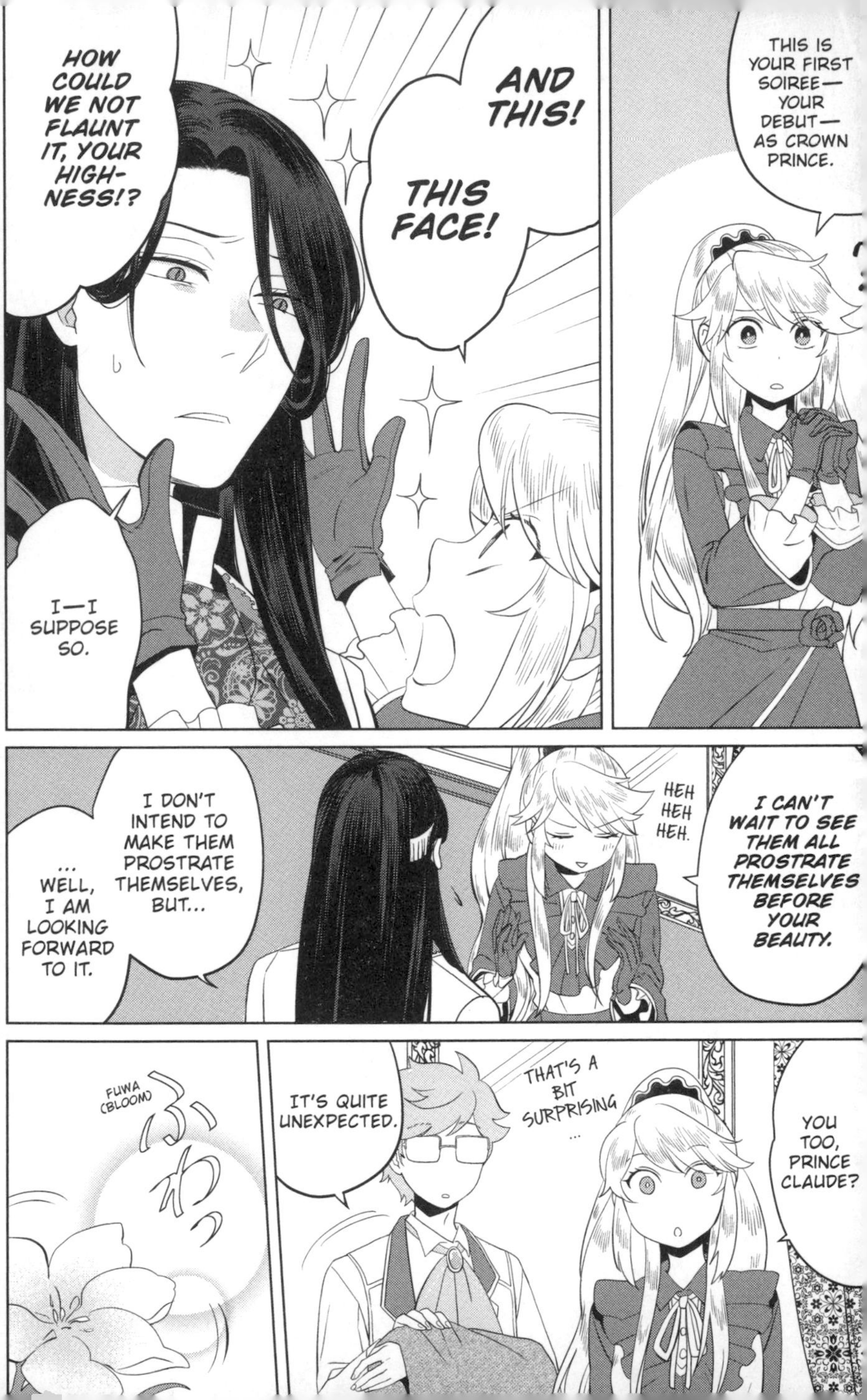
THIS IS YOUR FIRST SOIREE—YOUR DEBUT—AS CROWN PRINCE.
AND THIS! THIS FACE!
HOW COULD WE NOT FLAUNT IT, YOUR HIGHNESS!?
I—I SUPPOSE SO.
I CAN'T WAIT TO SEE THEM ALL PROSTRATE THEMSELVES BEFORE YOUR BEAUTY.
HEH HEH HEH.
I DON'T INTEND TO MAKE THEM PROSTRATE THEMSELVES, BUT...
...WELL, I AM LOOKING FORWARD TO IT.
YOU TOO, PRINCE CLAUDE?
THAT'S A BIT SURPRISING...
IT'S QUITE UNEXPECTED.
ふわっ
FUWA (BLOOM)

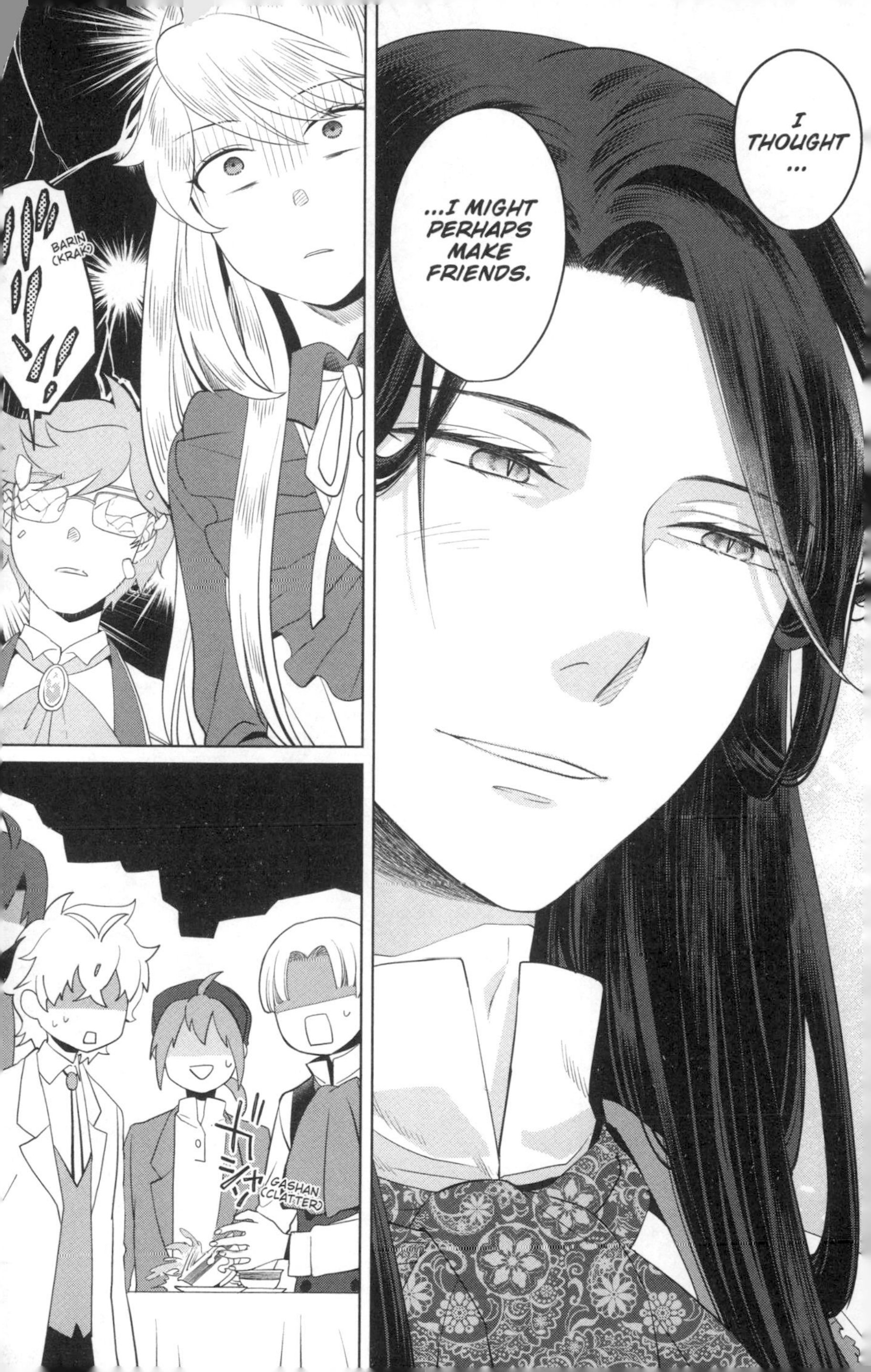
I THOUGHT ...
...I MIGHT PERHAPS MAKE FRIENDS.
BARIN (KRAK)
GASHAN (CLATTER)

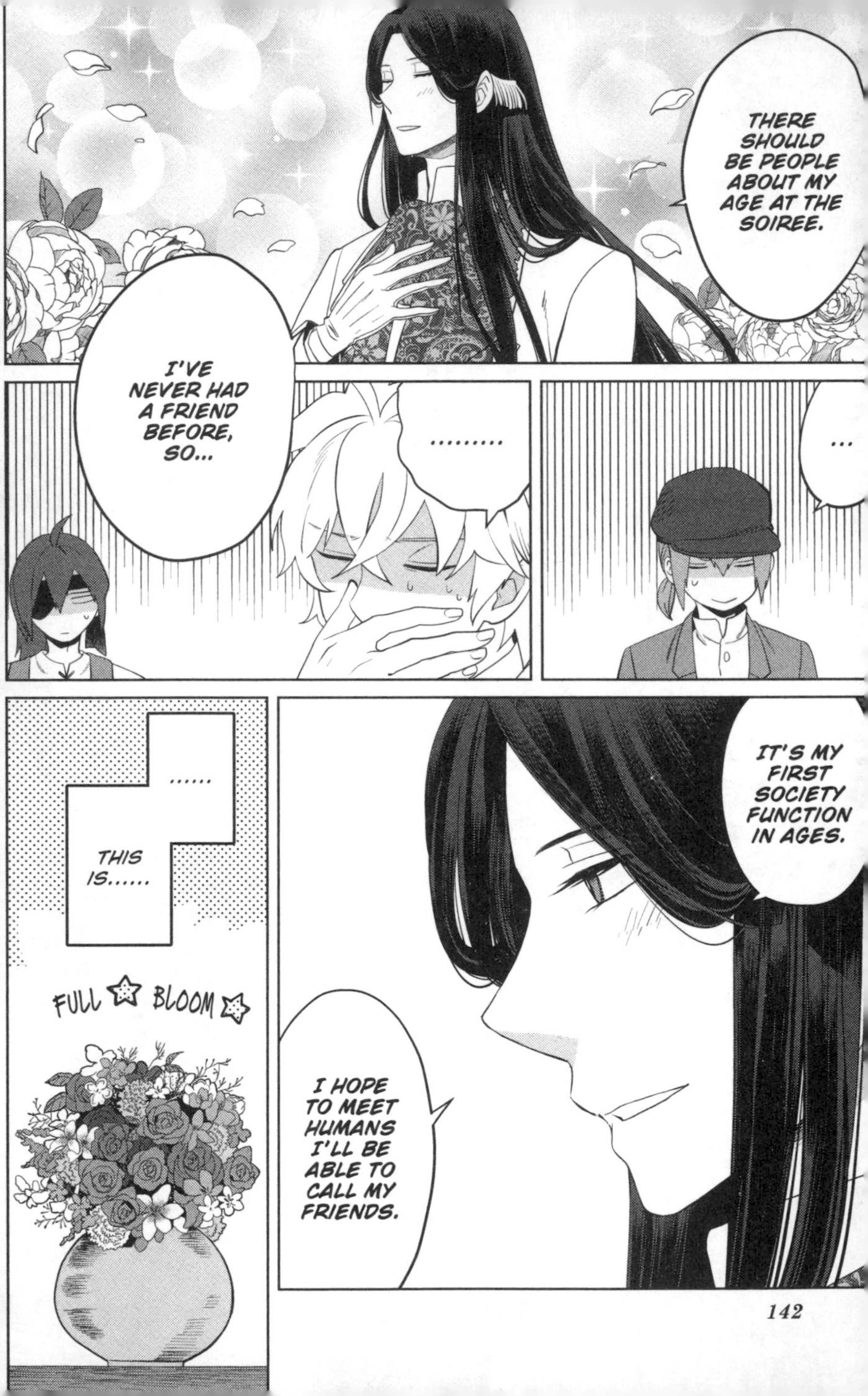
THERE SHOULD BE PEOPLE ABOUT MY AGE AT THE SOIREE.
I'VE NEVER HAD A FRIEND BEFORE, SO...
...
....
IT'S MY FIRST SOCIETY FUNCTION IN AGES.
I HOPE TO MEET HUMANS I'LL BE ABLE TO CALL MY FRIENDS.
......
THIS IS......
FULL BLOOM

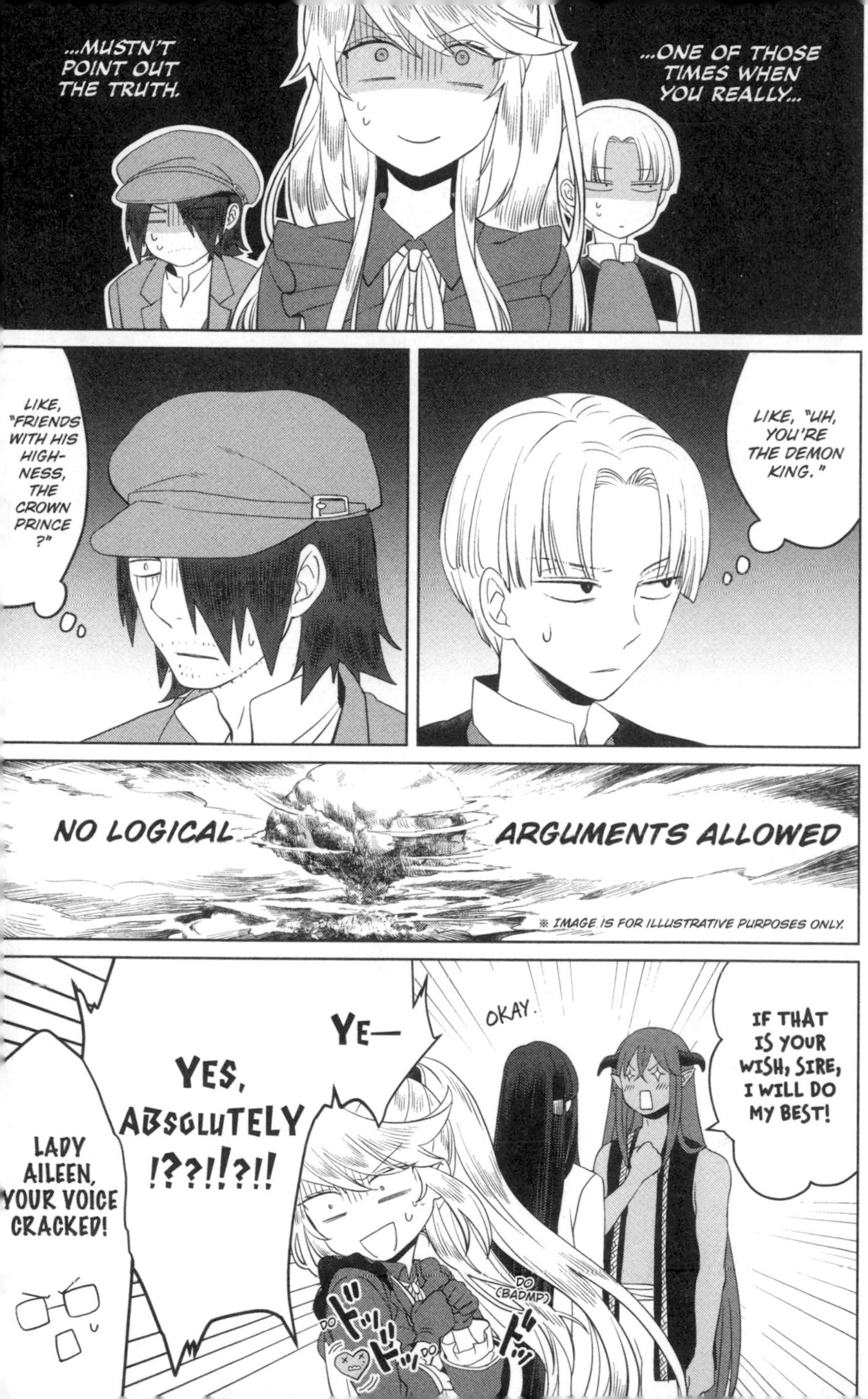
...ONE OF THOSE TIMES WHEN YOU REALLY...
...MUSTN'T POINT OUT THE TRUTH.
LIKE, "UH, YOU'RE THE DEMON KING."
LIKE, "FRIENDS WITH HIS HIGHNESS, THE CROWN PRINCE?"
NO LOGICAL ARGUMENTS ALLOWED
※ IMAGE IS FOR ILLUSTRATIVE PURPOSES ONLY.
IF THAT IS YOUR WISH, SIRE, I WILL DO MY BEST!
OKAY.
YE—
YES, ABSOLUTELY !??!!?!!
DO (BADMP)
DO
DO
LADY AILEEN, YOUR VOICE CRACKED!

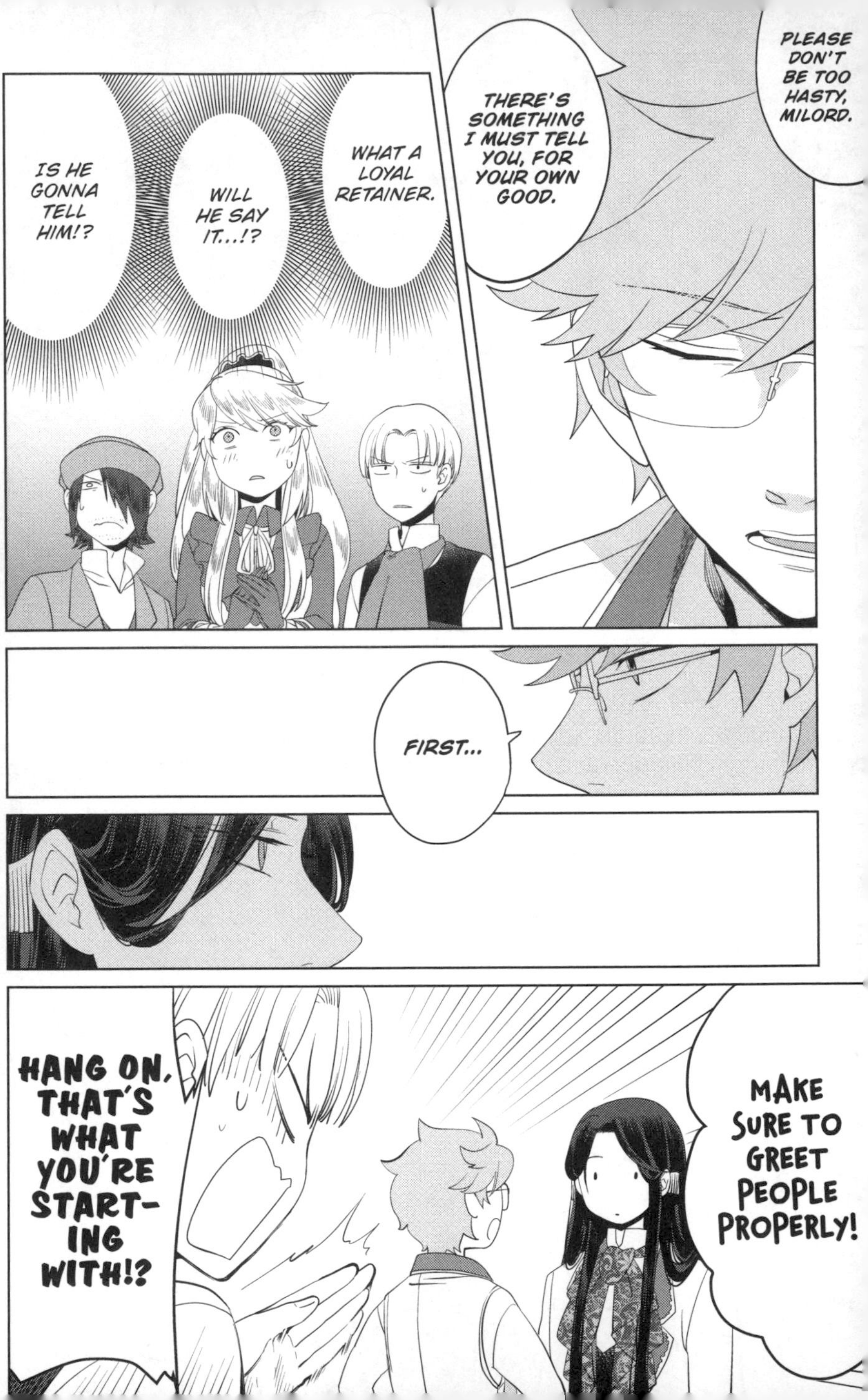
PLEASE DON'T BE TOO HASTY, MILORD.
THERE'S SOMETHING I MUST TELL YOU, FOR YOUR OWN GOOD.
WHAT A LOYAL RETAINER.
WILL HE SAY IT...!?
IS HE GONNA TELL HIM!?
FIRST...
MAKE SURE TO GREET PEOPLE PROPERLY!
HANG ON, THAT'S WHAT YOU'RE START-ING WITH!?

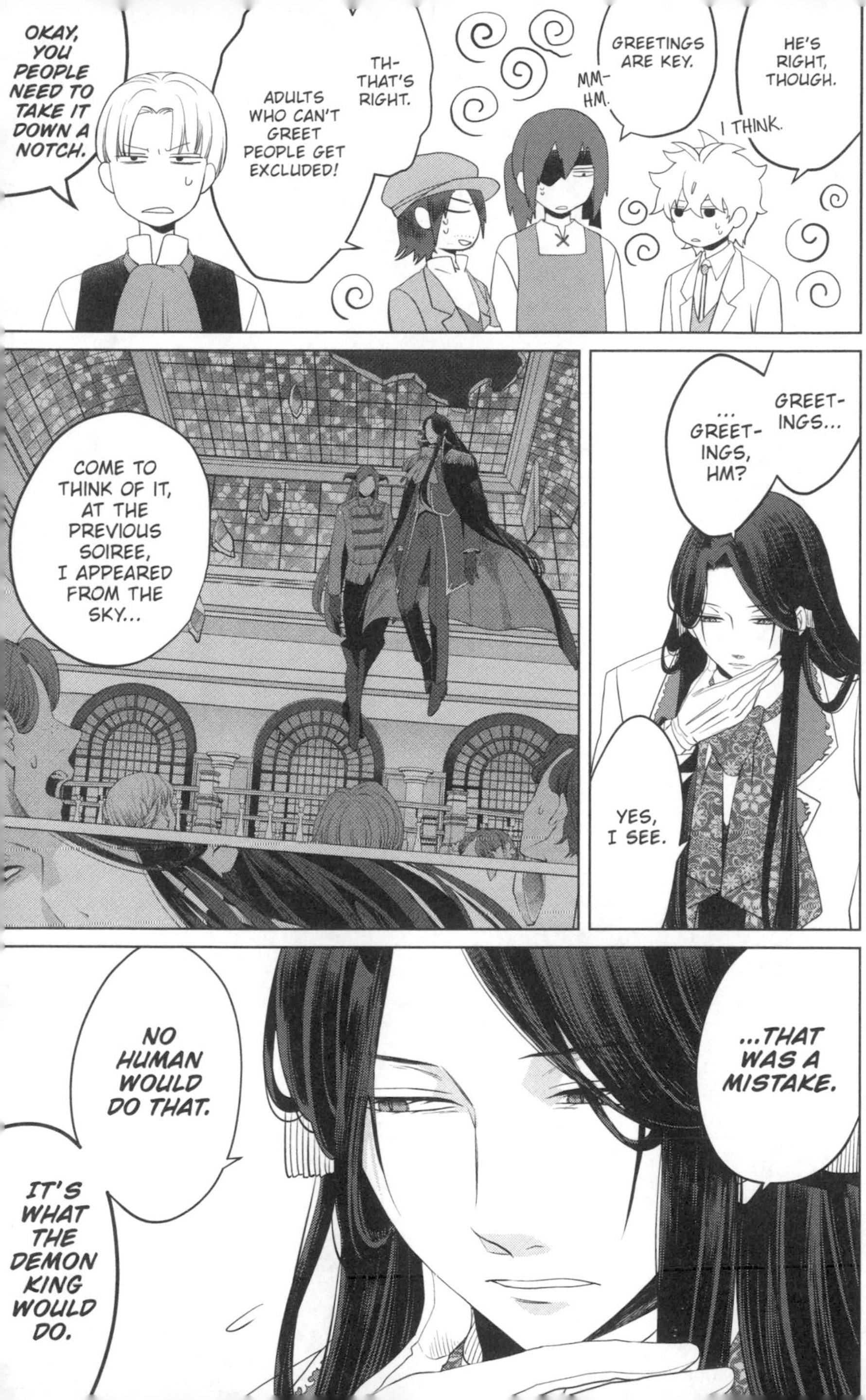
HE'S RIGHT, THOUGH.
I THINK.
GREETINGS ARE KEY.
MM-HM.
TH-THAT'S RIGHT.
ADULTS WHO CAN'T GREET PEOPLE GET EXCLUDED!
OKAY, YOU PEOPLE NEED TO TAKE IT DOWN A NOTCH.
GREET-INGS...
...GREET-INGS, HM?
YES, I SEE.
COME TO THINK OF IT, AT THE PREVIOUS SOIREE, I APPEARED FROM THE SKY...
...THAT WAS A MISTAKE.
NO HUMAN WOULD DO THAT.
IT'S WHAT THE DEMON KING WOULD DO.

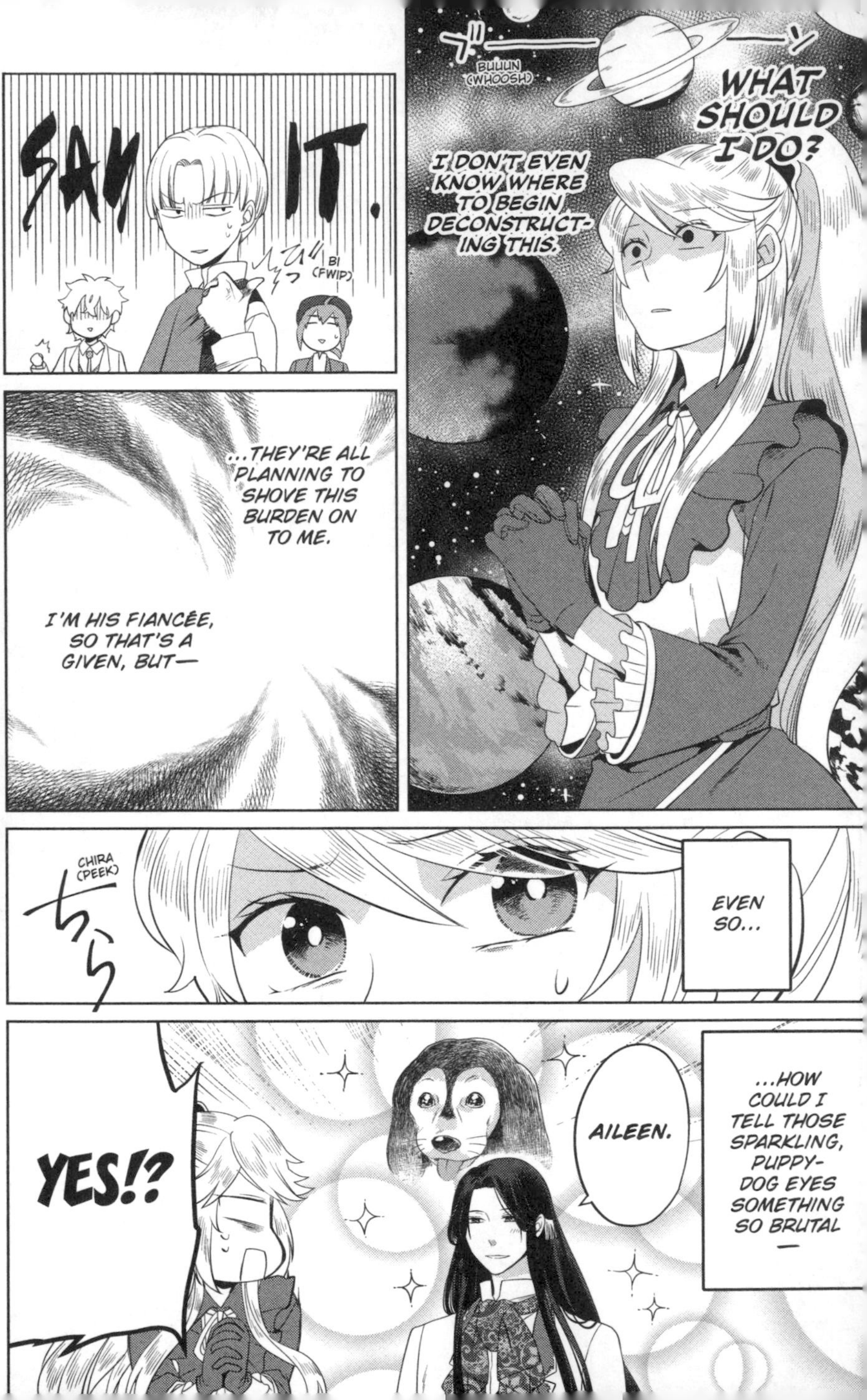
BUUUN (WHOOSH)
WHAT SHOULD I DO?
I DON'T EVEN KNOW WHERE TO BEGIN DECONSTRUCTING THIS.
SAY IT.
BI (FWIP)
...THEY'RE ALL PLANNING TO SHOVE THIS BURDEN ON TO ME.
I'M HIS FIANCÉE, SO THAT'S A GIVEN, BUT—
EVEN SO...
CHIRA (PEEK)
...HOW COULD I TELL THOSE SPARKLING, PUPPY-DOG EYES SOMETHING SO BRUTAL—
AILEEN.
YES!?

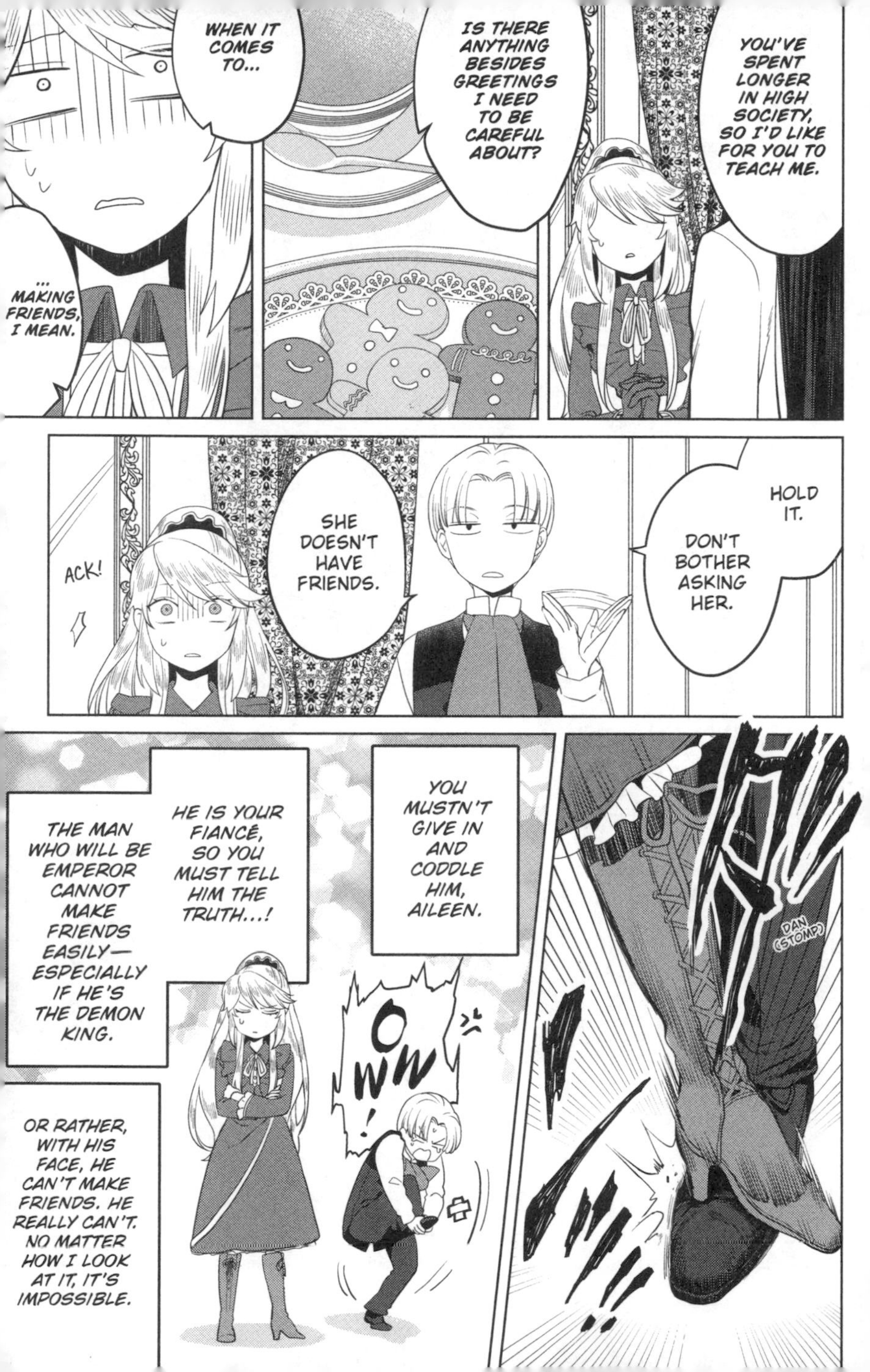
YOU'VE SPENT LONGER IN HIGH SOCIETY, SO I'D LIKE FOR YOU TO TEACH ME.
IS THERE ANYTHING BESIDES GREETINGS I NEED TO BE CAREFUL ABOUT?
WHEN IT COMES TO...
...MAKING FRIENDS, I MEAN.
HOLD IT.
DON'T BOTHER ASKING HER.
SHE DOESN'T HAVE FRIENDS.
ACK!
DAN (STOMP)
YOU MUSTN'T GIVE IN AND CODDLE HIM, AILEEN.
HE IS YOUR FIANCÉ, SO YOU MUST TELL HIM THE TRUTH...!
THE MAN WHO WILL BE EMPEROR CANNOT MAKE FRIENDS EASILY— ESPECIALLY IF HE'S THE DEMON KING.
OWW!
OR RATHER, WITH HIS FACE, HE CAN'T MAKE FRIENDS. HE REALLY CAN'T. NO MATTER HOW I LOOK AT IT, IT'S IMPOSSIBLE.

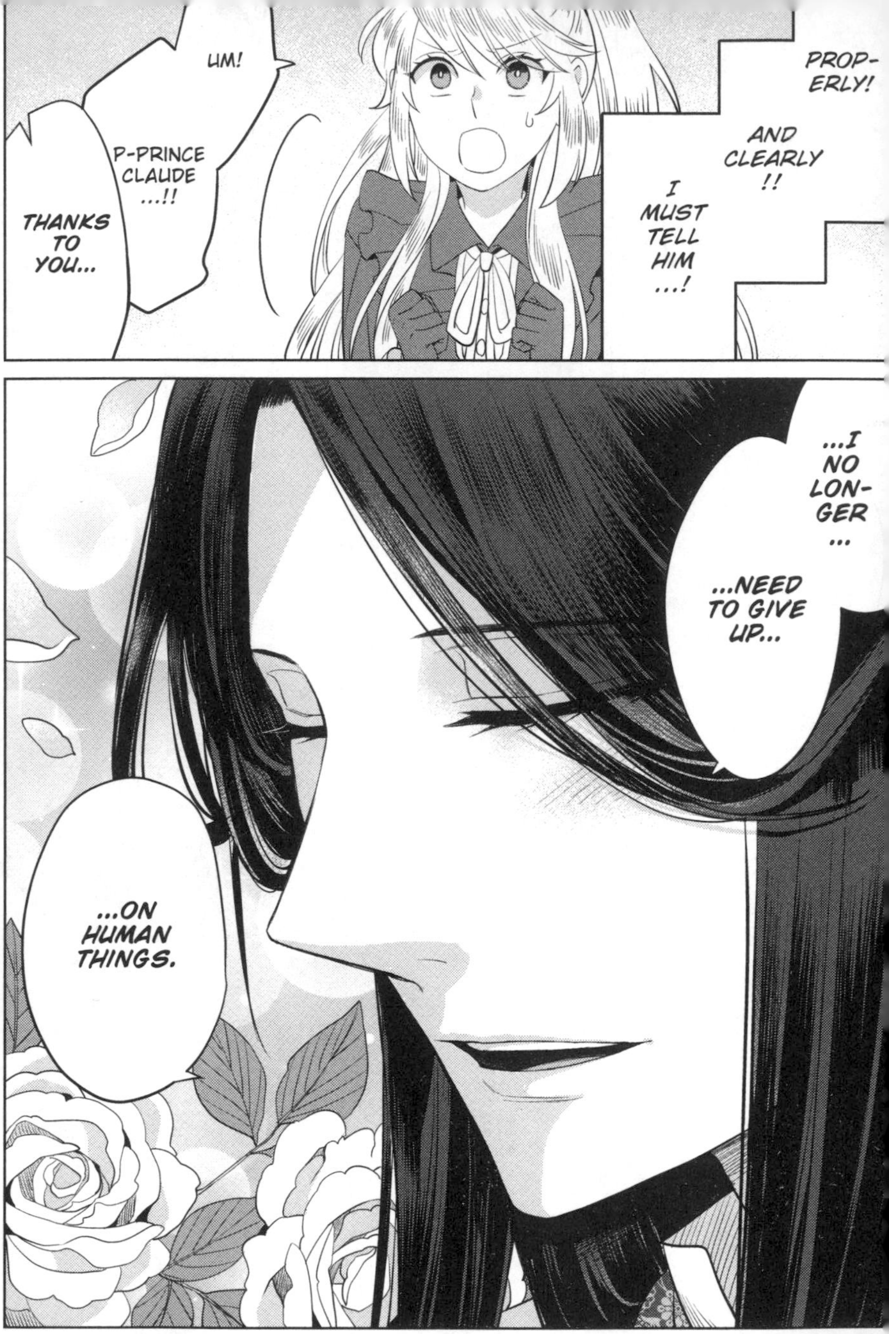
PROP-ERLY!
AND CLEARLY !!
I MUST TELL HIM ...!
UM!
P-PRINCE CLAUDE ...!!
THANKS TO YOU...
...I NO LON-GER ...
...NEED TO GIVE UP...
...ON HUMAN THINGS.

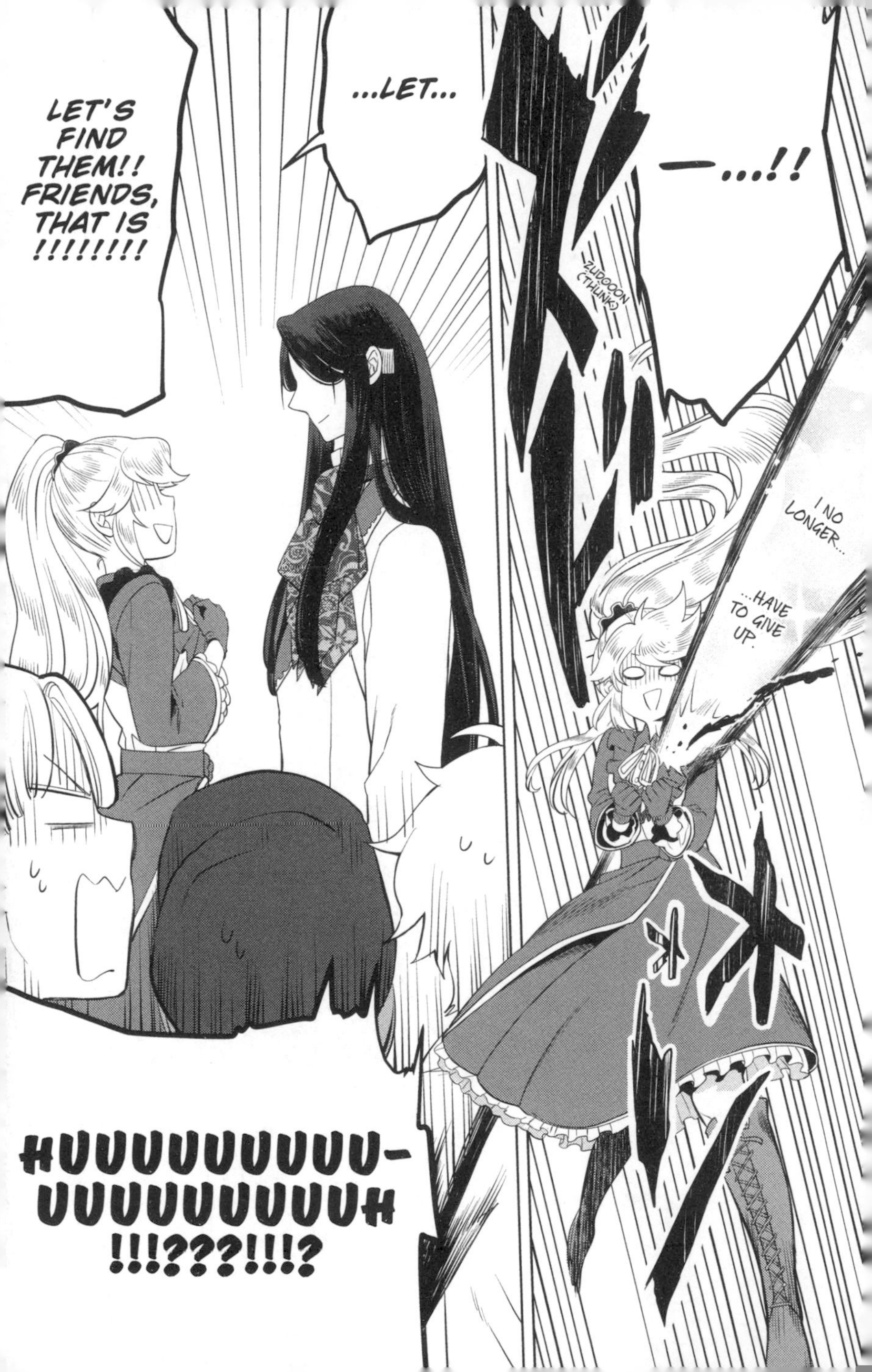
—...!!
ZUDOOON (THUNK)
I NO LONGER...
...HAVE TO GIVE UP.
...LET...
LET'S FIND THEM!! FRIENDS, THAT IS !!!!!!!!
HUUUUUUUUUU-UUUUUUUUUUUH !!!???!!!?

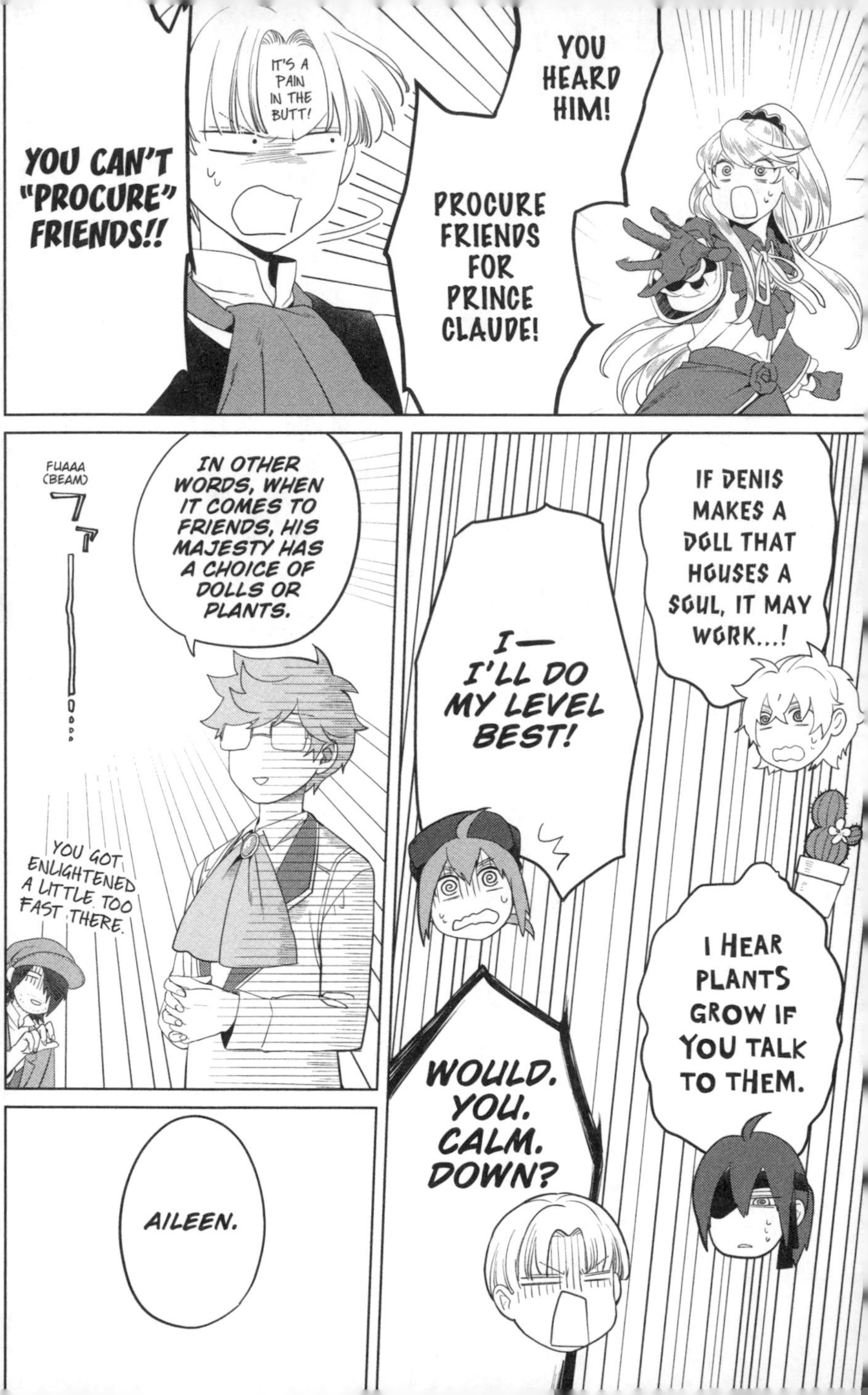
YOU HEARD HIM!
PROCURE FRIENDS FOR PRINCE CLAUDE!
IT'S A PAIN IN THE BUTT!
YOU CAN'T "PROCURE" FRIENDS!!
IF DENIS MAKES A DOLL THAT HOUSES A SOUL, IT MAY WORK...!
I— I'LL DO MY LEVEL BEST!
I HEAR PLANTS GROW IF YOU TALK TO THEM.
WOULD. YOU. CALM. DOWN?
IN OTHER WORDS, WHEN IT COMES TO FRIENDS, HIS MAJESTY HAS A CHOICE OF DOLLS OR PLANTS.
FUAAA (BEAM)
YOU GOT ENLIGHTENED A LITTLE TOO FAST THERE.
AILEEN.

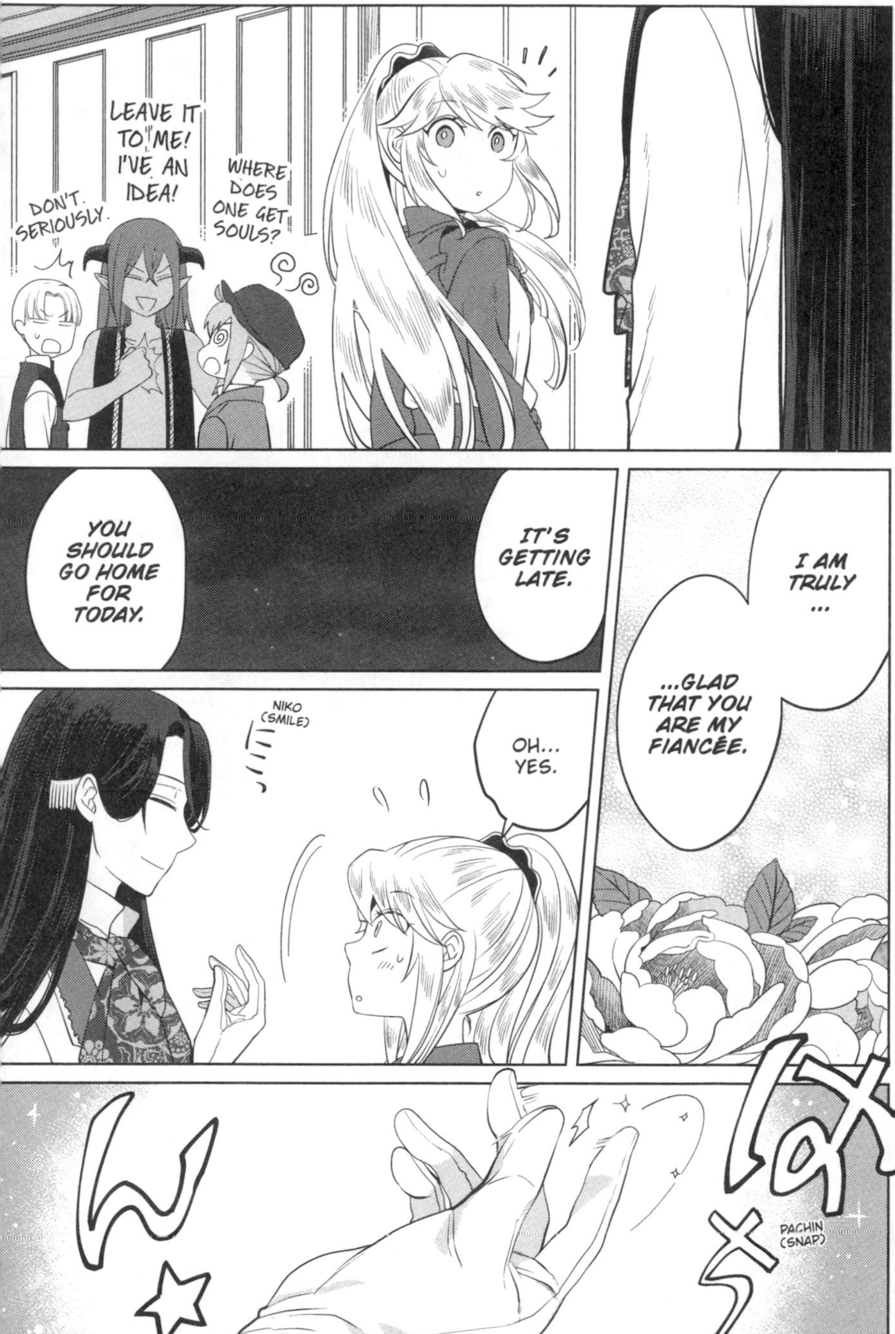
WHERE DOES ONE GET SOULS?
LEAVE IT TO ME! I'VE AN IDEA!
DON'T. SERIOUSLY.
I AM TRULY ...
...GLAD THAT YOU ARE MY FIANCÉE.
IT'S GETTING LATE.
YOU SHOULD GO HOME FOR TODAY.
OH... YES.
NIKO (SMILE)
PACHIN (SNAP)

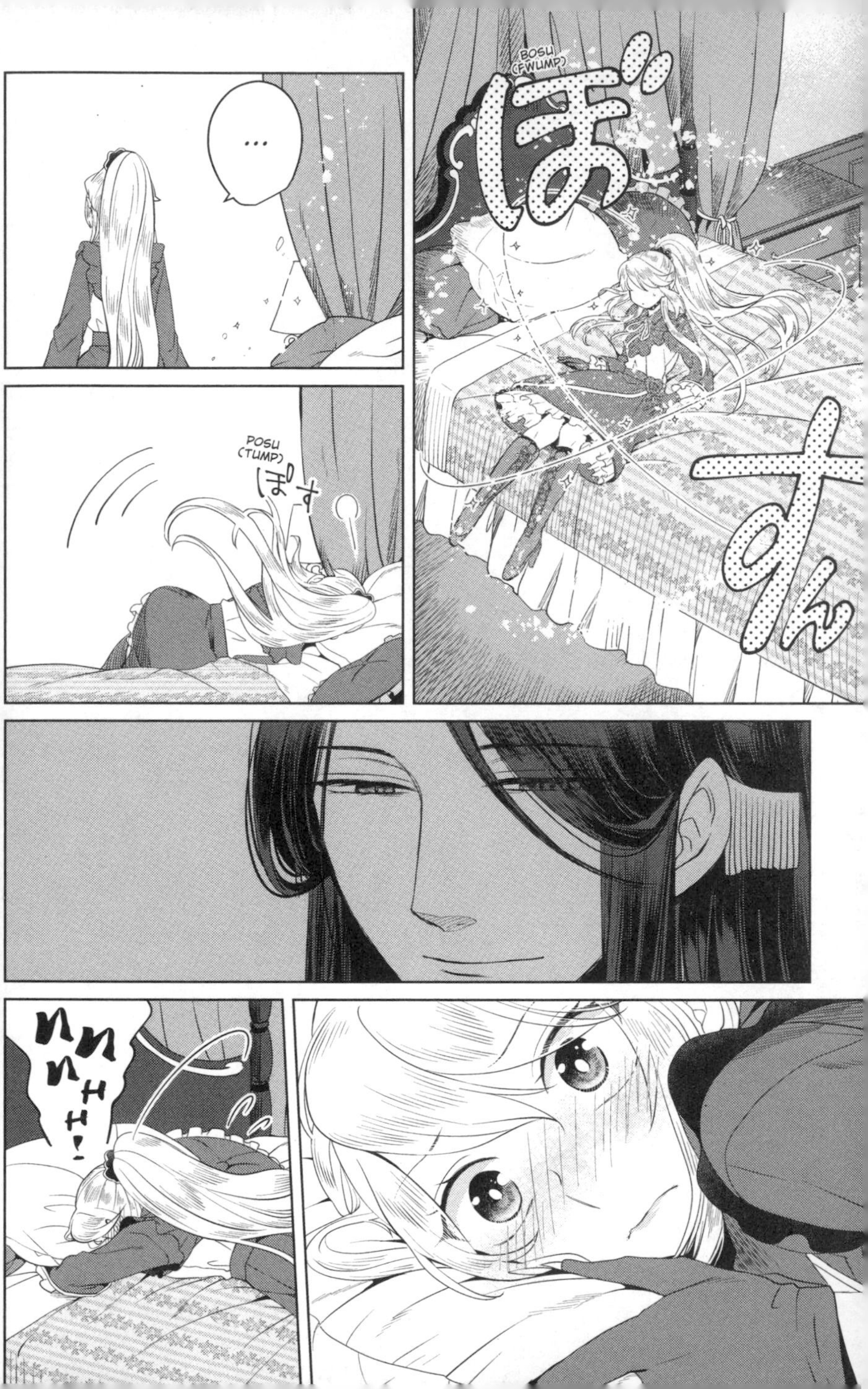
BOSU (FWUMP)
ぼすん
...
POSU (TUMP)
ぽす
NNNNHH!

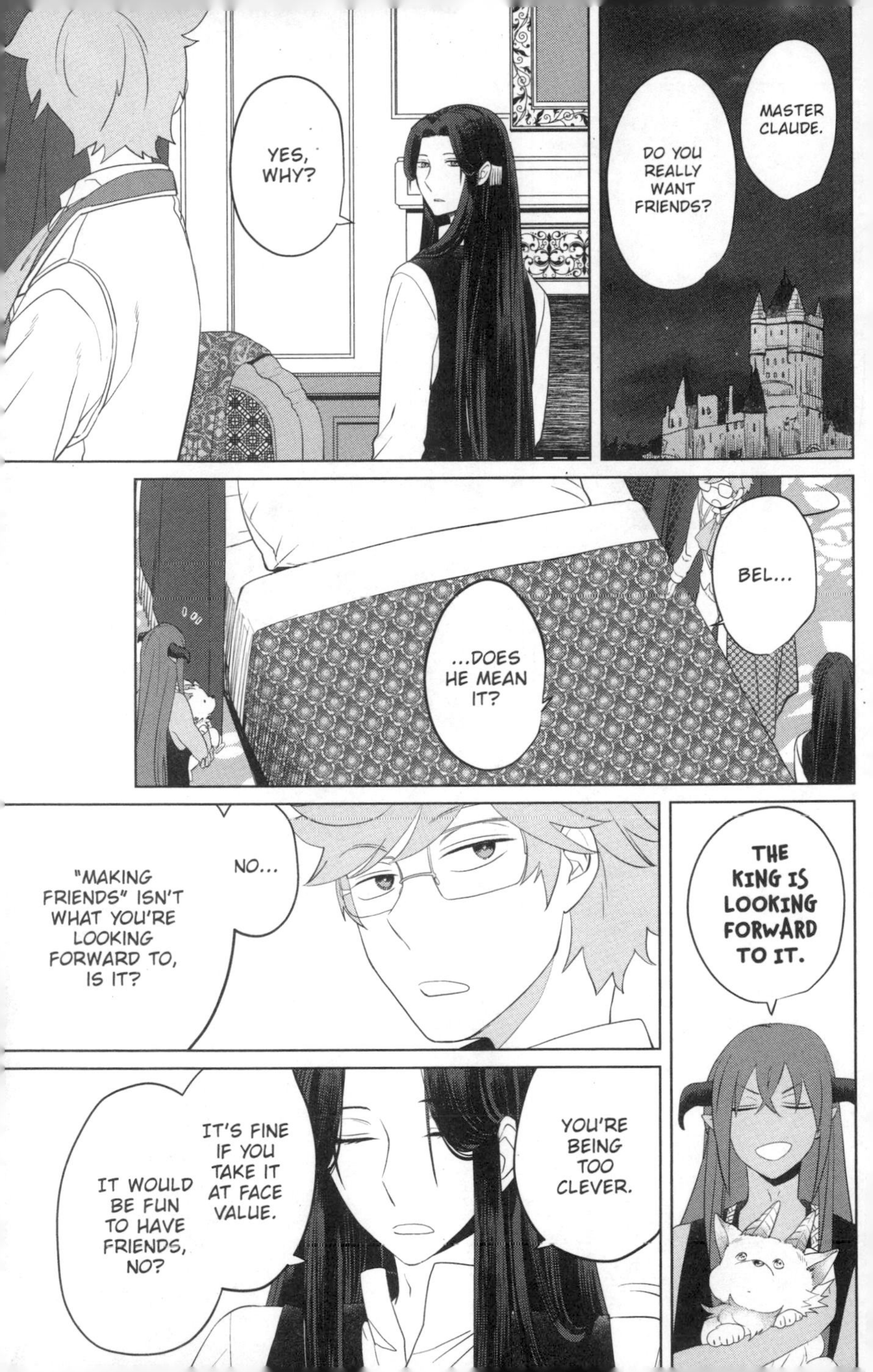
MASTER CLAUDE.
DO YOU REALLY WANT FRIENDS?
YES, WHY?
BEL...
...DOES HE MEAN IT?
THE KING IS LOOKING FORWARD TO IT.
NO...
"MAKING FRIENDS" ISN'T WHAT YOU'RE LOOKING FORWARD TO, IS IT?
YOU'RE BEING TOO CLEVER.
IT'S FINE IF YOU TAKE IT AT FACE VALUE.
IT WOULD BE FUN TO HAVE FRIENDS, NO?

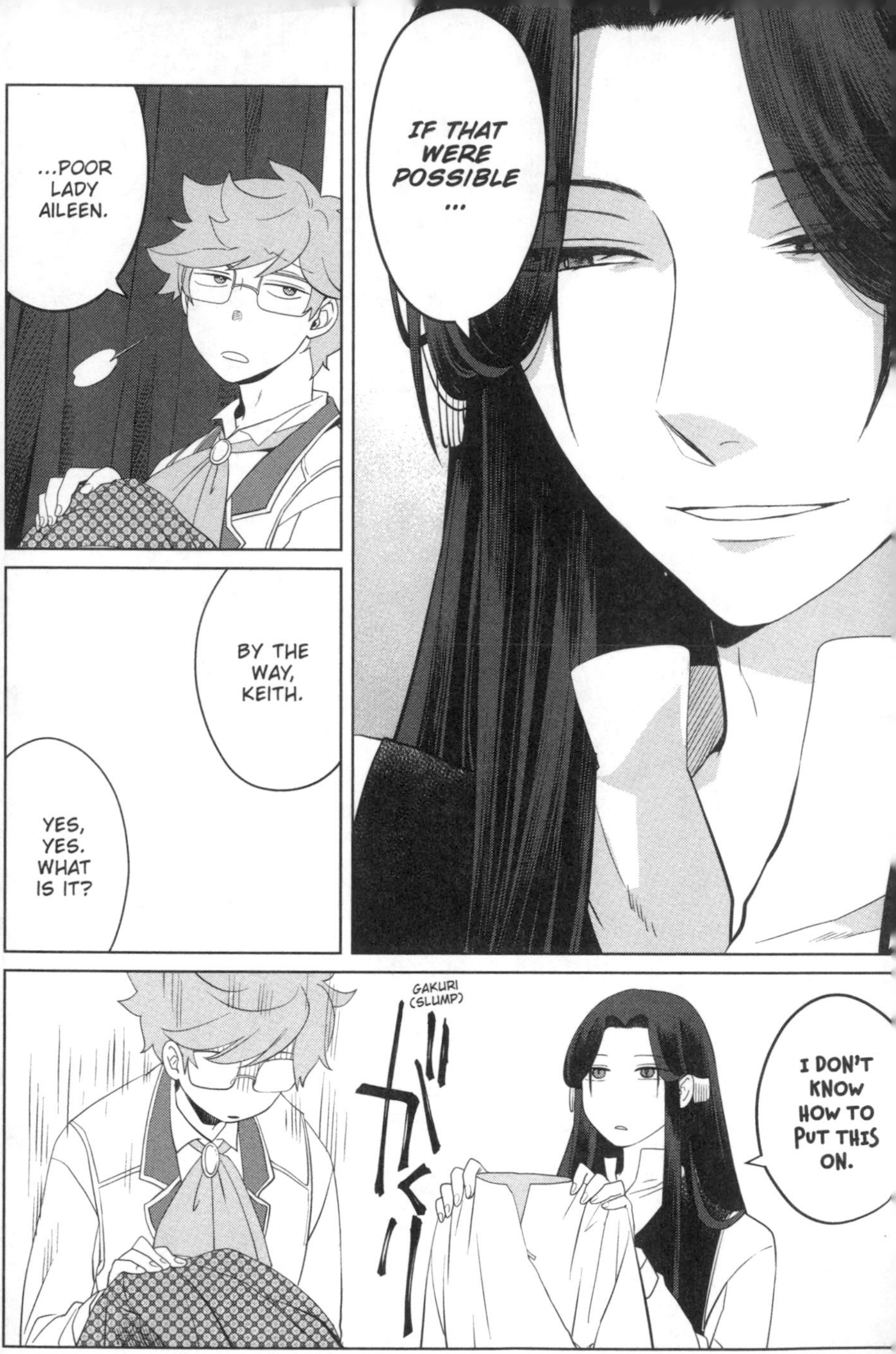
IF THAT WERE POSSIBLE ...
...POOR LADY AILEEN.
BY THE WAY, KEITH.
YES, YES. WHAT IS IT?
I DON'T KNOW HOW TO PUT THIS ON.
GAKURI (SLUMP)

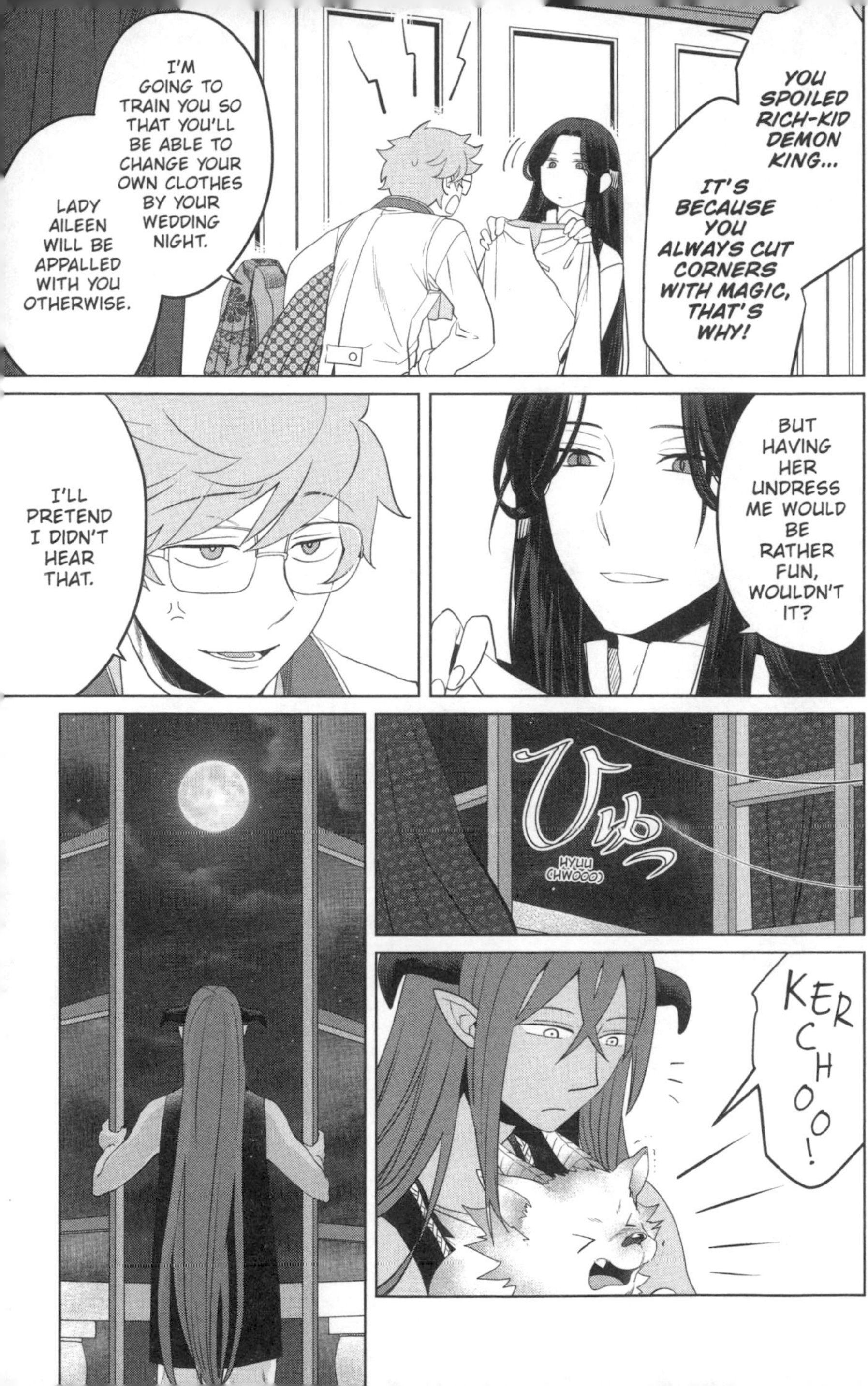
YOU SPOILED RICH-KID DEMON KING...
IT'S BECAUSE YOU ALWAYS CUT CORNERS WITH MAGIC, THAT'S WHY!
I'M GOING TO TRAIN YOU SO THAT YOU'LL BE ABLE TO CHANGE YOUR OWN CLOTHES BY YOUR WEDDING NIGHT.
LADY AILEEN WILL BE APPALLED WITH YOU OTHERWISE.
BUT HAVING HER UNDRESS ME WOULD BE RATHER FUN, WOULDN'T IT?
I'LL PRETEND I DIDN'T HEAR THAT.
ひゅっ
HYUU (HWOOO)
KERCHOO!

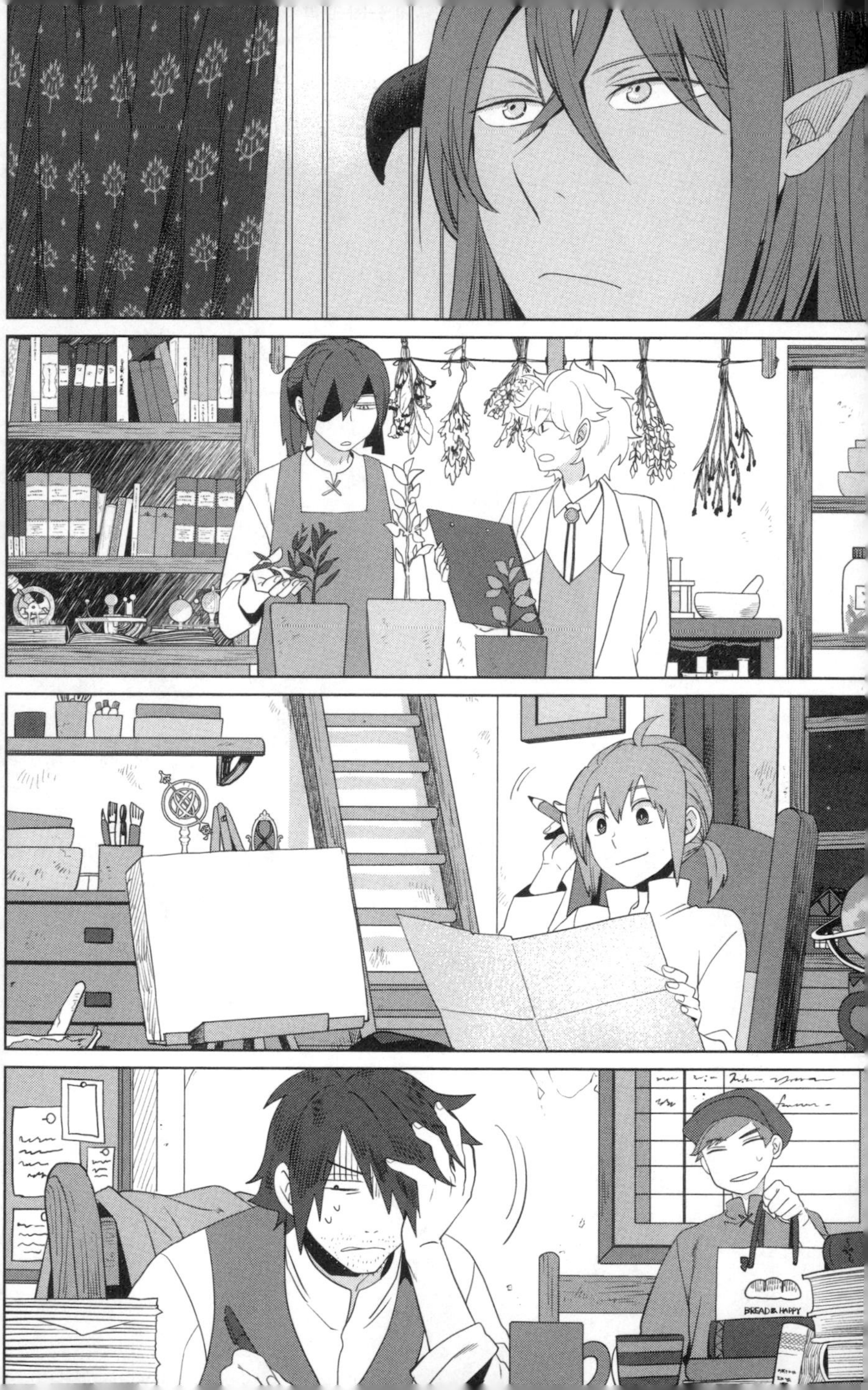
BREAD&HAPPY

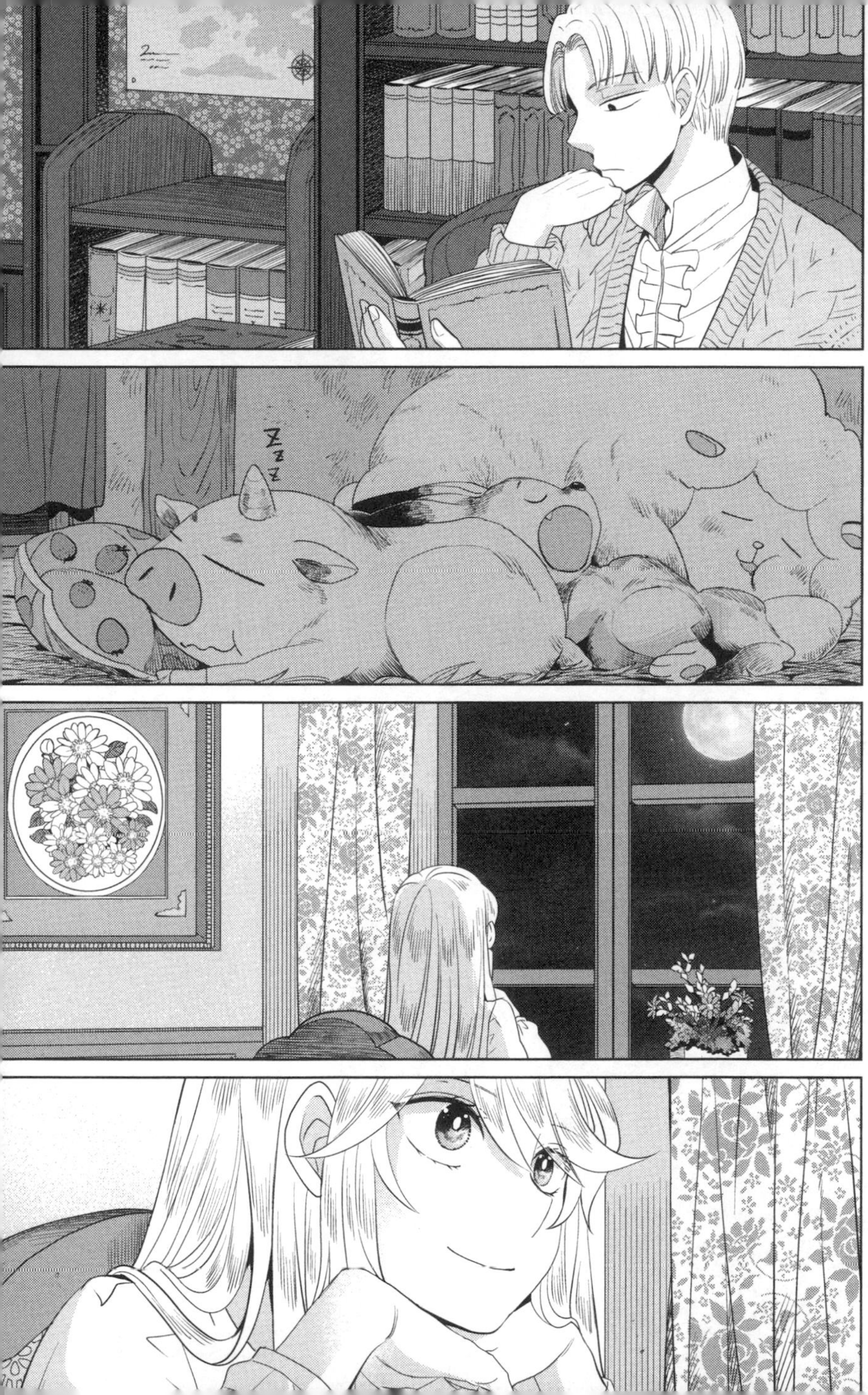
Zzz

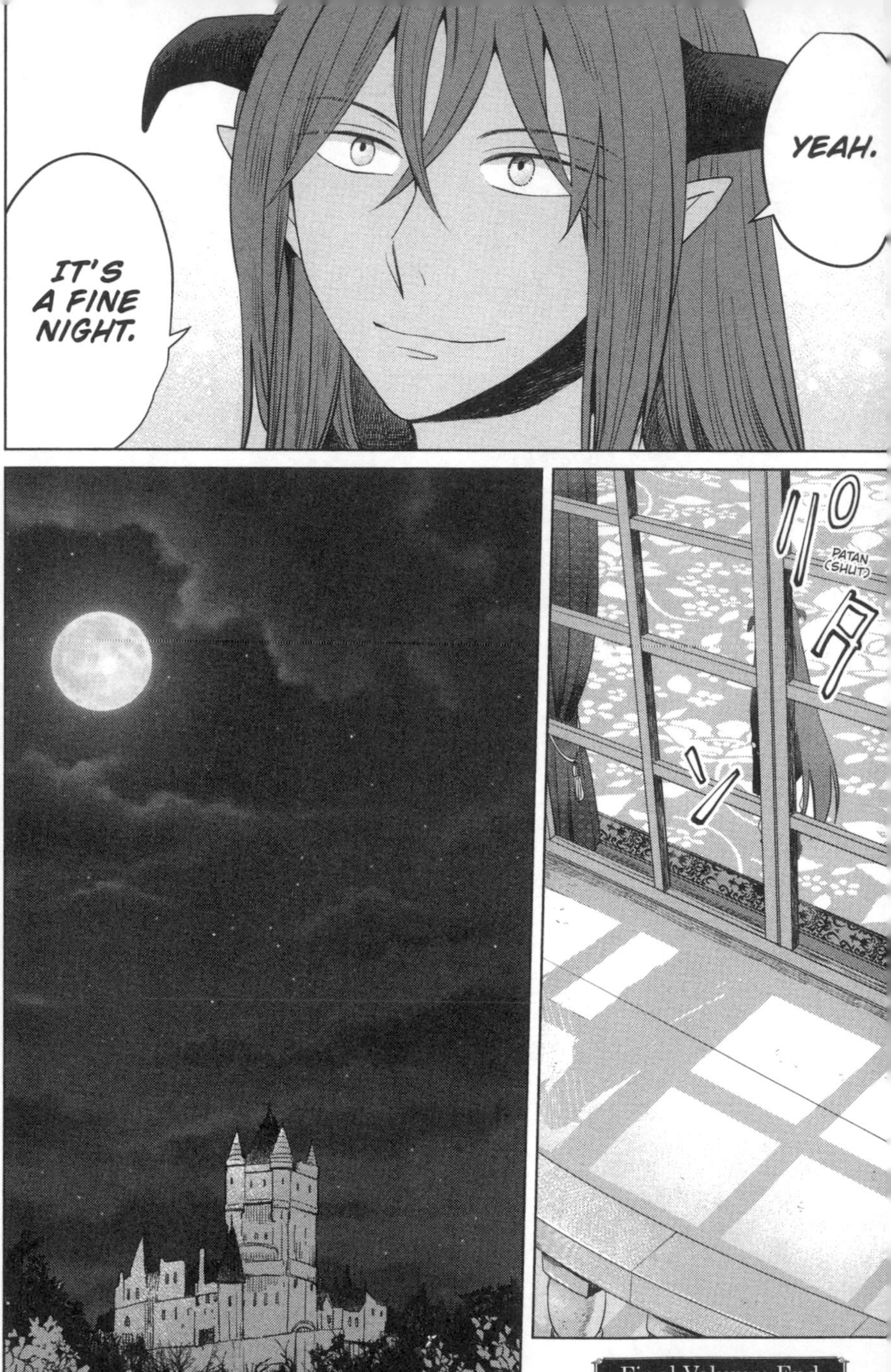
YEAH.
IT'S A FINE NIGHT.
PATAN (SHUT)

Final Volume: End

I'm the VILLAINESS, So I'm
Taming the Final Boss

I'm the VILLAINESS, So I'm Taming the Final Boss 3

Anko Yuzu
ORIGINAL STORY: **Sarasa Nagase**
CHARACTER DESIGN: **Mai Murasaki**

Translation: Taylor Engel   Lettering: Rachel J. Pierce

DISCARDED

AKUYAKU REIJO NANODE LAST BOSS WO KATTE MIMASHITA Vol. 3
© Anko Yuzu 2019 © Sarasa Nagase 2019
© Mai Murasaki 2019
First published in Japan in 2019 by KADOKAWA CORPORATION, Tokyo.
English translation rights arranged with KADOKAWA CORPORATION, Tokyo
and Yen Press, LLC through Tuttle-Mori Agency, Inc.

English translation © 2022 by Yen Press, LLC

Yen Press
150 West 30th Street, 19th Floor
New York, NY 10001

Visit us at yenpress.com • facebook.com/yenpress
twitter.com/yenpress • yenpress.tumblr.com
instagram.com/yenpress

First Yen Press Edition: February 2022

Yen Press is an imprint of Yen Press, LLC.
The Yen Press name and logo are trademarks of Yen Press, LLC.

The publisher is not responsible for websites (or
their content) that are not owned by the publisher.

Library of Congress Control Number: 2021935585

ISBNs: 978-1-9753-2123-9 (paperback)
978-1-9753-2124-6 (ebook)

10 9 8 7 6 5 4 3 2 1

LSC-C

Printed in the United States of America